FANTASY PIECES

DATE DUE

			PRINTED IN U.S.A.

Fantasy Pieces

METRICAL DISSONANCE
❦ IN THE ❦
MUSIC OF
ROBERT SCHUMANN

HARALD KREBS

New York ❦ *Oxford*
OXFORD UNIVERSITY PRESS
1999

Oxford University Press

Oxford   New York
Athens   Auckland   Bangkok   Bogotá   Bombay   Buenos Aires   Chennai   Calcutta
Cape Town   Dar es Salaam   Delhi   Florence   Hong Kong   Istanbul
Karachi   Kuala Lumpur   Madrid   Melbourne   Mumbai
Mexico City   Nairobi   Paris   São Paulo   Singapore   Taipei   Tokyo   Toronto   Warsaw

and associated companies in
Berlin   Ibadan

Copyright © 1999 Oxford University Press

Published by Oxford University Press, Inc.
198 Madison Avenue, New York, New York 10016

Oxford is a registered trademark of Oxford University Press

Library of Congress Cataloging-in-Publication Data
Krebs, Harald, 1955–
Fantasy pieces : metrical dissonance in the music of Robert Schumann / Harald Krebs.
p. cm.
Includes bibliographical references and index.
ISBN 0-19-511623-2 ISBN 0-19-516946-8 (pbk)
1. Schumann, Robert, 1810–1856—Criticism and interpretation.
2. Musical meter and rhythm.   I. Title.
ML410.S4K68 1999
781.2'26'092—dc21   98-12647

First issued as an Oxford University Press paperback, 2003

1 3 5 7 9 8 6 4 2

Printed in the United States of America
on acid-free paper

For Sharon

Préambule

In this book I investigate the pathology of musical meter—the manifold disruptive and distortive conditions that affect what we generally call "the meter" of a musical work. I have drawn most of my musical case studies from the works of Robert Schumann, which are particularly rich in "pathological" metrical states. I could just as well have based the book on the music of Beethoven, Brahms, or other composers (and I have included several analyses that demonstrate the occurrence of metrical conflict in works by composers other than Schumann). It seemed to me, however, that Schumann's music in general and his metrical structures in particular had been neglected in the music theory literature. Furthermore, I have always been fascinated by Schumann's music and personality, and was eager to spend some years in his company. I have not regretted my decision to do so; I have grown even more fond of his music, and even more intrigued by his personality.

I had begun to write this book as a "normal" academic study when my colleague, pianist Bruce Vogt, suggested that it would be appropriate to include some Schumannesque dialogues. His specific idea was that I should invent a new *Davidsbund* consisting of prominent twentieth-century rhythmic theorists, who would scintillatingly discuss issues relating to metrical conflict. Appealing though this idea was, I found myself reluctant to take the liberty of putting words into the mouths of living individuals. I decided instead to write a summary of nineteenth-century theories of metrical conflict in the form of a dialogue between Florestan, Eusebius, and various others, which became the first part of chapter 1. I then found myself unable to keep Florestan and Eusebius out of the later chapters, and the volume became a theoretical manuscript counterpointed by their commentary.

Some of the Florestan and Eusebius material is based on their writings, and some of it on the events of their last two years. The first six chapters "take place" in mid-January of 1854—a time when all of the interlocutors were still or already alive, and when Florestan and Eusebius were still able to walk about freely. The seventh chapter is set in April 1854, after their admission to the asylum in En-denich. The Epilogue, finally, is set shortly before their death in 1856. Many of the words and events are invented; hence the designation of the book as a set of "Fantasiestücke." I have not only put many words into Florestan's and Eusebius's mouths, but have frequently ascribed particular compositional intentions to them. I have, of course, no proof of these intentions, but my study of their music and their manuscripts leads me to believe that the intentions I mention *could have been* their actual ones.

I have organized the book as an alternation of theoretical chapters (to which Florestan, Eusebius, and occasionally Meister Raro and Clara contribute comments and musical illustrations), and "intermezzi" (in which the same interlocutors address issues peripheral to the theory of metrical conflict but central to an understanding of Schumann's use of such conflict). In the first chapter, I outline the thoughts of nineteenth- and twentieth-century authors on metrical conflict (with emphasis on writings that invoke a metaphor that pervades the book—the consonance-dissonance metaphor). I conclude that chapter with a summary of previous writings on Schumann's metrical anomalies. In the second chapter I describe various categories of "metrical dissonance" and set out a terminology and labeling system for the analysis of metrically dissonant passages. In the third chapter (the first intermezzo), Florestan discusses the music that influenced his metrical style. In the fourth chapter I investigate the operation of metrical dissonance within large contexts, particularly successions of metrical states and the types of processes in which they can be involved. In the fifth chapter (the second intermezzo), Florestan and Eusebius reminisce about the "metrical revisions" that played such a large role in their compositional process. The sixth chapter broadens the discussion of metrical dissonance by addressing its interactions with pitch structure, form and text, and considers the possible meanings of metrical dissonance in Schumann's instrumental works. The seventh chapter (the third intermezzo), couched in the form of a letter from Clara Schumann to a former piano student, addresses some issues relating to the performance of metrically conflicted passages. The eighth chapter is a collection of analyses of several works and movements by Schumann, alternating with shorter discussions of works by other composers. The volume concludes with an epilogue, which is an analysis of one of Schumann's very late works, as well as an attempt to suggest, with "dissonant" layers of prose and poetry, Schumann's mental state in the asylum at Endenich.

The "fantastic" portions of the book are disrupted by footnotes and musical example numbers. I apologize for these intrusive, but necessary elements. (As they form a "dissonant" layer within the imaginary discourse of Schumann's personae, they are, in a way, appropriate!)

I have included as many musical examples as possible, but readers who wish to follow each of my analyses in detail will need to consult scores at times. I have, for the most part, used the Clara Schumann-Brahms editions of Schumann's music, but have compared them to the Henle edition and to extant autographs where possible.

The book does not assume a great deal of prior theoretical knowledge. Some familiarity with recent writings about rhythm would be helpful but is not essential, as the relevant ideas are summarized in chapter 1. I assume some knowledge of Schenker's theory during a few of the analyses in chapter 6; most of the volume, however, can be understood without that knowledge.

Florestan and Eusebius have added much pleasure to the writing of this book. It is my hope that their presence will equally enhance the pleasure of readers.

Reconnaissance

I thank the Social Sciences and Humanities Research Council of Canada for a generous grant that enabled me to travel to Europe to study Schumann autographs and secondary sources not readily available in North America. I am grateful to the librarians and archivists at the following institutions, who graciously and generously assisted me: the Manuscripts Division of the Universitäts- und Landesbibliothek Bonn; the Schumann-Forschungsstelle at Düsseldorf; the Music Division of the Bibliothèque Nationale in Paris; the Manuscripts Division of the British Library in London; the Schumann-Haus in Zwickau; the Music Divisions of both houses of the Deutsche Staatsbibliothek zu Berlin — Preußischer Kulturbesitz, Musikabteilung mit Mendelssohn-Archiv; the archive of the Gesellschaft der Musikfreunde in Wien, and the Music Division of the Österreichische Nationalbibliothek in Vienna; the Music Division of the Bayerische Staatsbibliothek in Munich; and the Pierpont Morgan Library in New York. I must thank in particular Brigitte Berenbruch, former director of the Music Division of the Stadtbibliothek in Bonn, Dr. Gerd Nauhaus of the Schumann-Haus in Zwickau, and Dr. Matthias Wendt and Dr. Bernhard Appel of the Schumann-Forschungsstelle at Düsseldorf, all of whom gave me much valuable assistance and advice.

I thank Mekala Padmanabhan, Stephany and Gordon Wolfe, Donald McDougall, and Todd Harrop, graduate students at the University of Victoria, all of whom assisted me at some point during the preparation of this book. I am especially grateful to Donald and Todd for the many hours they spent in preparing musical examples.

I thank Amadeus Verlag, Belmont Music Publishers, European American Music, Heinrichshofen's Verlag, Peermusic Classical, and Theodore Presser Co. for permission to reproduce excerpts from musical works to which they hold the rights.

Some of the material in chapter 5 previously appeared in *Music Theory Spectrum*, vol. 19, no. 1 (Spring 1997): pp. 35–54 (© 1997 by the Society for Music Theory). I thank the University of California Press for permission to reuse this material. I also thank Walter Kreyszig, editor of *Austria, 996–1996: Music in a Changing Society, Proceedings of the International Millennium Conference, Ottawa, Canada, 2–7 January 1996,* for permission to include material that appears (albeit in a very different form) in volume 2 of that publication *(Issues in Music of the Late Eighteenth, Nineteenth and Early Twentieth Centuries)*.

I thank Richard Cohn, Peter Kaminsky, William Kinderman, Justin London, and John Roeder for their comments on material that I shared with them. John Daverio, William Rothstein, and a third, anonymous reader provided many extremely helpful comments on my manuscript, for which I am very grateful.

I thank Mark Franklin and Ajana, of Media Magic Inc., for conjuring up Florestan's and Eusebius's coffee beans, and Jill Michalski, Linda Sheldon, and Robert Malatest for their help with various technical matters.

I thank my parents and sister for their unfailing moral support. Special thanks, finally, to my wife, Sharon Krebs, for her assistance in innumerable ways—for her help during computer crises; for preventing me, with her infallible sense of direction, from getting lost (and thus wasting precious research time!) in European cities; and for exploring with me the wonderful *Lieder* of Robert Schumann.

Contents

FANTASY PIECES

ONE

Nineteenth- and Twentieth-Century Theories of Metrical Conflict

PROMENADE THROUGH THE TOWN OF EUPHONIA

Having already shown his guests Florestan and Eusebius many of the wonders of Euphonia, Hector led them, with an air of having something particularly amazing up his sleeve, toward an area of that town which, he informed them, was called the Rhythmic Quarter.[1] As they neared this area, their attention was caught by a throbbing and apparently chaotic din, which, however, they soon perceived to be composed of numerous noncongruent series of regular drumbeats. They walked slowly down one of the streets, briefly inclining their heads in a listening attitude before each house. From one of these there issued the simultaneous percussions of groups of three and four pulses, from another groups of four pulses against five, from another five pulses against six, from yet others even more exotic superpositions, such as five against eleven and eight against thirteen. Hector led them after awhile into a second street, from whose houses emanated combinations of equivalent but nonaligned groups of pulses. After sampling the sounds of a number of houses in this street, Florestan walked back to the point of intersection of the two streets and stood there for some time, listening to the intricate rhythms that resulted from the mingling of sounds from the two streets. When Florestan returned to his friends, shaking his head in wonderment, Hector said, "I must show you some of the performers." Together they entered one of the buildings—that from which there issued the sound of a superposition of five pulses upon seven. Inside, Florestan and Eusebius were overwhelmed, not only by the now deafening uproar of the drumbeats, but also by the recognition that the performers of these intricate rhythmic superpositions were very young children, who pounded away at their drums with intense concentration as well as ob-

EXAMPLE 1.1. *Excerpt from Michael Bergson's* Vier Mazurken, *op. 1, reproduced in Robert Schumann's review of the work*

vious enjoyment. They watched and listened for a time, then stepped back onto the street, where Hector explained, "Most systems of musical education neglect rhythm, or address only the most common and simple rhythmic devices; in Euphonia, however, the children are exposed to highly complex rhythms from an early age. *Within a few years, the children reach the point where the dividing of any beat in the bar, the syncopated forms, the blending of irreconcilable rhythms, and so on, hold no difficulties for them.* They learn to approach rhythmic complexities with excitement and joy rather than trepidation."[2]

Florestan said, "The Euphonian children are indeed capable of amazing rhythmic feats. Of course, rhythmic complexities and metrical conflicts are not of value in themselves. Look at the following excerpt from Michael Bergson's *Vier Mazurken* op. 1." On a sketchbook that he drew from his pocket, he quickly reproduced the measures shown in Example 1.1.[3] "The passage," he remarked, "is conflicted enough with its nonaligned duple groups of quarter notes within a triple meter. But the composer seems to have been carried away by a passion for complexity to notate the passage in a manner that makes it appear much more abstruse than it is. I hope that your young drummers are not similarly intoxicated by rhythmic complexity for its own sake." Hector replied, "It is our concern that every activity in this town be subservient to expression; *those who take pleasure in works that are false as to expression are inexorably banished, unless they consent to descend to some inferior employment, such as the making of catgut or the preparation of skins for kettledrums.* And this would, of course, apply to any who would worship rhythmic complexity for its own sake."[4] He added with a grim smile, "Michael Bergson, by the way, operates a little rosin factory on the outskirts of Euphonia."

Eusebius remarked, "Serves him right! The inexpressive use of rhythmical and metrical conflicts must result in tiresome compositions, overgrown with needless intricacies, or, as the worthy Moritz Hauptmann has written, in 'mere lawlessness, [in] a diseased rhythm in a healthy metre.'[5] Some critics, no doubt, feel that your music, dear Florestan, with its frequent usage of syncopation and other metrical conflicts, exemplifies these problems. Those, however, who inspect your music with due care must realize that all of your metrical complexities are subservient to the laws of expression. What comical effects, what breathless excitement you have communicated, for example, by the pages of syncopation in *Carnaval* and the *Davidsbündlertänze*! And at times your metrical incongruities

EXAMPLE 1.2A. *Excerpt from Beethoven's Symphony no. 7, third mvmt. (mm. 199–200), reproduced in Robert Schumann's essay "Das Komische in der Musik"*

EXAMPLE 1.2B. *Excerpt from Beethoven's Quintet op. 29, finale (mm. 124–28), discussed in "Das Komische in der Musik"*

seem to me to reflect the irreconcilable conflicts within your soul." His lips trembled with pain.

Hector, tactfully pretending not to notice Eusebius's emotion, took him and Florestan by the arms and guided them into as yet unexplored streets of the Rhythmic Quarter. As they walked, Florestan said, "It is quite true that I have often attempted to create comical effects and to express emotional conflicts with various rhythmical and metrical devices. And I am by no means the only composer to have done so." Again he took recourse to his sketchbook and notated two excerpts by Beethoven (Examples 1.2a and b), remarking, "The comical, bizarre effect of the first passage stems primarily from the semitone oscillations in the horns, which result in the intrusion of duple meter into the triple context. In the excerpt from the last movement of Beethoven's Quintet op. 29, the comedy stems from the struggle between two-four and six-eight meters.[6] Here is another more dramatic example by Beethoven of the effective employment of rhythmic and metrical conflict (Example 1.3); observe the *weighty pressing on weak beats*,[7] which produces a sense of duple meter that yields to the notated triple meter as the seventh chord is resolved. What perfect coordination between harmony and meter!"

Florestan and Eusebius had been noticing for some time that the din of the

EXAMPLE 1.3. *Excerpt from Beethoven's Symphony no. 3, first mvmt. (mm. 128–29), cited in Schumann's review of Christian Gottlieb Müller's Third Symphony*

EXAMPLE 1.4. *Fétis's first mutation type*

children's drums was receding into the distance. Hector told them, "We have now entered that part of the Quarter where the residents, including the children, are encouraged to speculate about rhythm and meter rather than just to perform complex patterns. I must introduce you to one of the masters who oversees their researches and pursues his own in his spare time—a man with whom you as well as I have had our disagreements, but who is nevertheless a fine musician.[8] I hope that we shall find him at home." He knocked at one of the doors, which was, after some delay, opened by a thoughtful-looking side-whiskered gentleman. "M. Fétis, I am sorry to interrupt your work," said Hector, "but I thought you would like to meet my two friends, Florestan and Eusebius, who are visiting this town for the first time." M. Fétis bowed and said, "Gentlemen, I am enchanted to see you. Please come in." He led them into his study and, by moving stacks of books and musical scores, made room for them on three chairs. Hector said, "We were just discussing rhythmic and metrical conflict—a subject which I know you have researched for some time." M. Fétis responded, "Indeed, I have. Just two years ago, I published a series of articles in the *Revue et Gazette musicale de Paris* in which I pondered how future generations of composers might make use of such conflicts."[9] Eusebius begged, "Pray unveil for us, Monsieur, what the future holds!" M. Fétis smiled and said, "There is much in the domain of rhythm that has not yet been exhausted, nor even broached, by the composers of today. Think, for example, about the possibility of 'mutation' or transformation of a meter that has been established within a piece of music. One type of mutation might take the form of the actual repositioning of the strong beat within the measure." He drew a rhythm on a blackboard that was mounted on his wall, then showed how the rhythm could be 'mutated' by shifting it in relation to the measure (Example 1.4). "This technique," he said, "could be applied within compositions as a form of variation, possibly during restatements of a theme."[10] M. Fétis continued, "In my articles, I also proposed another type of mutation, in which accentuation is modified *so as to create the effect of some new meter, even if the meter does not actually change.*" Again he drew two examples on the blackboard (Example 1.5). "Such mutation," he continued, "*could prepare the actual motion from one rhythm and metrical system to another.*"[11] In my example, I *take a passage in binary meter and superimpose ternary meter over it* ("*frappe de trois en trois sur un rhythme binaire*"), then actually change to a ternary meter.[12] The state of ambiguity that lies between the two meters prepares the actual establishment of the new meter. *The listener, still under the influence of the composition's overall meter, will preserve its impression in spite of the new superimposed meter; it is thus that the composer will be able to deceive his ear and actually pass into the*

EXAMPLE 1.5. *Fétis's second mutation type*

[new] *rhythm and meter. The music will have changed character, and the listener will not no-tice the moment of transition.*"[13] Hector nodded in agreement and said, "I, too, have, in a feuilleton in the *Journal des Débats* encouraged composers to explore as yet untried rhythmic and metrical effects, such as accentuation of the weak beat in-stead of the strong, the alternation of duple and triple groupings, the superim-posing of phrases *whose subdivisions bear to each other no compatible relation and have no points of contact other than the first beat*, the *episodic introduction of a melody based on a ternary rhythm into one based on four (or vice versa)*, and even *the intermittent use of sounds quite independent of both the main melody and the prevailing rhythm in the accom-paniment, sounds which are separated from one another by intervals that lengthen or dimin-ish in proportions not determinable in advance.*[14] There indeed remains much for future generations of composers to explore. But we must keep you no longer from your work." They all thanked M. Fétis and took their leave.

Outside, Florestan said to Hector, "I did not wish to embarrass you and our kind host while we were inside, but now I cannot resist pointing out that the very interesting techniques that M. Fétis and you have mentioned *are* already being used by composers today. In fact, I have frequently employed them myself." Eu-sebius smilingly interjected, "I remember one occasion on which you applied M. Fétis's first mutation type! Please pass me that sketchbook for a moment." When Florestan handed it to him, he jotted down the theme in Example 1.6a. "This was my idea for a passage near the beginning of the third movement of our Piano Sonata op. 11," he said. "I wrote it down and left it on the table while I went to the coffeehouse. When I returned, Florestan had 'mutated' the idea as follows" (and he wrote Example 1.6b). "Yes," said Florestan, "and since you approved, Eusebius, we used the mutated version in our sonata. Another passage that illus-trates this mutation type is found at mm. 26–27 of the 'Préambule' from *Carnaval*, where we shift a motive forward by one beat.[15] The second mutation type," Flo-restan continued, "plays a very large role in our works. Near the end of my very early Piano Quartet in C Minor, I transform triple meter into duple by first grouping eighth notes into twos, then actually altering the meter (Example 1.7a). There is also an example of such mutation near the end of the 'Préambule' from *Carnaval* (Example 1.7b)." Eusebius, meanwhile, had jotted down the passages that Florestan had mentioned and passed them to Hector. As Hector was study-

EXAMPLE 1.6A. *Sketch for the first Trio from Schumann's Piano Sonata op. 11, third mvmt., mm. 51–54, Deutsche Staatsbibliothek zu Berlin—Preußischer Kulturbesitz, Musikabteilung mit Mendelssohn-Archiv, Mus. ms. autogr. R. Schumann 35*

EXAMPLE 1.6B. *Later sketch for the same passage, Universitäts-und Landesbibliothek Bonn (ULB Bonn), Manuscripts Division, R. Schumann 14 (Sketchbook II), p. 5, brace 2*

ing them, Eusebius remarked, "Our young friend Johannes Brahms also seems to be very interested in exploring these mutation techniques. You remember the first movement of his Piano Sonata in F Minor, Florestan? It is in three-four time, but from the outset there are many duple groups of quarter notes. Just before the end of the exposition, there is another such duple passage, the duple grouping being achieved by a sequential pattern of falling fifths in quarter notes. All of these instances of the imposition of duple upon triple meter prepare the common time at the beginning of the development section" (see Examples 8.26 and 8.27).

Hector, having perused Eusebius's two examples, said, "You are right; these are examples of the procedures that M. Fétis mentions in his articles. The excerpt from *Carnaval* is a particularly effective mutation from what sounds like duple meter to triple meter, with a passage of powerful confrontation of the two meters beginning at the *fortissimo* marking. I find it interesting that while the first two bars sound as if they were in duple meter, you there maintain the notated three-four meter, whereas in the third bar you allow the duple meter to show itself undisguised." Florestan responded, "Much metrical conflict can be notated within the established metrical framework, but at times that framework must be overridden, or rather overwritten."

At this point, Hector said, "I must introduce you to one of the young residents of Euphonia who has been pondering the appropriate notation of metrical conflicts." He led them into a house within that same quiet portion of the Rhythmic Quarter in which a group of young people was engaged in a lively discussion about the opening theme of Beethoven's Piano Sonata op. 27 no. 1. Some of them argued that the theme should be rewritten so that the quarter notes became upbeats and the half notes downbeats, while others objected vociferously to any alteration of Beethoven's barring. A very young member of the group, apparently

EXAMPLE 1.7A. *Robert Schumann,* Piano Quartet in C Minor *(1828), ed. Wolfgang Boetticher, fourth mvmt., mm. 283–98. © 1979 by Heinrichshofen's Verlag, Wilhelmshaven, Germany. Ed. no. 1494. Used by permission of publisher.*

EXAMPLE 1.7B. *Robert Schumann,* Carnaval, *"Préambule," mm. 99–109*

no more than five years of age, piped up and said, "Even the greatest composers sometimes fall short of absolute precision of notation, and we should have no qualms about revising their notation in order to clarify the score for the performer. In the opening theme of Beethoven's Sonata op. 27 no. 1, the half-note chords are the most strongly accented events; they are the longest durations within the context, and some of them, moreover, act as appoggiatura six-four chords resolving to the dominant harmony. For these reasons, I support the renotation of these chords as downbeats."[16] Hector interrupted in order to introduce the boy, whose name was Hugo Riemann, to Florestan and Eusebius. He then

EXAMPLE 1.8A. *Chopin, Ballade no. 3, op. 47, mm. 69–73*

EXAMPLE 1.8B. *Riemann's renotation of the passage*

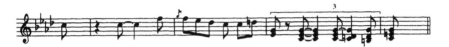

asked the young scholar to elaborate on his views on rebarring, particularly with reference to passages of metrical conflict.

Master Riemann complied with alacrity, saying, "I advocate renotation when it clarifies metrical conflicts that otherwise are likely to remain undiscovered by performers. In the Beethoven example, a subtle metrical conflict arises from harmonic ambiguity, that is, from the possibility of hearing the six-four chords either as unaccented continuations of existing tonic chords or as accented initiations of dominant harmony. Beethoven's notation conceals the conflict; performers playing from his notation will simply opt for the first of the two harmonic interpretations, tapering off each measure and deemphasizing the half-note chords. The rebarring brings the potentially accented nature of these chords into focus and forces performers to address the subtle conflict within the passage."

Florestan and Eusebius frowned during these comments, but Riemann continued without noticing their displeasure, "I have become aware of a type of metrical conflict that involves the intrusion of triple groups into duple contexts, the 'large triplet.'[17] Such triplets, easily overlooked by performers, can be rendered visually clearer by rebarring. There is a good example in the third Ballade of Chopin."[18] He shuffled through a sheaf of pages that lay before him—"notes for a book that he plans to write," Hector whispered to his friends—and drew out Example 1.8. "You will notice," Riemann continued, "that the large triplet in my renotation (Example 1.8b) is motivated by harmony; the triplet encompasses the duration of the cadential dominant.

"It would be wrong, however," he admitted, "to modify the composer's barring in all cases of metrical conflict. Imagine, for instance, a syncopated passage like this one." (He showed them Example 1.9a.) "If we were to turn the long durations into metrical downbeats, we would arrive at the following." (He showed them Example 1.9b.)[19] He continued, "This renotation implies that syncopation is nothing but an abrupt displacement (*ruckweise Verschiebung*) at 'NB. 1' followed by a realignment (*Wiedereinrenkung*) at 'NB. 2.' Syncopation is, however, actually a conflict between a basic meter (*Grundrhythmus*) and a simultaneously presented nonaligned meter that endures throughout the syncopated passage, as Herr Moritz Hauptmann has already stated.[20] The traditional notation, with its ties across the bar lines, makes that continuing conflict much clearer than the renotation.

EXAMPLE 1.9A. *Reconstruction of a syncopated passage discussed by Riemann*

EXAMPLE 1.9B. *Riemann's (deliberately) incorrect notation of a syncopated passage*

"Some metrical conflict," Riemann observed, "arises from the noncongruence of motivic lengths and metrical groups. Frequently, motives within a triple meter are two beats long; here is an example, Herr Florestan, from one of your own works (Example 1.10). The reverse, three-beat motives within a duple meter, is much less common.[21] When such conflicts appear in the music, we should by no means renotate the music in accordance with the conflicting elements. The notated meter remains in effect as a significant contender within the conflict, in fact, as the background without which the conflicting quality of other elements would be imperceptible.[22] Just as a harmonic sequence at times suspends the logic of harmonic progression on the surface while ultimately remaining subservient to it, so does this type of metrical conflict create a series of *pseudo-measures that for a time contradict the notated meter but that find their justification and motivation only through their continued subordination to the actual meter.*"[23]

When young Riemann paused, Eusebius said, "I find many of your arguments very convincing, Master Riemann. One of your ideas particularly intrigues me; aside from metrical conflict that occurs on the musical surface, you have also mentioned the possibility of larger-scale conflict—the 'large triplet,' which is actually a disturbance of phrase rhythm. The concept of large-scale metrical conflict is certainly worth exploring further." Florestan interjected, "Such large-scale conflicts, like those of smaller scale, must be used with care. I have reviewed a number of works in which there is at various points something missing or something superfluous in the phrase rhythm—that is, a conflict between the established phrase rhythm and shorter or longer units. In Amadeus Mereaux's *Grande Fantaisie*, for example, *in the first part of the third variation, there is, against all*

EXAMPLE 1.10. *Robert Schumann,* Novellette *op. 21 no. 4, mm. 108–14 (with grouping analysis by Riemann)*

norms of phrase rhythm, one measure too many.[24] Similarly, in Johann Friedrich Kittl's *Sechs Idyllen*, there is frequently a problem at section endings, *for example in no. 2, two measures before the end, the same in no. 3 and in no. 4, etc. The composer simply cannot finish at the right time.*[25] The same flaw can be found in this composer's *Drei Scherzi* op. 6, and in Ferdinand Hiller's *Etudes* op. 15."[26] Eusebius answered, "It seems to me that when such large-scale irregularities occur in the works of good composers, they are resolved at the appropriate time so that the listener is not left at the end of the work or movement with an unpleasant sense of incompleteness."[27] Florestan said, "In other works, the irregularity is so widespread that it becomes the norm and thus, again, has no unpleasant effect upon listeners once they become accustomed to it. I am thinking, Hector, of your works, especially of the *Symphonie fantastique.* The flexibility of large-scale meter seems to me to be *the most distinctive feature of your musical ideas. Your phrase rhythms appear to strive for the reestablishment of a primeval state in which the law of metrical accent* (Gesetz der Tactesschwere) *did not yet weigh upon music, and for the unfettered discourse* (ungebundene Rede) *and higher poetic punctuation* (höheren poetischen Interpunktion) *of Greek choruses, the Bible, and Jean Paul's prose. The novelist [Johann] Ernst Wagner's statement that the composer who completely veils and renders imperceptible the tyranny of meter will (at least apparently) liberate the art of music* seems to me to apply to your music."[28]

As Florestan concluded his remarks, the great organ that announces the hour to the Euphonians blared forth, and Florestan and Eusebius realized that it was almost time for them to begin their homeward journey. They bade farewell to young Riemann, and Hector led his friends back into the street. As they walked toward the coach-house, he thanked Florestan for his tribute, then said, "Master Riemann is an interesting youngster, is he not?" Florestan responded, "Yes, very interesting, though somewhat verbose. And I strongly disagree with his analysis of the opening theme from Beethoven's Sonata op. 27 no. 1. I find his hearing of the half-note six-four chords as accented appoggiaturas unconvincing. In m. 1, I hear an implied E♭ below the right-hand chord, and in m. 3, E♭ actually sounds in the bass; as a result, the right-hand chords do not suggest dominant, but tonic function to me, and I hear much less metrical conflict than does Master Riemann. I agree that the durational accents and harmonic changes in the passage are not coordinated, but that is not sufficient reason for a sweeping revision of Beethoven's notation!"

Eusebius, who had hardly been listening to Florestan's remarks, said, "The Rhythmic Quarter of Euphonia is a most fascinating place, and I have very much enjoyed our visits and conversations. I must share with you two ideas that have occurred to me here. First, it seems to me that metrical conflict can be reduced to two types of phenomena: to the association of unequal or noncongruent layers of motion on the one hand, and to the association of congruent but shifted layers on the other." Florestan interposed, "You are right. These two categories are implicit in Hector's description of rhythmic education in Euphonia; he mentions *the blending of irreconcilable rhythms* but also *the syncopated forms* (which, as Master Riemann stated, result from the conflict of simultaneously presented congruent but nonaligned layers). The two categories are also implicit in Hector's feuilleton. He writes of the alternation of duple and triple groupings, of the superimposing of phrases *whose subdivisions bear to each other no compatible relation and have no points of contact other than the first beat,* and of the *episodic introduction of a melody based on a ternary rhythm into one based on four (or vice versa)*, all of which techniques fit into the first category. He also mentions, however, accentuation of the weak beat instead of the strong, which would result in a conflict of the second type. M. Fétis's mutations also imply these two categories; those that involve the shifting of rhythms in relation to the bar line result in a conflict between two equivalent but non-aligned layers, whereas those in which a new grouping is superimposed onto the existing one result in a conflict between noncongruent layers." Eusebius said, "And young Hugo Riemann discussed conflicts engendered by the noncongruence of motive and meter and by the large-scale superimposing of duple and triple units, but also mentioned conflicts arising from syncopation or displacement.

"Second," Eusebius continued, "I have noticed suggestions of analogies between pitch and rhythm running like a thread through today's discourses on metrical conflict. Master Riemann's sequence analogy, which links the notions of surface and subliminal levels in the areas of pitch and rhythm, is an obvious example. Some of M. Fétis's mutations also imply such an analogy; his reference to motion from one meter to another, using passages of metrical conflict as a sort of pivot, recalls one of the most common techniques of modulation in the domain of pitch. My allusion to 'resolution' of large-scale conflicts hints at an analogy between metrical conflict and dissonance: the metrical conflicts are 'dissonances' that lead the listener to expect subsequent resolution."

Hector interjected, "I must tell you that I explicitly drew an analogy between rhythmic and metrical conflict and pitch dissonance in the feuilleton that I mentioned earlier, where I wrote: *'[Combinations of this sort] constitute in the domain of rhythm clusters and progressions analogous to the clusters and progressions that make up chords, melodies and modulation. There are such things as rhythmic dissonance; there are rhythmic consonances; there are rhythmic modulations.'*"[29] "A fascinating analogy," cried Florestan. "Here lies much food for thought for us and for later generations of musicians." They had now reached the coach-house, where Florestan's and Eusebius's conveyance was waiting. Having thanked Hector for acting as their guide and for introducing them to so many interesting people and ideas, they mounted their seats and waved to Hector as the coach moved off into the gathering dusk. Eusebius, fatigued from the promenade through Euphonia, almost immediately fell asleep. Florestan, who remained awake awhile longer, smilingly observed that the horses' hooves and Eusebius's soft, regular snores together produced a metrical dissonance of three pulses against four.

WALDSCENE: IDEAS OF METRICAL CONFLICT
IN THE TWENTIETH CENTURY

At dawn, they both awoke to sounds of scrabbling and thumping on the roof of the coach. The coachman apparently had noticed nothing out of the ordinary, for the vehicle continued to rumble through the snowy forest of the Harz. Florestan wrenched the window open and was about to stick out his head in an attempt to catch a glimpse of the roof when, with much flapping of wings and flying of feathers, a bird fluttered in and settled on Eusebius's shoulder. It was a bird of extraordinarily colorful plumage, but the men's attention was attracted primarily by a sheaf of paper which it carried in its beak and which, with an air of relief, it dropped into Eusebius's lap. They were even more astounded when, having released its burden, it began to speak. "Well met, my friends," it chirruped, "and thank you kindly for opening the window so promptly. It was cold out there, and landing on a moving coach is no simple matter, especially when one is burdened with a heavy theoretical manuscript." Florestan somewhat quaveringly asked the bird, "What manner of bird are you?" Their avian visitor chuckled and answered, "You two, of all people, should know me! I am a Prophet Bird." Eusebius, contorting his neck to catch a glimpse of the bird on his shoulder, exclaimed, "Of course! You look just as I imagined you many years ago." Meanwhile, Florestan had snatched the pages from Eusebius and had begun to leaf through them. "How uncanny!" he burst out. "This manuscript is concerned precisely with the issues that we were discussing in Euphonia." The Prophet Bird said, "Yes, I thought that it would interest you. Not only does the manuscript explore M. Berlioz's analogy between pitch and rhythm, but it makes mention of a large number of your compositions." When Eusebius inquired as to the author, the Prophet Bird said, "It is nobody you know—a music theorist from the late twentieth century." As Florestan and Eusebius gasped in amazement, the bird continued, "I see that you are eager to peruse the manuscript, so I shall leave it with you. I shall return someday to retrieve it. Farewell." The Prophet Bird fluttered out and soon disappeared in the depths of the forest.

The men might well have shrugged the episode off as a dream had the manuscript not remained in Florestan's hand. They stared at it in a daze for some minutes. Then Florestan shook himself and said, "Well, Eusebius, there is now sufficient light to read. Shall we?" Eusebius shut the window and moved to the seat beside his friend. They turned over the first leaf, and read:

Nineteenth-century references to metrical conflict are by no means numerous, and most of them are mere allusions to the topic rather than detailed discussions. In the twentieth century, the subject has been much more frequently addressed; most of the important large-scale studies of rhythm of the second half of the century discuss metrical conflict at least briefly. Grosvenor Cooper and Leonard Meyer, the authors of one of the earliest books of this century devoted entirely to rhythm, present brief analyses of conflicted passages by Brahms, Mozart, Dufay, and Beethoven, referring to the conflicts by a variety of terms, notably "metric crossing" and "rhythmic dissonance" (by which they mean superposition of nonequivalent layers), and "noncongruence" (by which they mean nonaligned statement of equivalent layers).[30] Conflict is much more central to Wallace Berry's discussion of meter. In his view, meter is "*not* to be equated with regularity" but is, "by definition, subject to fluctuation." Several of his analyses show how various determinants of meter move in and out of "accord" with the notation, and thus highlight the fluctuating, processive aspect of meter.[31] The term "in accord" implies the consonance/dissonance metaphor, and that metaphor is at some points explicitly invoked in Berry's discussion.[32]

Several studies of musical rhythm from the 1980s include interesting, though brief, investigations of metrical conflict. In *A Generative Theory of Tonal Music*, Lerdahl and Jackendoff, while hypothesizing a set of preference rules that listeners invoke when metrically interpreting tonal music, present some instances of passages where the musical evidence results in conflicting preferences and hence in metrical conflict.[33] In their presentation of preference rules for grouping structure (which they regard as separate from, but affecting meter), they also consider conflict; their designations of particular interpretations of grouping as "preferred" do not negate the possibility that some aspects of the music may conflict with those interpretations.[34] Joel Lester refers in *The Rhythms of Tonal Music* to a state of "nesting" of metrical levels, but also to the possibility of metrical levels that do not nest, and gives examples from Mozart, Schumann, and Brahms.[35]

Carl Schachter's articles on rhythm contain a considerable amount of discussion of metrical conflict.[36] Schachter analyzes excerpts containing "incommensurable levels," for example, a seven-against-two conflict by Mozart, a two-against-three conflict in a work of Beethoven, and similar conflicts from Schumann's *Davidsbündlertanz* op. 6 no. 1 (which he terms "rhythmic dissonances.")[37] He also gives examples of the nonaligned association of congruent layers; in his analysis of Schumann's op. 6 no. 1, for example, he shows that the music encourages two ways of parsing the passage into six-quarter-note and twelve-quarter-note groups. Schachter's discussion of Mendelssohn's "Song without Words" op. 102 no. 4 draws attention to a similar conflict; he demonstrates that the work is permeated by a struggle for supremacy between two metrical schemes, one (beginning on the notated downbeats) being strongly articulated by the accompaniment, the other (beginning on third beats) articulated by the melody. Schachter's durational reduction traces this conflict through the entire piece, showing the two layers of motion moving out of and back into phase.[38] Schachter's and Berry's demonstrations of the large-scale processes involving metrical conflict significantly influence the approach adopted in this volume. 🌸

Florestan sighed, "So far, this manuscript is quite boring." Eusebius agreed, but said, "Of course it is boring for us; we are not familiar with the writings that the author cites. But let us read on; perhaps it will become more interesting."

A number of the authors mentioned thus far allude to or actually employ the terms "consonance" and "dissonance" in connection with metrical conflict. These, and other twentieth-century applications of these terms to rhythmic and metrical structure to be mentioned below, do not seem to descend from those of the nineteenth century; to my knowledge, none of the numerous twentieth-century writers who have employed this metaphor has mentioned its origin in Berlioz's writings.

Not all twentieth-century writers have applied the metaphor in the same manner; three quite different usages can be discerned. One of the earliest, that of Henry Cowell, appears to be unique. Cowell's discussion of rhythm is based on his perception of its close relationship to pitch; he regards pitch as greatly accelerated rhythm.[39] Taking his departure from this basic assumption, Cowell develops numerous analogies between pitch and rhythm. He refers to combinations of "times" (essentially, meters) as rhythmic "intervals," and applies the term "in harmony" to rhythmic combinations based on ratios that produce pitch consonances, such as 2/1, 3/2, and 5/4. The wording "in harmony" hints at the consonance-dissonance metaphor. It is noteworthy that Cowell, rigidly following a pitch-rhythm analogy, regards as consonant rhythmic relationships that most other writers would deem "dissonant" (3/2 and 5/4!).[40]

Concurrently with Cowell, Charles Seeger also pursued analogies between pitch and rhythm, and specifically the consonance-dissonance metaphor.[41] Arguing that "rhythmic harmony" should be recognized "as a category on a par with tonal harmony" (p. 26), he proceeds to investigate the nature of "the rhythmic interval and chord" and to "classify the rhythmic consonances and dissonances." Although his terminology is similar to Cowell's, his application of the consonance-dissonance metaphor is quite different. Seeger defines rhythmic relationships such as "two against three" and "three against four" as "rhythmic dissonances," basing the definition of consonance and dissonance not on criteria derived from pitch theory but on the nature of the rhythmic phenomena themselves, namely on the degree of alignment of rhythmic layers. He complains that modern music still favors simple dissonances such as "two against three" and "three against four," and encourages composers to employ more complex "rhythmic intervals" such as 5/6, 5/7, or 6/7. He hints at a categorization of these intervals in terms of intensity of dissonance: "The classification of the rhythmic intervals in their chordal (vertical) sounding may be accorded the terms mild, medium and strong, starting with 2/3 and graduating toward such as 4/7 . . ." (p. 27).

The conception of rhythmic dissonance as an association of nonaligned layers underlies numerous later applications of the consonance-dissonance metaphor. Whereas Joseph Schillinger's theory of rhythm, as set down in his *System of Musical Composition*, does not include the terms "consonance" and "dissonance," the theory is based to a large extent on the notion of interferences of periodicities, which suggests conflict produced by the association of noncongruent layers.[42] Schillinger indicates how the interference of two or more noncongruent periodicities creates resultant rhythms and demonstrates, in a variety of meters, the resultants of three-against-two and four-against-three dissonance in the form of "vamps" (pp. 30–31). Schillinger's *Encyclopedia of Rhythms* expands upon these pages of the *System*; this book is a catalog of resultant rhythms of dissonances.[43] In the introduction to the latter volume, Charles Colin, one of Schillinger's students, explicitly designates superpositions of noncongruent layers as "dissonances." His use of the dissonance metaphor, then, is similar to Seeger's. Interestingly, Colin drifts into the Cowellian application of the metaphor at one point; his distinction between greater or lesser rhythmic dissonance depends on the degree of dissonance of the pitch intervals suggested by the ratios involved, recalling Cowell's rigid analogy between pitch and rhythmic intervals. Colin does not, however, follow through on this analogy: he classifies 3/2, for example, as a dissonance in the rhythmic domain.[44]

Other authors mentioned earlier, namely Cooper and Meyer, Berry, and Schachter, for the most part use the consonance-dissonance metaphor in the same manner as does Seeger. Maury Yeston's *Stratification of Musical Rhythm* is a larger-scale development of the Seegerian application of the consonance-dissonance metaphor.[45] Yeston describes a number of ways in which strata of motion can be produced in musical works; whereas he stresses stratification through pitch structure, devoting an entire chapter to it (chapter 3), he also considers attack point, timbre, dynamics, density, and pattern recurrence as delineators of layers of motion.[46] Yeston then defines rhythmic consonance and dissonance as products of the interaction of numerically congruent and incongruent layers, respectively.[47] The primary focus of his discussion of rhythmic dissonance is not on the dissonant states themselves, nor on the manner in which these states are deployed within musical works (Yeston analyzes no complete works or movements), but on the rhythms arising from the interaction of noncongruent layers, i.e., on resultant rhythms. Much of his discussion of metrical dissonance centers on the compositional exploitation of the resultant of two-against-three dissonance.[48] His final chapter explores other dissonant combinations in a more abstract manner.

Yeston and others who adhere to Seeger's application of the consonance-dissonance metaphor regard only associations of incommensurate layers of motion as dissonant. In other words, dissonance is defined by these authors in an arithmetical manner; if the constituents of a rhythmic relationship are based on incommensurate integers (integers that are not multiples or factors of each other), the relationship is deemed dissonant. Wallace Berry, however, begins to shift the definition of dissonance into the geometric rather than arithmetic domain when he refers to "metric asymmetries as horizontal and vertical *noncongruities* . . . in precise parallel to the geometric sense having to do with the potential for exact alignment (or nonalignment) of figures in superposition."[49] My article "Some Extensions of the Concepts of Metrical Consonance and Dissonance" expands upon the geometric model; nonalignment of layers is taken to produce dissonance, no matter what the arithmetic relationship between those layers might be.[50]

The shift from an arithmetic to a geometric approach brings a second type of metrical dissonance into play; dissonance may arise not only from the association of arithmetically incommensurate layers, but also from the nonaligned association of equivalent (congruent) layers. These are precisely the two types of metrical conflict at which nineteenth-century writers already hinted. Numerous twentieth-century writers show an awareness of the two types, applying to them a variety of terms. We have seen that Cooper and Meyer refer to "metric crossing" as well as "non-congruence," and that Schachter analyzes examples of both types. In two succinct articles, Karl Hlawicka discusses two rhythmic/metrical phenomena that correspond precisely to our two types of conflict: his "Verwechslung" (interchange or substitution—apparently used in the sense of substitution of noncongruent layers for potential and expected congruent ones) involves the superimposing of noncongruent layers, and his "Verschiebung" (displacement) the nonaligned presentation of congruent layers. He gives examples of "Verwechslung" in various ratios (3/2, 4/3, 5/2, 5/3, 6/5, 7/6, and 8/7) and categorizes them by the manner in which the antimetrical layers are produced (dynamic accents, melodic contour, harmony, etc.). His discussion of "Verschiebung" is similarly organized, involving a quantitative categorization of examples (by amount of displacement in relation to the notated meter) and a qualitative one (by origin of the displaced layers, such as register, ornamentation, melodic grouping, and stress).[51]

Hlawicka comes close to a conceptualization of the two types of metrical conflict as subcategories of a single broad phenomenon, a conceptualization that I brought to the surface in "Some Extensions." My manner of applying the consonance-dissonance metaphor has been taken up by a number of writers, including Peter Kaminsky and Richard Cohn. Cohn has formalized the definitions of rhythmic consonance and dissonance and has presented superb analyses showing how dissonance, particularly on large-scale levels, shapes entire movements by Mozart and Beethoven.[52] Kaminsky's work on the music of Robert Schumann will be discussed in detail below.

Florestan said, "Ah, the next section seems to include more names with which we are familiar!" They read on with renewed interest.

Aside from theoretical writings on rhythm, some books and articles dealing with composers in whose music metrical conflict plays a significant role have provided valuable insights into the nature of such conflict. Studies of Beethoven's music, including Andrew Imbrie's "'Extra' Measures and Metrical Ambiguity in Beethoven," David Epstein's study of the first movement of the *Eroica Symphony*, William Rothstein's investigation of numerous sonata movements, and my own analysis of the first movement of the *Ghost Trio*, among many others, have drawn attention to that composer's interesting usages of metrical conflict.[53] Writings about the music of Brahms, not surprisingly, furnish further examples.[54] Analyses of a number of other composers could be cited here.[55] Let us turn, however, to the Schumann literature, which is rich in relevant material, ranging from brief comments on Schumann's rhythmic inventiveness, through lists or detailed analyses of conflicted passages, to large-scale studies of Schumann's rhythmic style.

Virtually every author who has written about Schumann makes some mention of the fact that his music is particularly interesting from the standpoint of rhythm and meter. August Reissman already recognized in 1865 that the "most pleasing treatment of syncopation" was "a primary characteristic of Schumann's music." Early in the twentieth century, Walter Dahms similarly remarked that "it was in Schumann's [music] that syncopation assumed its reign." Wolfgang Gertler's study of Schumann's early piano works includes numerous insightful discussions of syncopation and other types of rhythmic conflict. Daniel Mason, writing about the early piano works, refers to the "whimsicality" expressed in the "boldness of their rhythms, especially their use of strong dislocations of accent and long-continued syncopations."[56]

One early-twentieth-century writer, Christian Knayer, ventures beyond mere recognition of Schumann's rhythmic ingenuity by identifying and categorizing a large number of relevant musical passages from Schumann's piano music. His first category, accentuation of upbeats and syncopation in one or both hands, corresponds roughly to our second type of conflict (association of equivalent layers in a nonaligned fashion). Knayer's second category includes actual changing of the meter through repeated insertion of asymmetrical motives in both hands (but with preservation of the meter on paper), as well as combination of two different meters; this category corresponds to our first type (association of noncongruent layers). Knayer proceeds to list many examples of each type (unfortunately by title only, not by measure number). Although his comments on the examples are rather superficial, it is obvious that he studied Schumann's metrical conflicts quite carefully—the first writer, to my knowledge, to do so. Aside from listing examples, Knayer makes some valuable, though brief, comments on the meaning of metrical conflict in Schumann, mentioning that it can suggest vagueness, dreaming, indecisiveness, and hovering, or that it can create humorous, witty effects.[57]

Later German writings on Schumann have continued to deal, in varying degrees of detail, with Schumann's metrical structures. Whereas meter is not the focus of Hans Kohlhase's investigation of Schumann's chamber music, he does make numerous remarks about metrical conflict. He refers to examples of the passing over of the downbeat by syncopation, the placement of the most significant harmonies on the weaker beats, and the consistent accentuation of weak beats, and draws attention to the fact that metrical conflict is the primary source of beauty and charm in many of Schumann's themes.[58] In a dissertation focusing on Schumann's *Humoreske* op. 20, Bernhard Appel refers to "metrical polyphony" and displacement, and comments on the relation of these phenomena to musical humor.[59] Arnfried Edler draws attention to metrical conflict in many of his analytical comments on Schumann's works.[60] Gerhard Dietel argues that Schumann approached the dissolution of "the tyranny of meter" by his rhythmic displacements ("rhythmischen Gegeneinanderverschiebungen").[61] 🎵

"It is gratifying to learn that our music will generate so much interest!" said Eusebius. "But not surprising!" countered Florestan. "Our rhythmic structures are unique, if I say so myself!" "True, true," Eusebius agreed smugly.

As they read the following sentence, their gratification gave way to horror:

The title of Dieter Schnebel's important essay "Rückungen — Ver-rückungen" puns on the double meaning of "verrückt" ("displaced" as well as "insane"), and the article draws a connection between Schumann's mental deterioration and his use of pervasive displacement. Schnebel analyzes conflicts of both categories in numerous works throughout Schumann's life and notes particularly sharp conflicts of the second type in works from periods during which Schumann suffered from severe mental disturbances and psychic strains. The idea that Schumann's metrical dissonances might be a symbol of mental illness will be further addressed in later chapters of this book.[62]

Discussion of Schumann's metrical conflicts is not restricted to the German literature. A sensitive recent account of displacement in Schumann's music is found in Charles Rosen's book *The Romantic Generation*. Rosen, as a fine performer, is able to perceive and to illuminate some of the visceral aspects of Schumann's rhythm: its "shock value," the sense of "competing system[s] of rhythm," and the effect of "dislocation." He writes eloquently on some of Schumann's reasons for pursuing "out-of-phaseness" — his desire to represent "anxiety" and his "idiosyncratic pleasure in hidden contradictions."[63]

There exist several studies of Schumann's metrical conflicts that fall more into the category of theory and analysis than those mentioned so far. Melitta Honsa's dissertation on syncopation, hemiola and meter change in Schumann's instrumental works and Mary Evans Johnson's dissertation on metrical anomaly both present categorizations of metrical conflicts and provide illustrations of the various categories from Schumann's works.[64] Honsa categorizes syncopation as follows: simple syncopation (a momentary breaking away from the metrical accentuation pattern); continuous syncopation (chains of syncopations); supported ("gestützt") syncopation (only one or some of the voices participate in syncopation); and unsupported syncopation (all voices take part in the syncopation). She categorizes hemiolas into those arising from syncopation and those arising from melodic grouping, then discusses actual meter change (in which area she feels Schumann was a pioneer). Johnson's categories of metrical anomalies are quite different from Honsa's. They include empty downbeats; lilt (where the role of the third beat in triple time as upbeat or afterbeat is ambiguous); consistent metrical displacement (our second category of conflict); oblique harmonic rhythm; metrical repositioning (which is equivalent to our first category of conflict); hemiola (which also falls within the first category); metrical flexing (brief insertions of noncompatible meters); and polymeter (by which she means superposition of lines with different time signatures). Johnson considers in some detail the performance problems created by these anomalies. Her dissertation is even richer than Honsa's in examples from Schumann's oeuvre. Both authors, however, present the examples out of context without investigating their role within the respective compositions.

Peter Kaminsky, using the conceptual framework from my article "Some

Extensions" with many useful additions of his own, does turn his attention toward the function of metrical dissonance within large contexts.[65] He provides a detailed analysis, for example, of the succession of metrical consonance and dissonance in the "Préambule" and the "Marche des Davidsbündler" from *Carnaval*, and broadens the context even further by pointing out that the "Marche" picks up and resolves some of the dissonances of the "Préambule." Through this and other analyses, Kaminsky is able to demonstrate that rhythm and meter participate both in the forging of coherent single movements and of unified cycles. Kaminsky's work is by far the most thoroughgoing investigation of metrical dissonance in Schumann's music thus far.

The above summary reveals that there has been a significant number of discussions, some brief, some detailed, of metrical conflict in the music of Schumann. In the present volume I attempt to go beyond these discussions in a number of ways. First, I take into consideration a larger body of Schumann's oeuvre than do earlier studies, in the hope that a clearer picture of Schumann's metrical ingenuity will thereby emerge. I discuss a large number of instrumental works, but also take vocal music into account. Second, I investigate Schumann's compositional process as it relates to metrical matters, an issue that has hardly been considered in print. Third, I attempt to put Schumann's rhythmic techniques into perspective by discussing similar (though usually less striking) techniques in the works of composers whose music he knew. Fourth, and most important, I investigate not only brief passages but entire works and movements in order to track, in greater detail than earlier authors, the roles of metrical conflicts within their actual contexts, and the relationships between metrical structure and other musical elements.

My basic theoretical tools in these endeavors are those hinted at in nineteenth-century sources and developed to some extent in earlier twentieth-century sources: pitch-rhythm analogies, in particular the consonance/dissonance metaphor and other concepts that grow out of it; and the notion of two classes of metrical conflict or dissonance. These elements of my approach are unfolded in a systematic manner in the following chapter. 🎜

They were about to read on when, glancing out of the window, Florestan noticed that they were entering the gates of Düsseldorf. Hastily, they stowed the manuscript in Florestan's bag and gathered their other effects together. At the coach-house, they dismounted and strode off toward the Bilkerstraße.

TWO

Metrical Consonance and Dissonance:
Definitions and Taxonomy

Florestan and Eusebius had intended to go home immediately to share their recent experiences with Chiarina, but as they approached their favorite coffeehouse, the enticing aroma of fresh coffee wafted over them, and they determined
that a few cups were just what they needed after their night in the coach. They
entered and sat down at their usual table. Having ordered, received, and sampled
their beverages, they propped the Prophet Bird's manuscript against the coffee
urn and continued to read where they had left off.

LAYERS OF MOTION

Several nineteenth-century theorists imply a conceptualization of musical meter
as a set of interacting layers of motion, each layer consisting of a series of approximately equally spaced pulses.[1] Fétis's wording *"frappe de trois en trois sur un
rhythme binaire,"* for example, implies a set of three layers: an underlying pulse
layer, a layer that groups those pulses into twos (resulting in the *rhythme binaire*), and a third layer that groups the pulses into threes. Hauptmann's (and
after him Riemann's) definition of syncopation as the interaction of two series
(*"Reihen"*) of durations, and Riemann's discussion of the imposition on a meter
of motives noncongruent with that meter, similarly suggest a model of superimposed layers of pulses.[2] This model, which has been explicitly embraced by a
number of twentieth-century theorists, particularly by Maury Yeston, Fred
Lerdahl and Raymond Jackendoff, Richard Cohn, and John Roeder, also underlies this study.[3] In the following paragraphs, I elaborate upon the model and
the numerous concepts that grow out of it. 🐦

22

Florestan mused, "The conception of meter as a set of interacting layers of motion appeals to me because it suggests a link between music and our lives. Our heartbeat is an uninterrupted pulse that spans our entire life. That pulse is overlaid with other more or less regular layers, some of them less continuous than our pulse, many of them much slower—for example, our breaths, our footfalls, our recurrent daily activities, and so on."

I define the meter of a work as the union of all layers of motion (i.e., series of regularly recurring pulses) active within it. The layers that contribute to the meter of a work can be divided into three classes: the pulse layer, micropulses, and interpretive layers. The pulse layer is the most quickly moving *pervasive* series of pulses, generally arising from a more or less constant series of attacks on the musical surface. (The omission of a few pulses here and there does not seriously disrupt the pulse layer once it is clearly established.) More quickly moving layers, or "micropulses," may intermittently be woven into the metrical tapestry of a work as coloristic embellishments. Of greater significance are series of regularly recurring pulses that move more slowly than the pulse layer. These allow the listener to "interpret" the raw data of the pulse layer by organizing its pulses into larger units. The pulses of each "interpretive layer" subsume a constant number of pulse-layer attacks; an interpretive layer can therefore be characterized by an integer denoting this constant quantity. I refer to this integer n as the "cardinality" of the layer, and to an interpretive layer of cardinality n as an "n-layer."

I conceive of interpretive layers not as components of an abstract, "given" metrical grid, but as perceptible phenomena arising from the regular recurrence of musical events of various kinds. Interpretive layers often arise from a regularly spaced succession of what Lerdahl and Jackendoff call phenomenal accents—"event[s] at the musical surface that give emphasis or stress to a moment in the musical flow."[4] Dynamic accent, shown in scores by markings like *sf, fz, rf*, and by various hairpins and carets, is a particularly obvious type of phenomenal accent. Such accentuation is, however, also produced by the placement of long durations among short ones (agogic or durational accents), thickly textured events among more thinly textured ones (density accents), by dissonant events among consonant ones, by registral high and low points (registral accents), by the affixing of an ornament to a note, by changes in harmony and melody (new-event accents)—in short, by any perceptible deviation from an established pattern.[5] A succession of accents occurring at regular intervals—that is, the highlighting of every nth member of the pulse layer—results in the establishment of an interpretive layer of cardinality n.

The following musical excerpts, drawn from the music of Robert Schumann, demonstrate the generation of interpretive layers by accentuation. In the left hand of Example 2.1, regularly recurring dynamic accents carve a 6-layer out of the sixteenth-note pulse (shown by the uppermost series of 6s). Registral (or contour) accents, created by the low points within the left-hand line, rein-

EXAMPLE 2.1. Intermezzo *op. 4 no. 4, mm. 8–9*

force this 6-layer. Another 6-layer, coinciding with the dotted-quarter-note beats in Example 2.1 (shown by the lower series of 6s), is created by durational accents (the longest note values in the right hand) and by new-event accents in the harmonic domain (i.e., by the harmonic rhythm). In Example 2.2, one 6-layer (1 = 8th) arises from a series of dynamic and durational accents; the dynamically accented attacks within the first violin part are also the longest durations. Durational and registral (low point) accents in the cello part, as well as new-event harmonic accents (harmonic changes), create another 6-layer whose attacks coincide with the downbeats of the notated meter. ❦

Florestan said, "I am suddenly seized by an irresistible urge to order a slice of *Torte.*" He beckoned to a waiter, and ordered a three-layer *Schwarzwälder-kirschtorte.* Carefully keeping the manuscript away from the icing, they continued their perusal.

Left-hand durational accents contribute to the creation of a clear 6-layer in Example 2.3 (1 = 8th). Regularly recurring density accents and new-event harmonic accents reinforce this layer. In the uppermost voice of the first two measures of the excerpt, melodic new-event accents establish a 3-layer, while the left-hand half- and quarter-note attacks suggest a 2-layer.[6] In Example 2.4, registral accents (low points) create one 6-layer (1 = 8th), and durational accents (the quarter notes immediately following the sixteenth notes) create another. ❦

EXAMPLE 2.2. *String Quartet op. 41 no. 3, second mvmt., mm. 193–96*

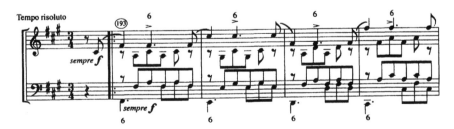

EXAMPLE 2.3. Davidsbündler *op. 6 no. 2, mm. 1–4*

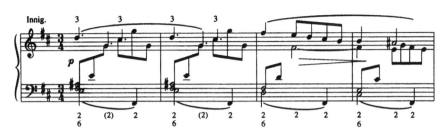

Eusebius interjected, "The latter 6-layer is enhanced by one's perception of the first quarter note in each measure as an appoggiatura." Florestan added, "True, but my crescendo markings detract from the appoggiatura effect since they prevent the pianist from tapering off in the usual fashion during the resolution. In fact, if the crescendo markings are followed, the second quarter note in each measure receives a dynamic accent, which results in yet another 6-layer." Eusebius said, "So many 6-layers! I think the pianist would have to choose to articulate just two of them; otherwise, every quarter-note pulse would be accented, and from these undifferentiated pulses *no* 6-layers would clearly emerge!" They continued to read:

The above excerpts raise a number of significant points about interpretive layers. Example 2.1 bears out the earlier statement that omission of some attacks of an interpretive layer does not significantly disrupt that layer; the 6-layer created by dynamic accents is perfectly perceptible although two expected accents are missing.[7] The examples also show that various accent types generally work together rather than in isolation to form interpretive layers. (I do not regard coinciding series of accents as distinct interpretive layers; rather, I regard them as collaborating in the creation of a single layer.)

Finally, the above examples show the importance of pitch structure, specifically of change in the harmonic or melodic domain, in the formation of layers;

EXAMPLE 2.4. Davidsbündler *op. 6 no. 1, mm. 1–4*

EXAMPLE 2.5. *Symphony no. 3, first mvmt., mm. 1–9*

new-event accents in these domains are among the most frequent producers of layers of motion. Not only surface-level melodic or harmonic change, but also change below the surface forms layers of motion.[8] A good example is found at the opening of Schumann's Third Symphony (Example 2.5), where subsurface melodic progression occurs at a regular rate; a rising arpeggiation of the tonic triad is succeeded by a descending stepwise line, each pitch of both the rising and the falling gesture occupying twelve eighth-note pulses.

The above examples also reveal that accentuation is not the only factor that can gather pulses together to form interpretive layers; a variety of musical grouping techniques independent of accentuation may be active as well.[9] Notational devices such as slurs and beams of consistent length, for instance, may suggest interpretive layers. In Example 2.1, slurring reinforces the 6-layer produced in the left hand by dynamic and registral accentuation. In Example 2.3, the left-hand slurs contribute to the 6-layer created by durational, density and harmonic new-event accents. ❦

Eusebius observed, "As the author states, slurring can reinforce layers produced by other means; it rarely, however, creates perceptible layers on its own. In Example 2.2, for instance, I would not regard the recurring slurs in the first violin part as forming a layer; there are so many other features that create prominent layers that the effect of these little slurs is negligible."

Repetition of various types frequently creates interpretive layers. In Example 2.1, a 2-layer (1=16th) arises from the regular recurrence in the left hand of particular pitches—of C, then A in the first measure, and of E, then C♯/D♭ in the second. The repetition of patterns rather than individual pitches, be they melodic, rhythmic, harmonic, or any combination of the three, contributes even more commonly to the creation of interpretive layers. Most of the passages cited above illustrate such pattern repetition. In Example 2.1, the rhythmic pattern "quarter-eighth" in the first two beats of the right hand reinforces the 6-layer created by harmonic change, as does the left hand's simultaneously presented pitch and contour pattern (a complete neighbor figure followed by a downward leap, an upward leap, then C-B). In Example 2.2, the repetition of rhythmic

EXAMPLE 2.6. *2-layers in the* Presto in G Minor

patterns in all instruments reinforces the 6-layers. The second violin and viola also establish 2-layers by repeated third- or fourth-oscillations in eighth notes. In the first two measures of Example 2.3, exact repetition of pitches and rhythm reinforces the 6-layer. In the next two measures, a repeated rhythmic pattern in the right hand (a quarter followed by four eighths) has the same effect. In Example 2.4, repetitions of rhythmic patterns reinforce the 6-layers, and in the first six measures of Example 2.5, repetition of a two-measure-long rhythmic pattern corroborates the 12-layer.[10]

Florestan, swallowing his last mouthful of *Torte*, commented, "In our works, we have fully explored the many ways of producing layers of motion that the author has mentioned. Do you recall our inventiveness with 2-layers (1=16th) in the original finale of our Sonata in G minor, op. 22? The generation of the 2-layer by dynamic accentuation is suggested in mm. 1, 2, 5, 6, 9, and 10, in all of which we stress the third sixteenth notes (Example 2.6a). In mm. 11–12 (Example 2.6b), we articulate the 2-layer more clearly by a series of dynamic accents, and reinforce that layer with slurs. In mm. 3–4 (Example 2.6a), 7–8, and 13–14, the attacks of an eighth-note melody create a 2-layer. The same is true in mm. 99–106

(Example 2.6c), and in the similar passages in mm. 129–36 and 337–44, where
the triplet eighths have exactly the same duration as the regular eighth notes in
mm. 3–4 and 7–8.

"In m. 14, the 2-layer arises not only from melodic attacks but also from density accents within the right-hand figure. Such accents also play a role in mm.
43–52, where every second sixteenth-note attack is thicker in texture (Example
2.6d). In these measures, pitch repetition in the uppermost voice is a second factor that contributes to the production of a 2-layer; the first two upper-voice duple
attacks in each measure are the same in pitch. Note repetition articulates the
2-layer even more clearly in mm. 107–18; in the sixteenth-note inner voice, such
repetition marks off duple durations (F's in m. 107, E♭'s in m. 108, etc.). Many
other passages in the movement are based on 2-layers—remarkably many for a
movement ostensibly in 6/16 time—but the variety of methods of layer production in the movement is, I believe, exhausted by those that I have mentioned."
Eusebius, who had been pursuing his own train of thought, now queried, "Given
the many different means by which interpretive layers can be produced, would
not any piece of music be absolutely riddled with them?" Florestan said, "You are
right. I see that the author addresses this issue."

Layers of motion are ubiquitous in pieces of music. As listeners, however, we inevitably focus on those interpretive layers that are most perceptible
and filter out those that are relatively hard to hear. In many cases, the most
perceptible layers are those that are articulated by the greatest number of musical features. A layer expressed, for instance, only by pattern repetition will
be less perceptible than one delineated by pattern repetition in conjunction
with accentuation. Thus, in Example 2.4, consideration of pattern repetition
alone would uncover four patterns, each six eighth-note pulses in length, and
hence each potentially suggesting a 6-layer; one pattern begins with the lowest bass notes, a second with the sixteenth notes, a third with the quarter
notes on the notated downbeats, and a fourth on the notated second beats. If
we take accentuation into account, however, as any listener would, two of
these layers move into the perceptual forefront: the layer formed by the recurring pattern beginning on the upbeats and by registral accentuation, and
the layer formed by the recurring pattern beginning on the downbeats in conjunction with durational accentuation (and the unnotated dynamic accentuation that most performers intuitively add to appoggiaturas and suspensions).
Similarly, in Example 2.2, two potential 2-layers arise from repeated patterns
in the inner voices. One, the pulses of which coincide with metrically weak
eighth notes, is formed by repetition of the vertical interval pairs F♯/A and
A/C♯, then E/G♯ and G♯/C♯, etc. The other, whose pulses coincide with quarter-
note beats, is formed by the repetition of the pairs A/C♯ and F♯/A, then G♯/C♯
and G♯/E, etc. The latter of these layers is much more perceptible, for it is at
least partially reinforced by accents (durational accents in the cello and dynamic accents in the first violin). 🎵

Eusebius observed, "The perceptibility of layers, of course, depends to a large extent on the performer, who must decide which layers to bring out. Frequently, the composer's notation will make clear which layers are intended to be prominent. In Example 2.2, our placement of one of the 2-layers on the metrical beats indicates that that layer is to be brought out. Had we wished the performer to emphasize the metrically weak 2-layer, we would have affixed dynamic accents to its pulses." They read on:

Not always is mere quantity of articulative musical features an indicator of perceptibility, for some features are more potent delineators of layers than others, and can form very clearly perceptible layers of motion independently of other factors.[11] One such feature is accentuation arising from harmonic change ("new-event" accentuation in the harmonic domain). In most pre-twentieth-century music, such change takes place in a regular fashion, sometimes on the surface level, sometimes below the surface. Layers of motion formed in this manner, often termed "harmonic rhythms," are very easy for us as Western listeners to hear, perhaps because we are conditioned to attend primarily to pitch. Also of great perceptual significance are dynamic accents. These are perhaps the most obvious of accents; many musicians immediately think of them when they hear the word "accent." Dynamic accents, like accents of harmonic change, often act in isolation to create prominent interpretive layers.[12] 🌿

Eusebius looked at his watch and said to Florestan, "Now that we have reached the end of a section, we should go home; Chiarina will be worried about us." Florestan responded, "We shall go very soon, but first I must wash down my *Torte* with one more cup of coffee." He placed his order, and while they waited for the coffee, they began the next section:

INTERACTION OF LAYERS

In the above examples, as in most tonal music, more than one clearly perceptible interpretive layer is active at once. These layers interact in one of two ways: they align (or "nest," to use Joel Lester's term) or they do not. A set of layers aligns when each pulse of each interpretive layer coincides with a pulse of every faster-moving layer. This state of alignment always exists when only one interpretive layer is imposed on a pulse layer. Two or more interpretive layers, however, may or may not align with each other. I refer to the metrical state resulting from the alignment of interpretive layers as "metrical consonance." The appropriateness of this metaphorical use of a term traditionally applied to pitch rests on the literal meaning of the word "consonance"; metrical consonance exists when pulses *sound together*. The metrical state arising when interpretive layers do not sound together can, applying the same metaphor, be termed "metrical dissonance."

Before we investigate these two states more closely, let us briefly consider the adjective "metrical." Its aptness is obvious when states of alignment or non-alignment result from the interaction of layers whose pulses are metrical beats, or beats above the level of the bar line (hypermetrical beats, or hyperbeats). But what of sets of layers whose pulses are submetrical, in some cases not even notationally present (for instance, the micropulse arising from superpositions of eighth notes and triplet eighth notes)? It might be argued that sets containing such layers should not be termed "metrical" consonances or dissonances. Since, however, I am defining meter as the union of all layers of motion active within a composition, I include even these submetrical interactions under the terms "metrical consonance or dissonance." In a later section, I introduce a series of more specific terms by which interactions of submetrical layers are distinguished from interactions of larger scale.

Consonance

Metrical consonance, the normal state of pre-twentieth-century tonal music, involves the aligned or nested presentation of interpretive layers whose cardinalities are multiples/factors of each other.[13] What is usually termed "the meter" of a work is in fact a particular consonance that functions as the normative metrical state of that work. Three-four meter, for instance, is a consonance consisting of a nested 6-layer and a 2-layer (1 = 8th) imposed on an eighth-note pulse, six-eight meter a consonance consisting of a nested 6-layer and a 3-layer imposed on the same pulse, nine-eight meter a consonance composed of a nested 9-layer and a 3-layer, and so on. I refer to the nested layers that form the normative metrical consonance of a work as "metrical layers."

In clearly metrical music, one of the metrical interpretive layers generally assumes particular significance for the listener, its pulses becoming reference points for all rhythmic activity in the given work. The layer formed by these pulses frequently, though not always, occupies a privileged position in the score, being rendered visually apparent by notational features such as bar lines and beams. I refer to this layer (as does Joel Lester) as the "primary metrical layer," and to the consonance that it creates in interaction with the pulse layer as the "primary consonance" of the work.[14]

Consonances can conveniently be labeled by ratios composed of the cardinalities of the interpretive layers involved, the highest number being stated first. Where the consonance arises from only one interpretive layer imposed on a pulse layer, the cardinality of that one layer suffices to characterize the consonance. Thus, in Example 2.2 the interaction of the metrical 6- and 2-layers produces the primary consonance 6/2 (1 = 8th). In Example 2.3, the 2-layer (1 = 8th) suggested in the bass in mm. 1–2 and clarified in mm. 3–4 (where it is created by subsurface, then surface melodic change) interacts with the metrical 6-layer to form the same primary consonance (6/2). The metrical 6-layer, however, also interacts with the 3-layer formed by melodic new-event accents to create the consonance 6/3.

Grouping and Displacement Dissonance

Although it contains two metrical consonances, Example 2.3 is by no means entirely consonant; the 3- and 2-layers do not align and hence result in a state of dissonance. In Examples 2.1, 2.2, and 2.4, a sense of dissonance arises from the superposition of nonaligned 6-layers. We turn now to a closer investigation of such dissonant states, which are the primary focus of this volume.

As nineteenth-century theorists already hinted, there are two basic ways in which nonalignment or dissonance between regular layers of motion can occur. First, dissonance can be formed by the association of at least two interpretive layers whose cardinalities are different and are not multiples/factors of each other.[15] In several earlier writings, I labeled this type of dissonance as "type A." Here I adopt Peter Kaminsky's term, "grouping dissonance"—an appropriate designation, for this dissonance type arises from the association of nonequivalent groups of pulses.[16]

Grouping dissonances may be labeled with a "G" followed by a ratio of the cardinalities of the layers involved, the larger cardinality being listed first. Thus, in the first two measures of Example 2.3, the dissonance formed by the 3- and 2-layers would be labeled G3/2 (1= 8th). If more than two interpretive layers are present, all of them can be listed in descending order in a similar format.

Florestan asked a passing waiter to bring some coffee beans. When the puzzled waiter had laid a handful of beans on the table, Florestan said to the equally puzzled Eusebius, "I thought we might find it easier to understand the author's descriptions if we constructed some little models. Why don't you build a coffee-bean model of the dissonance G3/2 while I build G5/3?"[17] They both laid out a row of closely spaced coffee beans, denoting the pulse layer, then placed additional rows of more widely spaced beans below to suggest the respective interpretive layers (Figure 2.1). After studying each other's models, they read on:

Grouping dissonance in pre-twentieth-century tonal music generally involves one of the metrical layers and one conflicting interpretive layer, or "antimetrical layer." Other situations are possible (and occasionally do occur in practice), for instance, dissonances composed of a metrical layer and more than one antimetrical layer (see the section on "compound dissonances" later in this chapter), or dissonances involving two or more antimetrical layers in the absence of metrical layers (see the unit on "subliminal dissonance").

Grouping dissonance invariably involves some alignment of attacks, the alignment occurring after a number of pulses generally determined by the product of the cardinalities of the interpretive layers. If in a grouping dissonance Gx/y, x and y have a common factor z, alignment will occur more frequently, namely after a number of pulses determined by the equation (xy)/z. Thus in the dissonance G9/6, alignment occurs at every 18th pulse (9 times 6, divided by 3, the common factor of 9 and 6), and in the dissonance G12/8, at every 24th pulse

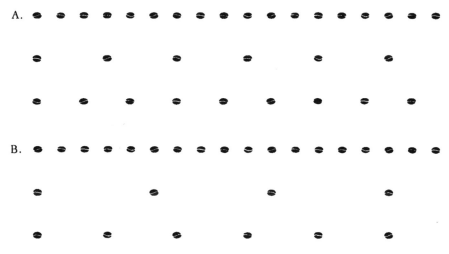

FIGURE 2.1. *Grouping dissonances (G3/2 and G5/3)*

(12 times 8, divided by the common factor 4). After Maury Yeston and Gretchen Horlacher, I refer to a segment demarcated by the points of alignment within a grouping dissonance as a "cycle."[18] ❦

"The cycles of our dissonances G3/2 and G5/3," said Florestan with a glance at the coffee bean diagrams (Figure 2.1), "would thus encompass six and fifteen pulses, respectively." Eusebius quickly verified these results, then said, "I wonder if the author's rule would work if there were three interpretive layers. If I add a 2-layer, for instance, to the five-against-three model, the cycle should by this rule comprise 30 pulses (5 times 3 times 2)." When he added a 2-layer to his diagram, he found that the length of the cycle indeed corresponded to the product of the three cardinalities. They read on:

> In spite of their characteristic periodic alignment, however, grouping dissonances are dominated by nonalignment. In a grouping dissonance Gx/y, there is for every point of alignment a number of nonaligning pulses determined by the formula $(x+y)-2$. In the dissonance G3/2, there are thus three nonaligning pulses for each point of alignment, in G4/3, five nonaligning pulses, and so on. ❦

They verified the author's statement about G3/2 by looking once more at Eusebius's coffee-bean model (Figure 2.1a). Florestan pointed out that in G5/3 (Figure 2.1b), there were $(5+3)-2$, or six nonaligning pulses between points of alignment.

Then Florestan remarked, "Grouping dissonance, which the author has discussed in such dry arithmetical terms, appears in interesting and exciting ways in

EXAMPLE 2.7. *G3/2 in the "Préambule" from* Carnaval, *mm. 28–32*

our music, especially in the specific form G3/2. The author has mentioned your poignant application of this dissonance at the opening of the *Davidsbündlertanz* op. 6 no. 2 (Example 2.3). In the tenth piece of op. 6, I employ the same dissonance, but in a much more impassioned vein. The passage beginning at m. 99 of the original finale of our Piano Sonata op. 22 (Example 2.6c) is another beautiful example of G3/2." Eusebius added, "You used this dissonance with humorous effect in the 'Préambule' from *Carnaval.* In that piece, the left hand's accompaniment pattern, suggesting a warped waltz, frequently establishes a 2-layer (1 = quarter), while repeated right-hand motives maintain a 3-layer. This occurs in mm. 28–34 (Example 2.7), more briefly in mm. 48–49, then at greater length in mm. 54–66. In most of the latter passage, you create the 2-layer not only with left-hand pattern repetition, but also with dynamic accents and harmonic changes. The dissonance G3/2 returns once more, with exhilarating effect, in the rising sequential passage that we discussed in Euphonia (Example 1.7b); at mm. 102–5, pattern repetition and durational accents in the right hand as well as recurring sforzandos delineate the metrical 3-layer, while left-hand pattern repetition and dynamic accents form a 2-layer." Florestan interposed, "We could both mention many more examples, but I am eager to read the author's description of the second type of dissonance."

The second basic type of dissonance involves the association of layers of equivalent cardinality in a nonaligned manner; that is, dissonance of this type does not depend on the association of noncongruent layers, but merely on the different positioning of congruent layers. For this type, I again adopt Kaminsky's term "displacement dissonance" rather than the term "type B" employed in my earlier studies.[19] Much displacement dissonance takes the form of "syncopation," which term, in its most common usage, designates a conflict between a metrical layer and an antimetrical layer formed by durational accents. The term "displacement dissonance," however, encompasses conflicts involving displacement produced in any manner. 🍂

Eusebius suggested, "Let us construct some models of displacement dissonances. I shall build a dissonance in which 2-layers are misaligned, and you could build one in which 3-layers are presented in nonaligned fashion." They left the

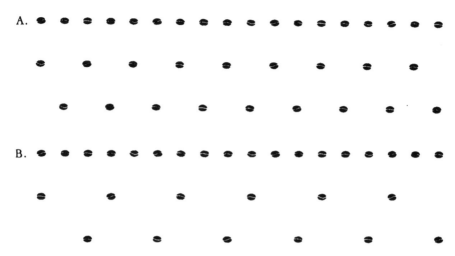

FIGURE 2.2. *Displacement dissonances*

pulse layers of their earlier models intact, but rearranged the coffee beans denoting interpretive layers as in Figure 2.2.
They read on:

> Whereas grouping dissonance involves periodic intersection of layers, displacement dissonance involves no intersection at all. No matter how long two identical but nonaligned interpretive layers are associated, they can never meet; each pulse of the metrical layer is contradicted by a pulse of the antimetrical layer. It is because of this very strong effect of nonalignment and contradiction that I consider such associations of layers dissonant (unlike Yeston, who considers them consonant on the basis of the numerical congruence of the constituent layers).
>
> Most displacement dissonance in tonal music involves a metrical layer and one antimetrical layer (although the possibility of larger numbers of constituent layers exists whenever the shared cardinality is greater than 2; see the section on compound dissonance later in this chapter). When a metrical layer is present within a displacement dissonance, we generally perceive the antimetrical layer or layers as a shifting out of the "normal position" designated by the metrical layer; the pulses of the metrical layer, in other words, function as a series of reference points in relation to which the pulses of the antimetrical layer are perceived as being displaced.[20]
>
> Given the referential function of metrical layers, it is appropriate to measure the amount of displacement within a particular dissonance in relation to those layers. I refer to the constant number of pulse-layer attacks that separates the metrical and antimetrical layers throughout a particular displacement dissonance as the "displacement index." The displacement index is an integer between 1 and x-1 (inclusive), where x is the value of the shared cardinality. (The amount of displacement must, of course, be smaller than the cardinality.)

EXAMPLE 2.8. Papillon *op. 2 no. 10, mm. 24–28*

Does displacement proceed in a forward or a backward direction from the pulses of a referential metrical layer? Measuring in the direction of musical flow from these pulses intuitively seems more reasonable; I believe that it is possible to hear virtually all displacements in a "forward" manner. There are, however, displacement dissonances that can also be perceived in a backward direction — dissonances whose antimetrical pulses can be heard as "early onset" in relation to the following metrical pulses.[21] This effect is most likely to arise when displaced pulses occur closer to the end than to the beginning of measures. It would be too hasty to conclude, however, that displaced pulses close to the end of a measure are *always* perceived in relation to the following downbeats. In the above passage from Schumann's tenth *Papillon* (Example 2.8), the accented third beats do not give the impression of "early onset" in relation to the following downbeats. There are two reasons why this displacement is more easily perceived in relation to the preceding downbeats. First, m. 25, separated from the preceding music by a rest, is clearly a beginning, and hence an obvious reference point for the displacement. Second, and more important, this displacement is more likely to be heard in relation to the preceding downbeats because the harmony during the displaced pulses is a continuation of that of the preceding downbeats. Harmony appears to be the main factor that can counteract our intuitive tendency to hear displacement in a "forward" direction.

My labeling system for displacement dissonances, though based on my assumption that "forward hearing" is more natural for the listener, does take into account the possibility of "backward hearing." I routinely assign to displacement dissonances labels of the form "Dx+a," where "D" stands for displacement, "x" is the shared cardinality of the interpretive layers, the plus sign denotes a shift in a forward direction, and "a" is the displacement index — the amount of displacement measured in pulse-layer attacks. When a backward interpretation is reasonable, I append a label of the form "Dx-a." Thus, in Example 2.1, I apply to the displacement dissonance created by two nonaligned 6-layers the label "D6+3" (1=16th); the points of initiation of the two 6-layers are consistently separated by three sixteenth-note pulses. In Example 2.2, two 6-layers lie two eighth-note pulses apart, measuring forward from the attacks of the referential metrical layer; I therefore label the dissonance as D6+2. There is no reason to hear either of these displacements in a backward direction. In Example 2.4, however, the label D6+4 (1= eighth), suggesting forward displacement from the

EXAMPLE 2.9. *"Paganini" from* Carnaval, *mm. 1–2*

downbeats, should be supplemented by D6-2. Unlike in the earlier examples, the registrally accented third beats harmonically anticipate the following downbeats, resulting in an effect of backward displacement.[22] ❦

Eusebius surveyed the coffee beans on their table (Figure 2.2) and noted, "The labels for the displacement dissonances that we have constructed would be D2+1 and D3+2, respectively, or, if the musical context justified a backward hearing, D2-1 and D3-1." Florestan said with some asperity, "I am growing tired of all of these numbers. Must every metrical state be labeled with numbers? Is metrical conflict only a matter of measurement and counting?" Eusebius calmly replied, "Whereas I, too, am not overly fond of numerical labels, I must admit that the author's labels nicely encapsulate some of the properties of the various metrical states. And perhaps the usefulness of the numerical labeling system will become clear later on in the manuscript." Florestan grunted and said, "Let us hope so."

At this point, Meister Raro walked in. They greeted him warmly, and urged him to join them. When he had done so and had ordered his coffee, Florestan briefly told him about their visit to the Rhythmic Quarter of Euphonia, about their mysterious acquisition of the manuscript, and about what they had read thus far. So absorbed did they become in their conversation that they completely forgot that Chiarina was awaiting them at home.

When Florestan had explained displacement dissonance and the author's labeling system, Raro said, "Innumerable dissonances of this type exist in your music. In 'Paganini' from *Carnaval*, the metrical 2-layer (1=16th) is articulated by the octave leaps in the right hand (Example 2.9), and in mm. 9–15, repetition of high notes adds further support to that layer. The dynamic accents and harmonic changes in the left hand, however, establish a strong antimetrical layer, and hence the dissonance D2+1 (which can here also be heard as D2-1). In the piece from *Carnaval* that you named after Chiarina (Example 2.10), you express the metrical 3-layer by harmonic change and by left-hand dynamic accents. A conflicting 3-layer arises from right-hand dynamic accents and new-event melodic accents on the upbeats, resulting in D3+2. In addition, you frequently associate the

EXAMPLE 2.10. *"Chiarina" from* Carnaval, *mm. 1–4*

pulses forming the displaced layer with strong pitch dissonance against the pre-vailing harmonies, a factor that further accentuates the displaced layer." Eusebius quietly interjected, "The melody notes on the upbeats belong to the harmonies initiated on the following downbeats. Do you not find that the displacement can therefore be heard in a backward direction, and that a label of the minus form — D3-1 — would be appropriate?" Meister Raro agreed, then proceeded to mention another example: "In mm. 151–57 of the sixth *Novellette* (Example 2.11), the har-mony changes on each downbeat, so that the metrical 2-layer (1=quarter) is clearly articulated. Dynamic accentuation, however, takes place on each upbeat, resulting in the dissonance D2+1."

Florestan said, "You have so far mentioned instances of displacement disso-nance from our early piano works. But there are many in our more recent com-positions as well. I included some exciting displacements in our Piano Quintet op. 44. Near the end of the first movement, there is an example of D4+3 (1=quarter). Each of mm. 320–23 (Example 2.12a) is based on a different triad, resulting in a clearly expressed metrical 4-layer (1=quarter). I set against it an antimetrical layer created by stabbing dynamic stresses of the final beats. In the *agitato* episode of the second movement of the same work (mm. 92–98), the har-monies again change at the beginning of each bar. All instruments, however, dy-namically stress the second quarter note, resulting in D4+1 (Example 2.12b). In the second Trio of the third movement (mm. 122–29), the dynamic accents

EXAMPLE 2.11. Novellette *op. 21 no. 6, mm. 151–54*

EXAMPLE 2.12. *Displacement dissonance in the Piano Quintet op. 44*

within the whirling sixteenth-note figure in the cello and violin articulate the metrical 4-layer (1=8th). The harmonies announced by the piano, however, consistently begin on the upbeats, establishing a strong antimetrical layer and hence the dissonance D4+2. In a passage in the fourth movement (mm. 21–29), I similarly pitted the strings and the piano against each other to form D4+2 (1=quarter). The dynamic stresses on the first of four repeated eighth-note chords in the strings articulate the metrical layer, while the piano establishes an antimetrical 4-layer by harmonic change, dynamic stresses, and a repeated melodic pattern of four rising steps."

Raro remarked, "Your symphonies, too, are rich in displacement dissonance. In the second movement of the First Symphony, mm. 55–66, harmonic change is precisely coordinated with the notated measure and thus articulates the metrical 3-layer (1=8th). In mm. 55–59 in the high strings and woodwinds, dynamic stresses and registral and durational accents on the second beats create an antimetrical 3-layer, which is continued in the following measures primarily by registral and durational accents; the result is D3+1. Similar passages are found in the first movement of the Second Symphony (mm. 50–57 and 174–202) and in the third and fourth movements of the Fourth Symphony (mm. 9–14 and mm. 39–57, respectively). At the opening of the second movement of your Third Symphony (Example 2.13), durational accents in the bass as well as a repeated rhythmic pattern express the metrical layer. The durational accents on second beats within the cello and viola melody, however, create the illusion that those beats are downbeats, resulting in subtle D3+1 (1=quarter)."

Eusebius, after pointing out that this passage illustrates the relative inconsequence of layers formed by slurs, suggested that they should have their beverages replenished and then continue their reading. As it was difficult for all three of them to see the manuscript at once, Florestan volunteered to read it aloud.

EXAMPLE 2.13. *Symphony no. 3, second mvmt., mm. 1–4*

"But please put a rein on your impetuosity and read slowly," begged Eusebius. Florestan promised to read "in tempo comodo," and began:

RESULTANT RHYTHMS

Any combination of interpretive layers generates a rhythmic pattern consisting of the summation of the attacks of the layers—a "resultant rhythm," or resultant for short.[23] The resultant, which can be expressed as a series of integers (where each integer represents a number of pulses) is a useful means of characterizing a given metrical state, for it encompasses the overall rhythmic information conveyed by that state. In consonant associations of layers, the resultant is always equivalent to the regularly spaced attacks of the fastest interpretive layer in the collection. The more complex and interesting resultants of dissonant combinations also exhibit regularity (the summation of regular pulses being, of necessity, regular as well). Resultant rhythms of grouping dissonances are recurrent palindromes, each palindrome occupying one cycle; the palindrome is the inevitable result of the superposition of layers of pulses equally spaced between points of coincidence.

Eusebius arranged the coffee beans so as to recreate the original grouping dissonances G3/2 and G5/3, and they all verified that in both cases the resultants within each cycle were palindromic (Figure 2.3). Florestan continued:

Resultant rhythms of displacement dissonances are merely recursive rather than palindromic. In a typical displacement dissonance, including the metrical layer and one antimetrical layer, each segment of the recursive series contains only two elements x and y, where x is the value of the displacement index and y is the difference between the displacement index and the shared cardinality. Thus, the resultant rhythm of D4+3 is "3–1–3–1 . . . ," and that of D5+2 is "2–3–2–3. . . ."

Eusebius nimbly reorganized the beans again to show these dissonances, and they together counted out the resultants (Figure 2.4). Florestan then said, some-

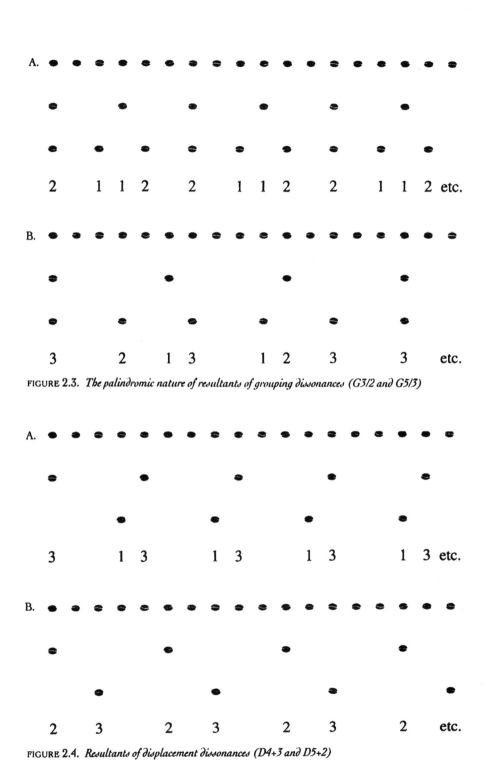

A.

2   1 1 2   2   1 1 2   2   1 1 2 etc.

B.

3   2   1 3   1 2   3   3   etc.

FIGURE 2.3. *The palindromic nature of resultants of grouping dissonances (G3/2 and G5/3)*

A.

3   1 3   1 3   1 3   1 3 etc.

B.

2   3   2   3   2   3   2   etc.

FIGURE 2.4. *Resultants of displacement dissonances (D4+3 and D5+2)*

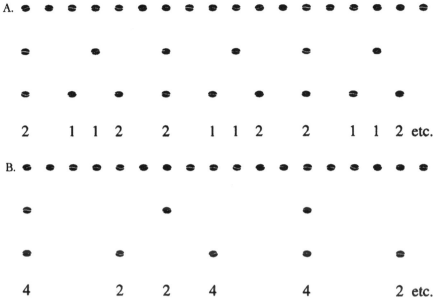

FIGURE 2.5. *The relationship between G3/2 and its augmentation, G6/4*

what hoarsely, "I need to wet my whistle. Eusebius, would you please take over?" Eusebius took the manuscript and read:

RELATIONSHIPS BETWEEN DISSONANCES

Dissonances may be related in various ways. All dissonances related in a particular way may be regarded as belonging to the same "family." Relationships between dissonances are frequently evident from a scrutiny of their labels. The degree of relatedness of two dissonances is best determined, however, by a comparison of their resultant rhythms; resultants, as encapsulations of the rhythmic activity of dissonances, are appropriate bases of comparison.

The labels of the dissonances G3/2 and G6/4, for instance, are composed of equivalent ratios, and thus suggest a close relationship between these dissonances. The relationship is clarified by comparison of the resultant rhythms, which reveals that the rhythms are the same, although that of G6/4 is augmented. 🌾

Florestan and Raro verified the author's claim by juxtaposing diagrams of G3/2 and G6/4 (Figure 2.5).

The same type of relationship exists between the displacement dissonances D3+2 and D6+4 — and again the obvious numerical relationship between the labels enables us to predict the rhythmic relationship. 🌾

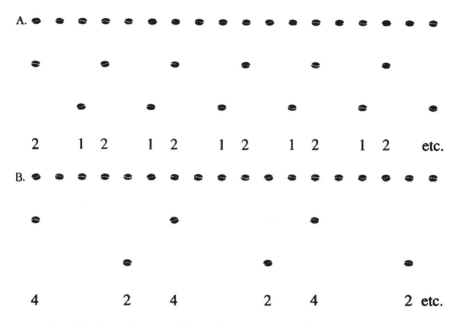

FIGURE 2.6. *The relationship between D3+2 and its augmentation, D6+4*

Again, Florestan and Raro constructed appropriate models (Figure 2.6).

In general terms, the grouping dissonances Gx/y, G2x/2y, G3x/3y . . . belong to
the same family. The same is true of the displacement dissonances Dx+a,
D2x+2a, D3x+3a. . . . I designate individual families of this type by the labels of
their simplest members (that is, the members whose labels are composed of the
smallest integers), placed within quotation marks to distinguish them from the
specific dissonance otherwise indicated by that label.[24]

   Certain relationships are relevant only to displacement dissonances. For
example, Dx+a and Dnx+a, where n is a positive integer, are closely related, the
resultant of the latter dissonance being a simplification of that of the former. ❦

By removing alternate coffee beans from the interpretive layers of the model of
D3+2, Raro created the dissonance D6+2 (Figure 2.7). He remarked, "The fact
that it is so easy to transform D3+2 into D6+2 certainly suggests that these dissonances are closely related." Eusebius read on:

   Just as closely related as Dx+a and Dnx+a are Dnx + (a+x), Dnx + (a+2x),
. . . Dnx + (a+[n–1]x). All of the latter dissonances are simplified, gapped versions of Dx+a; each of them can be created by eliminating equally spaced pulses
from the antimetrical layer of a displacement dissonance Dx+a. ❦

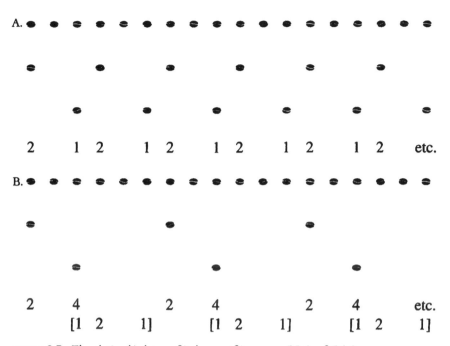

FIGURE 2.7. *The relationship between displacement dissonances D3+2 and D6+2*

Florestan, who had grown increasingly restive during these algebraic paragraphs, smashed his fist on the table, scattering coffee beans in all directions, and shouted, "Is this a manuscript about music or about mathematics? I am sick to death of these numbers and x's and y's!" Eusebius, furtively glancing at the other patrons who were staring in their direction, soothingly said, "Perhaps we can better understand this last passage, too, with the help of some coffee-bean models." Raro beckoned to the waiter to bring more coffee, then began to restore the coffee-bean model of D3+2 (Figure 2.8a). When he had done so, he again removed alternate beans from the metrical layer, then also removed from the antimetrical 3-layer those alternate beans that had remained in place during his construction of D6+2 (Figure 2.8b). They pondered the result, and Raro observed that the appropriate label for the newly created relative of D3+2 was D6+5. Eusebius smiled at Florestan and said, "Permit me to point out that we have just verified one of the author's formulas. The author stated that Dx+a and Dnx + (a+x) are closely related. We have before us the case where x is equal to 3, and n and a are both equal to 2; D3+2 is related to D(2x3) + (2+3), or D6+5." Florestan only frowned and motioned to Eusebius to continue his reading.

The members of such families of displacement dissonances differ in the number of antimetrical pulses sounding within any arbitrarily selected timespan, and hence also in the number of metrical pulses that are explicitly contra-

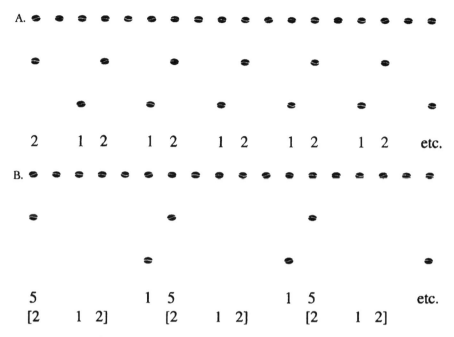

FIGURE 2.8. *The relationship between displacement dissonances D3+2 and D6+5*

dicted. I refer to displacement dissonances in which relatively many metrical pulses are contradicted as "tight" dissonances, and those in which relatively few metrical pulses are contradicted as "loose." I regard Dx+a as a "tight" relative of the other dissonances listed above, and those dissonances, conversely, as "loose" relatives of Dx+a.

    Given two displacement dissonances, relationships between them based on tightness and looseness may often be recognized from their labels by the existence of a constant difference between cardinality and displacement index. Thus, D12+7 and D6+1 may immediately be identified as relatives, because the differences between both their respective cardinalities and their respective displacement indices is 6. ❦

Eusebius observed, "The latter remark applies to the related dissonances D3+2 and D6+5 (Figure 2.8), the difference between both the cardinalities and the displacement indices being 3." Raro added, "And D6+5 is a tight relative of D3+2, D3+2 a loose relative of D6+5." Florestan, who, having begun to realize that the author's numerical labeling system had its advantages, was gradually regaining his composure, now guffawed, "No doubt old Wieck frequently applied the designation 'loose relative' to Eusebius and me!" Raro and Eusebius joined in his laughter, whereupon the latter continued to read:

final type of family of displacement dissonance is the entire group of possible displacements for a particular cardinality, from Dx+1 through Dx+n (where n is equal to x–1). Dissonances belonging to a family "Dx" are not related by virtue of similar resultant rhythms, but simply by their shared cardinality.

DISTINCTIONS BETWEEN DISSONANCES

It is important in musical analysis to be able to recognize relationships between dissonances; but it is equally important to be able to recognize differences between them. With the distinctions between grouping and displacement dissonance, and between tight and loose displacement dissonances, I have introduced two significant types of differentiation. In the following paragraphs, I draw attention to additional distinctions that are useful in the analysis of metrical dissonances.

Direct and Indirect Dissonance

So far, I have considered only dissonances formed by the superposition of layers of motion. It is also possible, however, for effects of dissonance to be achieved by the mere juxtaposition of layers. I refer to dissonance resulting from superposition as "direct dissonance," and that resulting from juxtaposition as "indirect."[25] Indirect dissonance exists because of our tendency as listeners to maintain an established pulse for a short time after it is discontinued in actuality.[26] When two noncongruent interpretive layers x and y, or two nonaligned congruent layers are juxtaposed, the listener inwardly continues the first layer as the second begins, so that there arises a brief but clearly perceptible conflict between the mentally retained first layer and the actually sounding second layer. The actual duration of indirect dissonance varies from passage to passage and from listener to listener. If the second layer persists, it will likely erase the memory of the first and hence dissolve the indirect dissonance after a few pulses. This adjustment is particularly easily made in the case of indirect displacement dissonance. The horizontal confrontation of a given layer of motion with a differently aligned but equivalent layer results in a brief effect of stammering or interruption, but the new layer, a mere repositioning of the earlier one, quickly effaces the memory of the original placement.

Indirect dissonance is inherent in all direct dissonances. At the inception of a direct dissonance, the antimetrical layer clashes not only with the portion of the metrical layer on which it is superimposed, but also with the pulses of the metrical layer that immediately precede it. Similarly, when a direct dissonance ends, the listener's mental maintaining of the antimetrical layer continues the dissonance indirectly for a few pulses. ❦

Eusebius looked up and said, "Direct dissonances, then, do not have sharp edges, so to speak; they do not end abruptly, but yield to consonance through an intermediate stage of indirect dissonance." Raro remarked, "The opening of your second *Davidsbündlertanz* illustrates this point (Example 2.3); the 3-layer is not articulated in m. 3, but the listener would likely maintain it at least through that measure, so that the direct dissonance G3/2 of mm. 1–2 would continue indirectly." Florestan said, "Indirect dissonances apart from those embedded in direct dissonances are common in our music. The *agitato* passage from the second movement of the Piano Quintet that I mentioned earlier (Example 2.12b) is a good example; the indirect dissonance created by juxtaposition of duple and triplet eighth notes adds even greater complexity to this displaced passage. Another relevant example is found in Eusebius's piece entitled 'Freundliche Landschaft,' the fifth of the *Waldscenen* op. 82. In mm. 14–15, you abruptly juxtapose the hitherto prevalent triplet-eighth-note pulse with duple eighth notes." Eusebius added, "And I render this indirect dissonance direct on the second beat of m. 16. But now let me read the next section, which appears to deal with a related topic."

Surface-Level and Subliminal Dissonance

Closely related to the idea of indirect dissonance is that of subliminal dissonance—a class of dissonance that is particularly common in Schumann's music. Subliminal dissonance arises when all musical features—accents, groupings, etc.—establish only one interpretive layer, while the context and the metrical notation imply at least one conflicting layer. The implied interpretive layer within such dissonances is usually the primary metrical layer, and the strongly articulated layer an antimetrical one. For instance, when in a work in three-four time there appears a passage in which accents and grouping organize the quarter-note pulse only into an antimetrical 2-layer, then the interaction between the notationally expressed 3-layer and the strongly articulated 2-layer results in the subliminal grouping dissonance G3/2. Similarly, if in a work in three-four time there appears a passage in which no musical features support the primary metrical layer, but many features express a nonaligned 3-layer, then there exists a state of subliminal displacement dissonance.

Subliminal and indirect dissonances are similar in that they involve no actual superimposing of conflicting interpretive layers. Furthermore, the categories overlap in that each subliminal dissonance must begin with an indirect dissonance arising from the intersection of a metrical and an antimetrical layer. Whereas indirect dissonance, however, is a short-lived surface-level phenomenon occurring at intersections of conflicting layers of motion, subliminal dissonance is a deeper-level conflict that may (although it need not) endure for long periods. Furthermore, whereas indirect dissonance arises from the listener's brief maintaining of an abandoned interpretive layer, subliminal dissonance cannot, except in brief instances, be assumed to result from such mental maintaining. As was mentioned above, it is a listener's tendency to maintain an abandoned layer for only a few pulses, and then to be captured by whatever new interpretive layer the composer has offered. It is unlikely that a listener would

EXAMPLE 2.14. Faschingsschwank aus Wien *op. 26, first movmt., mm. 87–90*

indefinitely maintain a layer—even the primary metrical layer—if it remained unarticulated for an extended period of time.

Because they involve only one obvious interpretive layer, subliminally dissonant passages can easily take on the semblance of consonances. It is the performer's duty to ensure that this does not occur. In many cases, the performer can subtly stress a heavily contradicted and otherwise unarticulated primary metrical layer; strongly stated antimetrical layers will certainly remain audible, and the performer's gentle reminders of the suppressed metrical layer will create a perceptibly dissonant effect. Obviously, the perception of subliminal dissonance depends to a much greater extent on signals sent by the performer than does the perception of indirect dissonance. The longer the subliminal dissonance lasts, the harder the performer must work to convey to the listener a sense of conflict and tension.

Some writers have suggested that there is in fact nothing that the performer can do to actualize subliminal metrical conflicts—that they are merely notational curiosities, symbolic rather than real.[27] Composers who so tortuously notated such conflicts, however, surely did not mean them to be a secret between themselves and the performer, but rather wished performers to communicate them. The performer must encourage listeners to join him or her in sensing a subliminal metrical dissonance instead of simply giving themselves over to the new and different state of consonance that the musical surface suggests.

Florestan said, "The author is right. We took great pains to notate subliminal dissonances. For instance, in the first movement of the *Faschingsschwank aus Wien*, I could so easily have notated mm. 87–126 in recurrent metrically consonant alternations of half notes and quarter notes (see Example 2.14). And in the finale of the Piano Concerto op. 54, I could have notated mm. 188–228—surely my most celebrated example of subliminal dissonance—in three-two meter. But instead, I employed in both cases a much more cumbersome notation involving numerous ties and bar lines that conflict with the apparent meters. I would certainly not have wasted so much time and ink if I had desired the performer to play, and the listener to hear, metrically aligned chords."

Eusebius said, "The examples of subliminal dissonance that you have just mentioned are among the most extensive in our oeuvre. There are, however, as the

EXAMPLE 2.15. *Subliminal dissonance in the Piano Sonata op. 11, fourth mvmt.*

author points out, a great many other instances of such dissonance in our works. At the beginning of the coda of the finale of our Piano Sonata op. 11 (mm. 407–28), I take care to establish the primary consonance 6/2 (1=8th) very clearly by reiterating a dotted figure occupying two eighth-note pulses, thus setting up Florestan's subsequent indulgence in some striking metrical dissonance." Raro interjected, "The obsessive repetitions of rhythmic patterns that are so common in your music surely occur for just such reasons: to establish the metrical layers strongly enough that subsequent conflicts against them will be more easily perceptible." Eusebius continued, "In this case, the conflict takes two forms: first, a subliminal displacement dissonance (D2+1), then a subliminal grouping dissonance (G3/2), where 1 is equal to an eighth note. In mm. 429–37 (Example 2.15a), Florestan ceases to articulate the metrical 2-layer, while establishing a displaced 2-layer by harmonic changes and sustained melodic attacks in both hands. In mm. 438–49, he alternates segments of metrically uninterpreted eighth-note scales with two-measure arpeggiating segments, within which dynamic accentuation and melodic patterns organize the eighth-note pulse into a 3-layer. In mm. 450–57, he vehemently and continuously announces the 3-layer; these measures, governed on the surface by the consonance G6/3, are subliminally dissonant (Example 2.15b). The cadential V-I harmonies that Florestan places on the downbeats of mm. 458–61, though they strongly assert the metrical 6-layer, are noncommittal with respect to its subdivision into a 2- or 3-layer, and only the pair of eighth notes on the upbeat to the final chord reestablishes the metrical 2-layer—too late fully to wipe out the subliminal dissonance!"

"Ha, Eusebius, that was a bold ending!" shouted Florestan. He continued,

EXAMPLE 2.16. *"Grillen" from* Phantasiestücke, *mm. 61–72*

"One of my favorite instances of subliminal and also indirect three-against-two dissonance occurs in 'Grillen' from the *Phantasiestücke* (Example 2.16). Before m. 61 the metrical 3-layer is quite clearly perceptible. In the new section beginning at that measure, however, I no longer articulate the metrical layer. The new-event harmonic accents suggest a 2- rather than a 3-layer (1 = quarter), resulting in subliminal G3/2. Beginning with the last beat of m. 66, I hint at a resurrection of the 3-layer; pattern repetition (pitch and rhythm) suggests two pulses of a 3-layer (which is not, to be sure, aligned with the notated measure). But I do not allow this layer to come to full fruition; I dynamically stress the last quarter note of the second group of three (m. 68), thus curtailing it to a duple group. The result is additional subliminal G3/2.[28] I continue the 2-layer begun with the dynamic accent, and the subliminal dissonance, until the last two bars of the phrase, where the final cadence of the section firmly reestablishes the metrical 3-layer." Eusebius interjected, "You paradoxically change the time signature to two-four near the first attempt at reassertion of the metrical 3-layer (m. 68), and revert to three-four notation while the 2-layer is, for the moment, being confirmed (mm. 69–70) — a typically Florestanian 'Grille'!"[29]

"Do you remember the third of the *Nachtstücke*, op. 23?" Eusebius continued. "It is metrically a straightforward piece, except for a brief interlude moving in steady quarter notes (mm. 165–204), which contains much subliminal dissonance. A rising scalar passage leading to fanfare-like cadences (Example 2.17a) continues the metrical 3-layer that was so clearly in effect in the preceding section. We answer this section by another, based on falling scales, during which a 2-layer is established by harmonic changes and reinforced by slurring; the

EXAMPLE 2.17. *Subliminal dissonance in* Nachtstücke *op. 23, no. 3*

3-layer disappears from the musical surface (Example 2.17b). This passage thus illustrates the subliminal dissonance G3/2. After we restate the rising scalar passage (and reassert the metrical 3-layer), we continue with a segment that fuses elements of the preceding two, combining rising scales with a 2-layer (Example 2.17c); the rising scales are imitated at two-beat intervals, and groups of two quarter notes are slurred together. Nothing within this segment articulates the metrical 3-layer, resulting in a continuation of subliminal G3/2. A final statement of the original rising passage concludes the interlude." Raro pointed out, "The fact that the clearly triple rising passage recurs throughout the section reminds listeners of the metrical 3-layer and thus facilitates the perception of the subliminal dissonance during the duple passages."

Raro continued, "Eusebius mentioned Florestan's usage of subliminal dissonance very close to the end of a work—the Sonata op. 11. Even bolder are the situations where you start a work with subliminal dissonance, that is, without establishing what is to become the primary metrical layer. The opening of the finale of the Piano Sonata op. 11 is an example; it could give the impression of being in two-four time, because the main harmonic changes take place at two-quarter-note intervals (see Example 5.10). The notated 3-layer does not make a clear ap-

EXAMPLE 2.18. *Symphony no. 3, fifth mvmt., mm. 46–54*

pearance until the second section (m. 17). The subliminal dissonance at the end of the movement belongs to the same family as that with which it begins ('G3/2'), resulting in a pleasing unity." Florestan interjected, "You mentioned that the opening 'could give the impression of being in two-four time.' You are right; but a good performer should ensure that the primary metrical 3-layer, and hence the G3/2 dissonance, is audible. A very slight stress on the downbeats would allow the listener to perceive a delicious hovering between two meters rather than stodgy, square duple time."

Eusebius said, "Additional movements that begin with subliminal dissonance are the second movement of the Piano Sonata op. 14, the Scherzo of the String Quartet op. 41 no. 2 (see Example 5.9b), and the Scherzo of the Piano Quintet. In the latter movement, the scale figures sound like upbeats, and the chords, because they carry new-event harmonic, density, and durational accents, sound like downbeats. These apparent downbeats are not coordinated with the notated ones, which always fall in the midst of the 'upbeat' scales. The resulting subliminal dissonance, using the author's labeling, is D12+9 (1=8th). In the coda (m. 258), we for the first time align one of the thick chords with the notated downbeat to create a sense of triumphant resolution—an effect which would not have been possible without the subliminal displacement dissonance earlier." Florestan remarked, "Do you recall how Chiarina used to place subtle stresses on the notated downbeats at the opening of this movement, and how the string players followed suit in their subsequent scale figures? I felt that these stresses were appropriate as long as they remained subtle; I would have objected if they had been so powerful as to suggest that they were notated dynamic accents!"

Eusebius resumed, "I must mention one of your more recent examples of subliminal dissonance. In mm. 45–46 of the finale of the Third Symphony (Example 2.18), you establish a displaced 4-layer (1=quarter), and the dissonance D4+1, by durationally accenting the second quarter-note pulse of each measure. At m. 47, you supply a dramatic cadence on a downbeat, but even as the cadence occurs, you initiate a new theme in the horns, whose durational and dynamic accents continue the displaced 4-layer and the dissonance. You confirm the antimetrical layer in the full orchestra at mm. 48–51 and push the metrical layer mercilessly below the surface. At m. 52, you abruptly bring that layer into play again by placing durational and harmonic new-event accents on the notated downbeats."

EXAMPLE 2.19. Faschingsschwank aus Wien *op. 26, fifth mvmt., mm. 23–29*

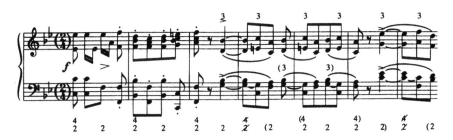

They listened inwardly, with smiles of admiration, to Florestan's thrilling passage, whereupon Raro said, "I wish to return once more to the subject of subliminal grouping dissonance. As the examples that we have mentioned indicate, associations of 2- and 3-layers are especially common in your works, both on the surface and subliminally. But you do occasionally indulge in associations of layers of other cardinalities. I recall one subliminal example from the last movement of the *Faschingsschwank* op. 26 (Example 2.19). The movement begins with the primary consonance 4/2 (1=8th). You present the metrical 4- and 2-layers with particular insistence at mm. 17–25; surface harmonies alternate in two-eighth-note pairs, and in mm. 21–25, the larger-scale harmonic changes occur at four-eighth-note intervals, on the notated downbeats. At m. 25, you whimsically increase the length of the surface pattern of harmonic change by one eighth note, and simultaneously eliminate the metrical layers, resulting in a 3-layer and in the indirect and subliminal dissonances G4/3 and G3/2." Eusebius said, "Another subliminal grouping dissonance involving layers of cardinalities other than 2 or 3 occurs in the Study op. 3 no. 4 (Example 2.20), where a 5-layer created by dynamic accents abruptly intrudes on a passage that has adhered to the metrical 6-layer. The metrical 6-layer is abandoned during the section containing the 5-layer, so that the dissonance (G6/5, 1=8th) is indirect and subliminal. Of course, we cannot take credit for this passage: the conflict is already present in the Paganini Caprice on which our study is based. But we should continue with our reading. Meister Raro, would you please take a turn?" And Raro read:

EXAMPLE 2.20. *G6/5 in Study op. 3 no. 4, mm. 9–13*

Low-level, Mid-level, and High-level Dissonance

We can distinguish different levels of metrical dissonance on the basis of the relative durations of the pulses that are organized by the constituent layers. Low-level grouping dissonances are formed by the association of noncongruent subdivisions of metrical beats. In many cases, the "micropulse" underlying such dissonances is not articulated within any single voice but is merely the resultant of the pulses of different voices. Low-level displacement dissonances are those whose shared cardinality is smaller than the value of a metrical beat. Even such low-level displacement dissonances are more than minor rufflings of the metrical surface: each pulse of a metrical layer is contradicted (whereas in low-level grouping dissonances the conflicting layers merge at some of the metrical beats).

"Eusebius" from *Carnaval*, with its seven-against-two conflicts, is a good example of low-level grouping dissonance. The implied micropulse is one-fourteenth of a half note; the right hand frequently organizes this implied pulse into groups of two (eighth-note septuplets), while the left hand presents groups of seven (quarter notes). Some measures present a low-level indirect grouping dissonance based on an implied micropulse of one-fifteenth of a half note, i.e., juxtapositions of quintuplet sixteenth notes and triplet eighths. Further interesting examples of low-level grouping dissonance are found in the last movement of the *Fantasy* op. 17 (mm. 72–79), where Schumann follows a metrically consonant chordal passage with eight measures of delicately traced two-against-three, four-against-three, and five-against-six dissonances. 🌱

"Such effects are by no means restricted to our piano music," Florestan said. "At the recapitulation of the slow movement of the First Symphony (m. 78), the violins and violas engage in a three-against-two conflict at the thirty-second-note level. In the first episode in the second movement of the Piano Quintet (mm. 29–61), the first-violin melody is accompanied by persistent eighth notes in the second violin and viola combined with triplet quarter notes in the piano, resulting in low-level three-against-four dissonance. The piano part contains low-level three-against-two dissonance as well; harmonic change determines a 3-layer (especially from m. 32 onward), and density accents, occurring on every second triplet, determine a 2-layer."

Raro drew their attention to a low-level displacement dissonance in the finale of the Piano Quintet (see Example 4.12). "In mm. 224–28," he pointed out, "there are two nonaligned layers moving in quarter notes (i.e., twice as fast as the primary metrical 2-layer). The displacement index is a mere eighth note, and the resultant rhythm moves in eighth notes as well." Florestan reminded them that many of their song accompaniments consisted of slightly displaced quickly moving layers. "'Schöne Wiege,' op. 24 no. 5," he stated, "begins with such a pattern. The left hand expresses the metrical layer while the attacks of the right consistently occur an eighth note later. During a later section, at 'Wahnsinn wühlt in meinen Sinnen'. . . ." Florestan abruptly sank into brooding silence. Raro and Eusebius gazed at him sympathetically; then the former picked up where Florestan

EXAMPLE 2.21. *Piano Trio op. 80, first mvmt., mm. 404–14 (piano part)*

had left off, saying, "During that later section (see Example 6.12), the displacement moves to an even lower level; the two hands state the same line a sixteenth note apart." Eusebius continued, "Florestan placed a particularly complex low-level dissonance near the end of the first movement of our Piano Trio op. 80 (Example 2.21). The duplet eighth-note layer beginning in m. 402 results in low-level indirect grouping dissonance against the established triple eighth-note pulse; this dissonance can be labeled as G3/2 (1=16th). At m. 406, Florestan initiates low-level displacement dissonance, the two hands of the piano part stating the same melody in duplet eighth-note durations, a sixteenth note apart. Florestan momentarily resolves this dissonance (D3+1.5) at m. 410, but reinstates it after one measure."[30] Raro said to the still silent Florestan, "At m. 410, you set into motion a somewhat higher-level dissonance—a dissonance involving different groupings of the duplet eighth-note pulse; you juxtapose the established 6-layer (1=16th) with a 9-layer, created by slurring three duplet eighth notes together, and by dynamic stress and melodic pattern repetition. The resulting dissonance, G9/6, is an augmentation of that at m. 402. Indirect G9/6 reappears when you reestablish the 6-layer at m. 418."

Florestan remained unresponsive. Raro shrugged and began to read the next section of the manuscript:

Dissonance at high levels could be termed "hypermetrical," as it involves layers moving more slowly than the primary metrical layer.[31] In Schumann's

EXAMPLE 2.22. Waldscenen *no. 1 ("Eintritt"), mm. 1–8*

music, hypermetrical dissonance seems to be relatively rare; like much nineteenth-century music, his is dominated by undisturbed four-bar hypermeter. Some of his works do, however, contain indirect and subliminal dissonance at high levels. The beginning of the first piece of the *Waldscenen* op. 82 (Example 2.22) illustrates subliminal hypermetrical displacement dissonance.[32] The second four-bar hypermeasure is expected to begin with m. 5. Instead, it begins two beats earlier, in the middle of m. 4, the point of early onset being dynamically accented. We could label this dissonance between expected and actual four-bar hypermeasures as D16+14, or D16-2 (1=quarter), the minus sign designating the effect of premature initiation of the second hypermeasure. The dissonance continues through the first ending; the second hypermeasure, which "should" conclude at the end of m. 8, actually ends in the middle of that measure. The second half of m. 8 appears to initiate a repetition of the first hypermeasure, two beats too soon. The actual restatement of the first measure reestablishes, with a surprising stammer, the original hypermetrical 16-layer. 🌿

Florestan, who had emerged from his gloom, said, "If this excerpt is simply an example of backward displacement by two quarter-note pulses, why is the cadential melody of m. 7 not displaced in relation to that of m. 3?" Eusebius briefly mulled over the music, then responded, "I believe it is because of the presence of an 'extra' chord at the beginning of m. 7. The dotted portion of the cadential motive could easily have begun during the F major harmony in the second half of m. 6 (with the notes C and F in the melody); the C major harmony with the eighth-note turn figure above it could then have followed directly at the beginning of m. 7, and the resolution to F major could have occurred on the third beat of that measure, resulting in a displacement with respect to m. 3."

EXAMPLE 2.23. *Symphony no. 4, fourth mvmt., mm. 75–85*

Raro said, "Not all of your metrical and hypermetrical manipulations, then, can be explained by the author's theories." He continued, "Another high-level dissonance is found in the passage from the finale of *Faschingsschwank* that we discussed earlier (Example 2.19). In m. 25, the subliminal dissonances G4/3 and G3/2 (1=8th) coincide with a subliminal and indirect hypermetrical dissonance: four-bar hypermeasures yield to three-measure hypermeasures (mm. 25–28, 28–31, 31–34, and 34–37), whereupon four-bar groups are reinstated. The result is a nice correspondence between the mid- and high-level four-against-three dissonances—or, to use the author's labeling, between two members of the family 'G4/3' (G4/3 and G16/12)."

Eusebius said, "I must mention one more indirect hypermetrical dissonance, from the finale of our Fourth Symphony. The exposition is dominated by two- and four-bar hypermeasures. Near its end, we present rocketing rising-scale sequences in two-bar waves (mm. 67–68, 69–60, 71–72, and 73–74). The final, cadential hypermeasure of the exposition, however, is three measures long, the "extra" measure being our repetition of m. 75 an octave lower (Example 2.23).[33] A measure of silence after m. 77 would have rendered the end of the exposition much more stable. The instability (or high-level grouping dissonance) resulting from the three-bar unit is appropriate for it propels the music across the double bar line, either back to the opening of the exposition or onward into the development section. I find the latter continuation especially effective. Whereas the return of the opening at the first ending immediately restores unambiguous two- and four-bar hypermeter (because the listener already knows how to parse this familiar music), the first bar of the development section has an ambiguous status;

it is not certain whether it belongs with the previous three bars as the final bar of a four-bar hypermeasure, or whether it is to be interpreted as the beginning of a new hypermeasure. The possibility of the former interpretation welds the opening of the development section onto the end of the exposition."

Florestan interjected, "By m. 82, the ambiguity is resolved; in retrospect it is clear that the first four bars of the development section form a four-bar hypermeasure. The succeeding fugato passage, however, introduces additional hypermetrical conflict: the fugal entries take place at three-measure intervals. Thus we pick up on the three-bar layer of motion suggested at the end of the exposition. The juxtaposition of three- and four-bar hypermeasures results in clearly perceptible indirect hypermetrical dissonance."[34]

They sipped some coffee as they let this striking passage move through their minds. Then Raro continued his reading:

Most of Schumann's metrical dissonances lie at levels between the two extremes of micropulse and hypermeter; they are formed by the interaction of metrical and antimetrical layers, as defined above. It is on these mid-level dissonances that I focus in this study, although I also refer to higher- and lower-level dissonances where they are significant within the overall metrical structure of a given work.

Strong and Weak Dissonance

Whereas it is intuitively obvious that metrical dissonances are not all of equal intensity, it is by no means obvious precisely how the intensity of dissonances should be ranked. I make no attempt to rank the intensity of dissonances of different types (i.e., grouping and displacement dissonances); there is no reason to assume that grouping dissonances are inherently more dissonant than displacement dissonances, or vice versa. Individual dissonances within each basic type can, however, be said to be more or less inherently dissonant than others. One factor that determines inherent intensity of grouping dissonances is length of cycle; the more pulses elapse before attacks of the constituent layers coincide, the more intense the dissonance. Thus, G5/4, with a 20-pulse cycle, is inherently more dissonant than G3/2, with a 6-pulse cycle.[35]

A basic principle governing inherent intensity of displacement dissonances appears to be proximity to consonance; the more closely a given dissonance approaches a state of alignment, the more strongly dissonant it is.[36] In numerical terms, dissonances whose displacement indices are 1 or x-1 (where x is the shared cardinality) are the most intense. Another factor that affects inherent intensity of displacement dissonance is relative tightness. Since tight dissonances contradict the metrical layers more frequently, they are perceived as more intensely dissonant than loose dissonances.

The inherent intensity of a given dissonance is also determined in part by the number of pairs of noncongruent layers that it contains; the more such pairs there are, the more intensely dissonant the given collection. This statement applies primarily to grouping dissonances[37] but is, to some extent, also relevant to displacement dissonances. Within a work in six-eight time, for instance, a combination of displacements by two and by three eighth notes, resulting in the dissonances D6+2 and D6+3, would be more intensely dissonant than either of those dissonances alone. Paradoxically, however, a combination of all possible displacements of a given cardinality is not as intensely dissonant as any of the less exhaustive combinations. The association of all possible displacements results in accentuation of all members of the pulse layer, and hence in the virtual elimination of an effect of nonalignment or dissonance. ❦

Florestan remarked, "I am reminded of our earlier discussion of the first *Davids-bündlertanz* (Example 2.4), where the abundance of 6-layers could produce the result that the author mentions." Eusebius added, "Is the middle section of 'Estrella' from *Carnaval* perhaps another illustration of the latter statement? In your effort, Florestan, to render the displacement dissonance particularly intense by multiplying the displaced layers, did you nullify the dissonance entirely?" Florestan answered, "I do not believe so. Although each beat is accented, my use of distinct registers should make possible the perception of three conflicting layers." He motioned to Raro to read on:

Of more musical significance than inherent intensity is contextual intensity —that is, intensity determined not by the inherent properties of a given dissonance but by its manner of presentation. The general principle determining contextual intensity is perceptibility or prominence of the dissonance, which in turn depends mostly on the prominence of antimetrical layer(s).

Various aspects of presentation influence the prominence of antimetrical layers, and hence contextual intensity of dissonance. To some extent, contextual intensity is dependent on the number of accent types that contribute to the formation of antimetrical layers. If, for instance, an antimetrical layer is produced only by durational dissonances, the resulting metrical dissonance will be much weaker than if dynamic *and* durational accentuation collaborate to form that layer. Measuring intensity exclusively by the number of active accent types, however, is problematic because some accent types—dynamic and new-event harmonic accents—create more perceptible interpretive layers than others. When an antimetrical layer is formed by either of the above accent types, I consider the resulting dissonance intense, no matter whether other accent types are present or not.

Dissonances whose antimetrical layers are formed by accentuation are more intense than those formed by grouping alone. Accentuation is based on the prominence, on the marking for consciousness, of particular events, and thus has a greater capability of rendering dissonance intense than does grouping. If, however, accentuation and grouping collaborate in the formation of antimetrical layers, the resulting dissonance will be more intense than one whose antimetrical layers are formed by either of those factors alone.

The degree of sustention of pulses within constituent layers plays a role in contextual intensity. A displacement dissonance in which the antimetrical pulses are released before the next metrical pulse is considerably less intense than one in which antimetrical pulses are sustained during the metrical pulses. As in a dialogue, the sense of contradiction and conflict is much greater when the utterances of the interlocutors overlap.[38]

The prominence of the voices involved in antimetrical layers may be a factor in the contextual intensity of a dissonance. If only one voice of a multivoiced texture participates in the establishment of such a layer, the resulting dissonance will be less intense than if a number of voices participate. If only an inner voice participates, the dissonance will again be less intense than if an outer voice does so.[39]

The number of antimetrical attacks within a dissonance affects its contextual intensity. One or two antimetrical attacks may suggest a particular dissonance, but that presentation of the dissonance will necessarily be weaker than one in which the antimetrical layer is announced at greater length. By the same token, when an antimetrical layer is sporadic (i.e., some pulses are not articulated), the resulting dissonance will be weaker than one in which all pulses are present.

A final feature that seems to be of importance in determining the degree of intensity of a dissonance is the extent to which the antimetrical layer is formed by a consistent event type. As was mentioned above, layers of motion are not necessarily generated by just one event type; the occurrence of some event at regular time intervals, no matter what type of event it is, generates a layer of motion. The more similar the type of recurring event, however, the more perceptible is the layer of motion; similarity of event type invites the listener to perceive the events as a connected series. 🎵

Eusebius observed, "The dissonance G3/2 in my second *Davidsbündlertanz* (Example 2.3) is, then, much less intense than your G3/2, Florestan, at the opening of the tenth piece of that set; you render your antimetrical 3-layer particularly prominent by using dynamic accents. Furthermore, your piece as a whole is much more intensely dissonant than mine, for your dissonance goes on for no less than 60 measures, whereas mine occurs only in two- or four-measure bursts."

Raro now begged Florestan to continue to read out loud. Florestan consented, and read:

Simple and Compound Dissonance

I refer to metrical dissonances composed of the minimum number of layers—a pulse layer plus two conflicting interpretive layers—as "simple" dissonances. When more than two noncongruent interpretive layers are combined, "compound" grouping dissonances may result. If a 3-layer, a 4-layer, and a 7-layer were combined, for instance, the compound grouping dissonance G7/4/3, including the simple dissonances G4/3, G7/3, and G7/4, would be created.[40]

Compound displacement dissonances are also possible. It could be argued that all displacement dissonances are, in a sense, compound dissonances; each displacement dissonance Dx+n includes D2x+n, D4x+n, and so on (D2+1, for instance, includes D4+1, D8+1, etc.). Such inclusions can often be disregarded as trivial. Sometimes, however, superpositions of the type Dx+n/ax+n are perceptible as compound dissonances. ❦

Florestan looked up and said, "I believe mm. 102–5 of the first movement of our First Symphony demonstrate the difference between trivial and nontrivial combination of D4+1 and D2+1. Syncopation in the viola, cello, and wind parts keeps D2+1 active throughout the passage, and D4+1 is therefore present as well. In mm. 102–3, however, dynamic accents on the second eighth note make possible the perception of D4+1 against the continuing background of D2+1, so that one could refer to the passage as a genuine compound dissonance."

He continued to read:

The most striking compound dissonances are those that contain both grouping and displacement dissonance. Example 2.1 illustrates such compound dissonance; the passage contains not only the dissonance D6+3 mentioned earlier, but also G3/2. The right hand suggests a 2-layer (1=16th), while the contour of the left hand line implies a 3-layer, the complete neighbor figure forming one triple group, the dynamic accent and downward leap initiating another. ❦

Raro interjected, "The author could also have mentioned the compound grouping/displacement dissonance in mm. 29–31 of the Préambule of *Carnaval* (Example 2.7). Your 'oom-pah' accompaniment pattern expresses a 2-layer, against which the motive in the right hand articulates two 3-layers. The metrical 3-layer is created by sforzandos as well as durational accents (quarter notes after eighth notes). The antimetrical 3-layer, displaced by one beat, arises from grouping; since the motive's first announcement in m. 26, you have conditioned the listener to hear the first eighth note as the beginning of a group, and a layer of motion is therefore formed by recurrences of that initial note. At four-measure intervals, you reinforce this second triple layer with a dynamic stress, as in mm. 27, 31, and 35. Two dissonances emerge from this mélange, namely G3/2 and D3+1." Florestan pointed out that similar compound dissonances occur in the first Trio of the third movement of the Piano Sonata op. 11 (see Example 4.8c) and at the beginning of the Scherzo from the op. 32 piano pieces.

Eusebius had been punctuating the remarks of Florestan and Raro by hearty yawns, and now said, "I am having trouble staying awake; our journey has fatigued me. And what must Chiarina be thinking?" Florestan, who had regained his usual ebullience, slapped him on the back and responded, "No doubt you are also fatigued by this manuscript; a little of it goes a long way! There is only one more paragraph in this chapter; I shall read it, and then we shall break off for today and go home to put Chiarina's mind at ease." He read:

> In this chapter, I have described a wide variety of metrical states, have set out a system of terminology and labeling for these states, and have applied the terminology in the analysis of short musical excerpts. In the following chapters I demonstrate how various metrical states operate within larger contexts, and how the terminology unfolded here is helpful in the analysis of such contexts. 🌱

Florestan closed the manuscript and called for their reckoning. As the waiter brought it to the table, Clara entered the coffeehouse. She stared at the litter of plates, cups, and coffee beans on the table, then said reproachfully, "Robert! I have been looking for you for hours." He stammered an apology and an elaborate explanation involving the town of Euphonia, the Prophet Bird, and a theoretical manuscript. She could make neither head nor tail of his story. With tears in her eyes, she took his arm and led him toward the door. He resisted, saying, "First I must pay my reckoning." He looked over the bill and expressed surprise at the lowness of the total, which came to exactly one-third of what he expected. But Clara assured him that everything was in order. They paid, and walked homeward together.

Intermezzo 1

THREE

Influences on Schumann's
Metrical Style

At home, Clara excused herself, as she needed to practice. Florestan, Eusebius, and Meister Raro entered the drawing room and, after helping themselves to brandy and cigars, settled into comfortable easy chairs. Eusebius had barely lit his cigar when he nodded off. The cigar fell from his grasp and would have burned the carpet had not Florestan stooped to retrieve it. He and Meister Raro sipped and smoked in silence for a time, smiling indulgently at the sleeping Eusebius.

Then Raro inquired, "I assume that the interest in metrical dissonance, so clearly evident in your works, did not arise spontaneously, but was triggered by the music of others. Do you recall which composers influenced you in this respect?" As Florestan gazed pensively into his glass, there arose before him a vision of himself at the age of eight at a concert in Karlsbad, staring in awe at a man seated behind him, who had just been pointed out to him as the great Ignaz Moscheles.[1] Smiling at the memory, he turned to Raro and said, "Like all young pianists of our time, I first studied the works of pianist-composers like Moscheles, Hummel, Cramer, and Kalkbrenner, and performed some of them as early as 1821. I continued to play their works during the period when I had the ambition of becoming a virtuoso pianist; in 1828 through 1830 I was engaged, under Wieck's guidance, in practicing the studies and a few other works of Hummel and Moscheles, and in 1831 I worked hard on the études of the latter composer.[2]

"It was in the works of these composers that I first encountered metrical dissonance. Their music was, for the most part, rhythmically uninteresting; all the more striking, therefore, were the few instances of metrical conflict, which almost always took the form of displacement dissonance. I remember a few exam-

EXAMPLE 3.1. *Metrical dissonance in Ignaz Moscheles's Twenty-Four Studies op. 70*

ples that intrigued me. The fifth of Moscheles's Twenty-Four Studies op. 70 begins with left-hand syncopation, resulting in D2+1 (1=quarter). At mm. 8–9, antimetrical slurs and dynamic accents intensify this dissonance (Example 3.1a),
and at m. 21 harmonic changes and dynamic accents produce yet another flash of
intense dissonance; this one could be heard as D2–1 (Example 3.1b). Occasional
dynamic accents on the second beats of the common-time measures result in the
closely related, looser dissonance D4+1. This variant appears within the major-
mode middle section as well, providing a subtle link between sections. The eighth
study of the same set features much D2+1 (1=8th). At first, the antimetrical layer

EXAMPLE 3.2. *Metrical dissonance in Johann Nepomuk Hummel's Piano Concerto op. 85*

is articulated merely by attacks on offbeats (m. 12—Example 3.1c). At mm. 18–20 (Example 3.1d) and 25–27, the notes that form the antimetrical layer are sustained through the metrical beats, so that the antimetrical layer is reinforced, and in mm. 28 and 46–49, Moscheles writes some antimetrical dynamic accents. In mm. 36–38, the related looser dissonance, D4+1, is produced by dynamic accents as well. The study is thus spanned by a gradual intensification of displacement dissonance.

"In April 1829 I performed Hummel's Piano Concerto in A minor, op. 85, a work in which I noted a few fairly prominent displacement dissonances.[3] Within the orchestral introduction of the first movement, three consecutive measures contain second-beat dynamic accents, resulting in D8+2 (1=8th). A few measures later, antimetrical slurs and dynamic accents create the tighter dissonance D4+2. Near the end of the first movement, piano and orchestra dynamically accent the fourth beats of two measures, then both weak beats of the next measure. Finally, the piano and orchestra part company, the latter dynamically accenting the metrical beats, and the former, the weak eighth notes. The result is a progression from D8+2 to the tighter dissonance D4+2, then to the diminution of the latter, D2+1. This successive 'contraction' of displacement dissonances renders the approach to the final cadence of the movement quite dramatic. Occasionally Hummel's pianistic figuration contains displacement dissonance. In mm. 95–98 of the Rondo, for instance, Hummel places dynamic accents on weak eighth notes of two measures (Example 3.2a), then registral accents on the third sixteenth-note triplets for two measures. At one and only one point in the work, there is a prominent grouping dissonance (low-level, to be sure): within a brilliant passage based on dominant harmony, just before a big cadence, the left hand plays bro-

EXAMPLE 3.3. *Metrical dissonance in Hummel's* Pianoforte Method

ken octaves in triplet sixteenths, the octaves superimposing a duple layer upon the established triplet pulse (Example 3.2b).

"Even the musically most arid études that I was forced to practice contained a few crumbs of metrical dissonance. In Hummel's *Pianoforte Method*, for instance—a work that contains much that is useful, but just as much that is pointless[4]—I encountered in the twenty-fourth exercise a triple/duple conflict, the metrical 2-layer being created by pitch repetition in the lower voice, the antimetrical 3-layer by pitch repetition in the upper voice and by registral accentuation (Example 3.3a). A similar conflict occurs in exercise no. 263, where registral and density accents superimpose an intermittent 2-layer on the triplet pulse (Example 3.3b). Another example of grouping dissonance is found in that perennial companion of budding pianists, Clementi's *Gradus ad Parnassum*. The fully notated version of Study no. 68, with its eighth-note neighboring motions in *alla breve* time, is metrically consonant. Clementi's suggested variant, however, forces the neighboring motion into a twelve-eight context (Example 3.4). The dotted quarter-note beats are to be dynamically accented, so that the metrical 3-layer remains clearly perceptible; the oscillations of the neighboring motion, however, maintain the duple layer that was consonant within the fully notated version, but that creates grouping dissonance within the variant.

"All of the passages that I have mentioned are flashes in the pan—isolated events within compositions or sets of studies that are otherwise rhythmically rather monotonous. Nevertheless, my ears pricked up at such passages, and I believe that I began to learn certain lessons from them beyond the pianistic ones that they were intended to teach. The climactic usages of grouping dissonance in Hummel's Concerto, for instance, taught me that metrical dissonance is an ef-

EXAMPLE 3.4. *Metrical dissonance in Muzio Clementi's* Gradus ad Parnassum

EXAMPLE 3.5. *Metrical dissonance in Niccolò Paganini's* Caprice for Solo Violin *op. 1 no. 13*

fective means of increasing tension within a work, and some of Moscheles's studies alerted me to the possibility of generating musical processes using metrical dissonance."

As Florestan paused to sip some brandy, his eye fell upon the looking glass above the mantel. To his consternation, the glass reproduced not his image, but showed instead the figure of a slim, demonic violinist standing within a magic circle, playing for a merry group of dancing skeletons.[5] He forced himself to turn away from the horrifying vision toward Meister Raro. "Another virtuoso-composer," he continued somewhat tremulously, "influenced me more deeply than those whom I have mentioned so far, namely Niccolò Paganini. I was fascinated with his playing (I heard him in Frankfurt in 1830), and I was equally impressed with his Caprices for Solo Violin op. 1."[6] Florestan glanced furtively at the mirror, where, to his relief, he now saw only his own features. He went on, "I began in 1832 to transcribe some of the Caprices for piano and, in the process, gained an ever greater appreciation of their rhythmical and metrical finesse. Metrical dissonance takes many forms in these works. At the coffeehouse, we discussed the opening section of Caprice no. 13, with its indirect G6/5—not at all a common grouping dissonance in the music of our time (Example 2.20). At m. 17 of this Caprice, a different dissonance follows (Example 3.5); registral accents in each group of six sixteenth notes in mm. 17–18, 21–22, 25–27, etc.—low-point accents on each fourth note and high-point accents on each fifth note—render the grouping of the sixteenth notes ambiguous and result in G3/2 (1=16th). The 3-layer is enhanced by the alternation between contrasting articulations (slurred and detached triplets of sixteenth notes), and by the ringing of open-string G's on the fourth sixteenth.

"The sixth Caprice is also riddled with metrical conflict. The opening material (Example 3.6a) and numerous later passages hover uneasily between triple and duple grouping of eighth notes. The slurring generally suggests a 3-layer (1=8th), and accentuation at times clearly expresses this layer; there are registral accents (high points) on the fourth eighth notes of mm. 1, 3, 39, and 41, and dynamic accents at the corresponding points of mm. 32–34. A number of harmonic changes, however, corroborate the 2-layer suggested by the notated meter. In m. 3, for instance, that layer is reinforced by the appearance of a new harmony on the third of the notated quarter-note beats. In m. 4, the resolution of a cadential six-four, and in m. 5 the motion to C minor harmony, coincide with duple pulses. In each of mm. 32–35, the main harmonic changes occur on the second duple

EXAMPLE 3.6. *Metrical dissonance in Niccolò Paganini's* Caprice for Solo Violin *op. 1 no. 6*

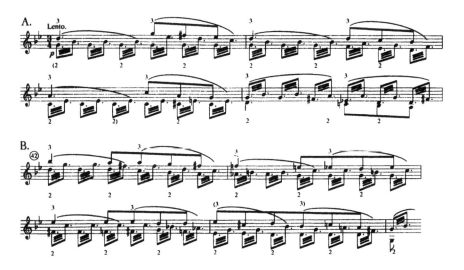

pulse, so that the 2-layer, and its conflict against the 3-layer created by slurring and accentuation, become quite pronounced.

"Paganini resolves the metrical conflict at several significant points of the work. At the strongest cadence in the first section, for instance (mm. 10–11), he brings the chord changes into alignment with the 2-layer and (in m. 10) reinforces that layer with the slurring and dynamics as well. Similarly, at the end of the first section (m. 18), Paganini coordinates harmonic change and slurring with the 2-layer. After the double bar, G3/2 returns. At the recapitulation (m. 39), the dissonance is resolved in favor of the 3-layer, which predominates just as it did at the opening. Soon thereafter, however, Paganini initiates a definitive resolution in favor of the 2-layer. Harmonic changes are particularly active in asserting that layer; from m. 42 onward (Example 3.6b), significant harmonic changes appear almost consistently on quarter-note beats, so that the metrical 2-layer is prominent. After m. 45, the slurring suggests the 2- rather than the 3-layer. In mm. 48–49, a dynamic accent falls on one of the duple pulses, and, in the final two measures, quarter-note repetitions of the tonic note further clarify the 2-layer. The Caprice, in short, is permeated by G3/2, which is resolved at the end of the first section, reinstated, then resolved definitively at the end of the work.

"I could mention many other instances of metrical conflict in Paganini's op. 1 —the displacement by one sixteenth note in Caprice no. 3, mm. 58–61 and 67–70, and in no. 16, mm. 46–49; the displacement by an eighth note in no. 12, mm. 24 and 32–33, in no. 16, mm. 13–20 and 50–51, in Variation 7 of no. 24, and so on."

Florestan sipped some brandy, then continued, "My discussion of the Caprices reminds me of another significant influence on my rhythmic style: Pa-

EXAMPLE 3.7. *Metrical dissonance in J. S. Bach's* French Suite *no. 2, Courante, mm. 46–49*

ganini could, of course, never have written these works had he not learned the art of writing for solo violin from Johann Sebastian Bach. I, too, learned a great deal from old Bach, including some aspects of the treatment of metrical conflict. I became very familiar with the master's keyboard works in the early 1830s, at which time I was not only playing but also assiduously analyzing them.[7] These works, particularly the various dance movements of the suites, are filled with examples of both grouping and displacement dissonance. Some of the dissonances arise from traditions associated with particular dances. Sarabandes, for instance, often involve durational accentuation of the second beats, and hence the weak displacement dissonance D3+1 (1=quarter). Many of Bach's dances in triple meter are rich in hemiolas (or G3/2 dissonances); like other composers of his time, he frequently uses these dissonances to highlight cadences. At times, however, he employs G3/2 in a striking manner within phrases—that is, in locations where they are not traditionally found. In mm. 3–5 of the second Courante of the first *English Suite*, and in mm. 5–6 of the Courante of the second *English Suite*, Bach superimposes on the metrical 2-layer (1=quarter) a 3-layer formed by harmonic changes. In mm. 46–48 of the Courante of the second *French Suite*, harmonic changes and new-event melodic accents in the bass result in a 4-layer (1=8th) within three-four meter (Example 3.7)." Raro, who knew the works of J. S. Bach just as well as Florestan, interposed, "In the latter passage, there is also grouping dissonance at the eighth-note level; a contour pattern divides the right-hand figuration into groups of three eighth notes, which conflict with the metrical 2-layer (1=8th)." Florestan nodded and continued, "At the end of the first section of the Sarabande of the second *English Suite*, grouping dissonance similarly occurs on two levels. In mm. 9–10, registral accents and harmonic change together organize the eighth-note pulse into threes, resulting in G3/2 in interaction with the metrical 2-layer. In mm. 10-11, harmonic changes occur at four eighth-note intervals; the interaction of the resulting 4-layer with the metrical 6-layer produces G6/4. The Gigue of the third *English Suite* includes a fine example of higher-level grouping dissonance. In mm. 13-15, harmonic changes result in a 9-layer (1=8th), and hence in subliminal dissonance against the metrical 6- and 12-layers." Raro interrupted once more, saying, "My favorite example of grouping dissonance from the works of Bach is the 'Tempo di Minuetta' from the fifth *Partita*, in which the steady eighth notes are grouped into threes by a recurring contour pattern, and in which the 2-layer expected in three-four meter is apparent only at cadences." Florestan said, "A superb example! These and many other metrical dissonances in Bach's keyboard music revealed to me how metrical conflict can be generated within steadily moving passages, even without dynamic accentuation (for Bach does not use the latter)."

Florestan paused to puff on his cigar. As he gazed up into the cloud of smoke that hovered above him, he was visited by another vivid vision: he saw himself bending down to pick up a pen near the graves of Beethoven and Schubert—a pen which he was to treasure as if it were a gift from the two masters.[8] He turned to Raro and said, "Also of great significance for the development of my rhythmic style were the compositions of Schubert and Beethoven.[9] Schubert's chamber works, with which I was occupied intensely in late 1828, and which strongly influenced my own first efforts at writing chamber music, contain some metrically dissonant passages that interested me.[10] For example, at the end of the first section of the slow movement of the Piano Trio in B♭ Major, Schubert creates the displacement dissonance D6+2 (1=16th) by dynamically accenting syncopated octaves in the piano part. During the following section, he presents the related dissonance D3+1, at first even employing syncopated octaves to forge a clear connection between two sections that are otherwise strongly contrasted. In the finale of the E♭ major Trio, Schubert quite frequently superimposes a 2-layer on the metrical 3-layer by placing density and dynamic accents at unexpected points.

"Among other works by Schubert that had an impact on my 'metrical education,'" Florestan continued, "were his waltzes for piano. Their significance for me must be clear to anyone who plays my early sets of piano pieces (particularly the *Papillons*), and to anyone who reads my writings; I reviewed the dances of Schubert's op. 9 and op. 33 in the *Neue Zeitschrift* in 1836.[11]

"The Viennese waltz in general, with its duple steps within a triple metrical framework, is conducive to metrical conflict—this is one reason why I was always drawn to this dance.[12] Schubert's waltzes, however, contain more displacement than grouping dissonance. The first few waltzes in op. 9, for instance, are perfectly consonant, in fact, predictable and somewhat square. The second section of no. 7 begins with a hint at D3+1 (1=quarter); the second beat of m. 9 is dynamically accented. In op. 9 no. 8, Schubert expands upon this dissonance, accenting the second beats of mm. 1, 2, 5, and 9. The dissonance is absent in nos. 9 to 11, but reappears in nos. 12, 16, 17, 18, and 21, where half notes on second beats result in durational accents (which are at times reinforced by dynamic accents). In no. 20, accents on the third beats of mm. 5–6 and 13–14 create the dissonance D3+2, which is also present in the first half of no. 21, throughout no. 22, in the first half of no. 23, in no. 25, and in the first half of no. 26. Nos. 27–30 are consonant. In no. 31, accentuation of alternate third beats in the first half and accentuation of alternate second beats in the second half results in loose relatives of D3+1 and D3+2 (D6+1 and D6+2). No. 33, dominated by D3+2, also contains incursions of D3+1 (m. 3, 11), and no. 34 begins with D3+2 (mm. 3-14) but ends with D3+1 (Example 3.8). The final two dances of the set restore consonance at the quarter-note level." As Florestan paused for some brandy, Raro remarked,

EXAMPLE 3.8. *D3+1 and D3+2 at the end of Schubert's Waltz op. 9 no. 34*

"From what you have said, it appears that the succession of metrical dissonances in op. 9 is planned; Schubert introduces D3+1 and D3+2 gradually and separately, then juxtaposes them within individual dances (first in no. 21, then in three dances near the end of the set)." Florestan agreed, and added, "This and other sets of waltzes by Schubert thus taught me how metrical dissonance could aid in the construction of a unified work out of a collection of short piano pieces written at different times — a problem with which I was often confronted in those years.

"Beethoven's music," he continued, "influenced my rhythmic style even more profoundly than did Schubert's. I heard some of Beethoven's symphonies in the late 1820s, notably the *Eroica* and the Seventh, and during my pianistic studies and my later critical endeavors became increasingly familiar with his piano sonatas. I mention but a few passages from Beethoven's piano sonatas whose metrically conflicted quality fascinated me: the opening theme of the slow movement of op. 7, in which durational accents and new harmonies fall on second beats until m. 4, creating a shifted 3-layer that strongly collides with the metrical layer in m. 5; the accents on third beats in mm. 9–15, and on second beats in mm. 55–65 in the second movement of op. 10 no. 2; the accents on the last quarters of mm. 75–77, 79–81, and 83–85 in the first movement of op. 10 no. 3; the displacements by a sixteenth note that permeate the first movement of op. 31 no. 1; the contraction, in mm. 67–71 of the first movement of op. 31 no. 3, of a three-beat cadential gesture (in three-four time) to a two-beat gesture, resulting in indirect grouping dissonance; the sforzandos on the final eighth notes of two-four measures in the scherzo of the same sonata; the strong displacement dissonance in the poignant passage at mm. 142-58 of the finale of op. 57, created by dynamic accentuation of the second eighth notes of two-four measures; mm. 47–50 of the first movement of op. 90, where right-hand durational accents and new harmonies fall on second beats (in mm. 55–58 and 61–64, durational accents on second beats continue the dissonance); the first movement of op. 101, where the displacement dissonance D3+2 (1=8th), created both by durational and dynamic accentuation, is used frequently, particularly dramatically at climactic passages (mm. 48–49 and 85–87); mm. 10–13 of the *Molto Allegro* movement of op. 110, where sforzandos and melodic repetition result in a shifted 2-layer. In the latter movement, the dissonance D2+1 (1=quarter) is augmented to D4+2 in the coda, where dynamically accented triads consistently fall on the weak bars within four-measure groups."[13]

EXAMPLE 3.9. *Metrical dissonance in Beethoven's* Eroica Symphony, *first mvmt.*

EXAMPLE 3.9. (*continued*)

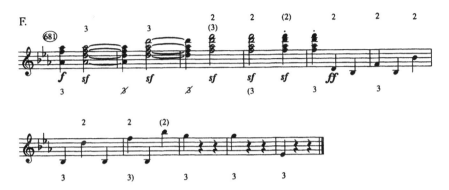

As Raro gaped in astonishment at Florestan's deep familiarity with the piano sonatas of Beethoven, the latter puffed smugly on his cigar, then continued, "Beethoven's use of metrical dissonance is not, of course, restricted to his piano sonatas. Let me remind you of just one relevant movement that I have mentioned in my writings:[14] the first movement of the *Eroica* Symphony, in which Beethoven exploits the dissonances G3/2, D3+1, and D3+2 (1=quarter). Within the first twenty-five measures, the only dissonance is the striking syncopation at the eighth-note level in mm. 7–8. Thereafter, Beethoven emphatically introduces G3/2 and D3+2. In mm. 25–32, sforzandos in all instruments and registral accents in the first violins mark off a 2-layer, resulting in G3/2 (Example 3.9a). In mm. 32–34, G3/2 is replaced by indirect and subliminal D3+2; sforzandos and registral accents now articulate a displaced 3-layer rather than a 2-layer. In the final measures of the first theme area (mm. 35–36), Beethoven restores the metrical 3-layer and metrical consonance. During the transition, D3+1 makes its first appearance (mm. 45–54, Example 3.9b); the motivic fragments tossed from instrument to instrument, each beginning with a durational or dynamic accent, establish a 3-layer shifted by one pulse, while the metrical 3-layer is intermittently expressed by the cellos' and double basses' reiterations of the note F on notated downbeats. In mm. 55-57, as the second theme begins, consonance is reestablished.

"Later in the second theme area, however, Beethoven brings back D3+1. The second beats are emphasized by instrumental entrances (density accents) in mm. 83–87, 91–93, and 95–98, and by initiations of new harmonies in mm. 99-101, so that a clear antimetrical layer shifted by one quarter-note pulse is established. The metrical 3-layer is intermittently expressed by durational accents (mm. 86 and 96) and changes of harmony (mm. 91 and 97). Beethoven also hints at D3+2 in this passage by placing sforzandos on third beats in mm. 85 and 89.

"D3+1 becomes unprecedentedly intense at the beginning of the closing group in mm. 109–16 (Example 3.9c). In mm. 109–12, dynamic and density accents on the second beats and, in mm. 113–16, initiation on the same beats of a repeated rhythmic figure beginning with a durational accent (reminiscent of mm. 45–54) result in a clear antimetrical 3-layer. The metrical 3-layer is to some extent maintained by harmonic changes in this passage. Two measures of consonance (mm. 117–18) lead in mm. 119–27 to a reappearance of G3/2, absent since mm. 32, the antimetrical layer resulting from sforzandos on alternate beats. Beethoven reiterates the progression D3+1 to G3/2 with different music in mm. 124–31. The motivic displacement dissonances each make one more brief appearance within the exposition; dynamic accents in the violas and second violins form D3+1 in mm. 145–46, and in mm. 135–39, ties initiated on beat three result in durational accents and hence in weak D3+2. Otherwise, the final measures of the exposition are primarily consonant.

"In the development section, Beethoven continues to play the three motivic dissonances off against each other. D3+2 in mm. 160–65 (durational accents on beat three versus bass attacks on beat one) yields to D3+1 in mm. 166–77 (which recall mm. 45–54). Measures 198–202 contain D6+2, a loose relative of D3+2; sforzandos fall on alternate third beats rather than on each third beat. Subtle G3/2 appears in mm. 208–9 and 212–13, where pattern repetition in the first violins creates a duple layer. D3+1 is featured in the passage leading up to the main climax of the development section (mm. 220–49), the antimetrical layer being formed by displaced motivic groups (as in mm. 45–54) and, after m. 236, by sforzandos on beat two (resulting in an effect of intensification). In mm. 248–53 (Example 3.9d), D3+1 is answered by G3/2, and regular alternation between the two dissonances—two bars of D3+1 followed by four of G3/2—continues until m. 271. In mm. 271–79, the climactic measures, one gains the impression that D3+1 and G3/2 are forced into even closer association—compressed or crushed together, so to speak. (How appropriate is this gesture for these particularly intense measures!) In mm. 270–75, for instance, the duple layer is expressed without interruption by the accented attacks of the winds and high strings. Harmonic change at m. 272 and 274, however, results in clear articulation of notated downbeats, and thus in hints at D3+1 (although G3/2 continues as well). In mm. 276–78 (Example 3.9e), D3+1 is emphatically articulated as the strings and winds shriek at each other, but in mm. 278–80, where the 2-layer predominates, D3+1 merges into G3/2. Measures 280–84 gradually resolve the metrical dissonance (just as they resolve the intense pitch dissonance). Some listeners might hear the first chord in m. 280 as the downbeat, and the resolution of the ninth in m. 282 might similarly be heard as a metrical accent. These prominent second beats imply a shifted 3-layer and hence, continuing D3+1. Full metrical resolution takes place at m. 284, beautifully coordinated with harmonic resolution. Most of the remainder of the development section is metrically consonant. Hints at D3+2 appear at mm. 305, 307, 309, and 317 (where sforzandos appear on third beats), and the climactic G3/2 is weakly echoed at mm. 338–64 (where the rising notes of string arpeggiations establish a duple layer while durational accents in the winds maintain the metrical 3-layer).

"The coda (beginning at m. 551) brings some interesting new developments. Beethoven begins it with consonance, then states G3/2 in the same fashion as at the end of the development section (cf. mm. 603–14 and 338–64). In mm. 615–20, Beethoven superimposes D3+1 and G3/2. The metrical layer, expressed by the durational accents in the horns, is set against a duple layer formed by pattern repetition in the low strings, and against a 3-layer displaced by one beat, which is created by durational accents in the winds. Beethoven resolves this compound dissonance in two steps: the shifted 3-layer and hence D3+1 disappears after m. 620, and G3/2 resolves as the duple layer is abandoned in m. 631. Whereas the motivic dissonances are absent in most of the final, triumphant, tonic-prolonging passage, Beethoven does grant them one more appearance each (Example 3.9f): the V7 within the final cadential progression (mm. 681–88) is associated first with D3+1 (the shifted 3-layer being expressed by syncopation and dynamic accents), then G3/2 (the duple layer being articulated by the attacks of a rising arpeggiation within the first violin melody). This final gesture not only reviews the two motivic dissonances, but also recalls the close associations between them earlier in the movement.

"Beethoven's metrical dissonances opened my eyes and ears to the immense dramatic possibilities of metrical conflicts deployed across large musical expanses. In Beethoven's music, I also discovered the effectiveness of simultaneous pitch and metrical dissonances (as at the climax of the development section of the *Eroica* and at the beginning of the coda of the first movement of op. 101).

"Of course," Florestan remarked as he refilled his glass, "I did not immediately absorb all of the techniques that I have mentioned into my earliest works, in which metrical dissonance is uncommon. Individual movements and passages, however, demonstrate that I was even at this early stage beginning to employ metrical dissonance in interesting ways. In one unfinished work—the Piano Concerto in F from 1830–31—the use of metrical dissonance is much the same as that in the music of Moscheles and Hummel; amid virtuosic arpeggiations and scales, there appear occasional brief passages of displacement dissonance and, even more rarely, some striking grouping dissonance.[15] In one passage, in *alla breve* time, I form three-quarter-note groups by repeating a melodic pattern of that duration. A dynamic stress on a fourth beat is at first heard as the inception of a final group of three, although later events do not bear out that hearing (Example 3.10). Another unfinished project that grew out of my early preoccupation with virtuosity was a collection of finger exercises, intended for a treatise on piano technique; I incorporated a number of these into my Foreword for the op. 3 studies after Paganini.[16] Many of these exercises contain displacement dissonance, particularly the set of nine that appears at the end of the Foreword. Here I force the pianist to accentuate points other than the metrical beats, in order to 'strengthen the individual fingers and to make them independent.'

"In some of my unpublished exercises, grouping dissonance arises from the repetition of scale segments within a metrical context with which they are incongruent. In one exercise, for example, I reiterate a pair of five-note scale segments in sixteenth notes within common time, with the result that the segments travel through several metrical positions before cycling back to their original one (Example 3.11).

EXAMPLE 3.10. *Excerpt from sketches for Schumann's Piano Concerto in F, ULB Bonn, Manuscripts Division, Schumann 15 (Sketchbook I), p. 25*

"My Piano Quartet in C Minor (1828–29) occupies a particularly important position in my development as a composer.[17] Whereas I ultimately felt that the work was not worth publishing, I valued portions of it very highly, and it contains my first serious compositional engagements with metrical dissonance. The first movement contains not only a great deal of low-level dissonance but also an interesting treatment of the displacement dissonance D2+1 (1= quarter). During the first portion of the movement, I render this dissonance progressively more perceptible. At the very opening, I suggest D2+1 by placing density accents on the offbeats (Example 3.12a). At m. 48, I imply the same dissonance by antimetrical slurring of quarter notes, and at mm. 58–59 intensify it greatly by writing dynamic accents on the offbeats. Echoes of the dissonance in the form of the rhythm 'quarter-half-quarter' pervade the remainder of the movement.

"In the third movement, there is little striking dissonance, but at m. 104 indirect grouping and displacement dissonance abruptly appear simultaneously (Example 3.12b). The durational accents in the melody result in a 2-layer (1=quarter) that forms G3/2 in conjunction with the previously established 3-layer, and imitation of the melody a quarter note later results in D2+1 as well. This sudden piling up of metrical dissonance effectively heightens the sense of climax. At mm. 106-7 the dissonance resolves, and the remainder of the movement remains consonant.

"In the fourth movement, repetitions of the progression I-V at mm. 40–42 and 48–51 result in an antimetrical duple layer and in indirect and subliminal G3/2 (Example 3.12c). In mm. 283–98 (a passage that Eusebius and I discussed

EXAMPLE 3.11. *Metrical dissonance in one of Schumann's unpublished piano exercises, ULB Bonn, Manuscripts Division, Schumann 15 (Sketchbook III), p. 23*

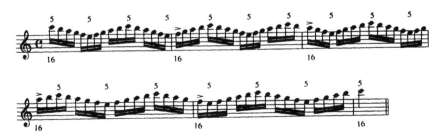

EXAMPLE 3.12. *Metrical dissonance in Schumann's Piano Quartet in C Minor (1828), ed. Wolfgang Boetticher, first, third and fourth mvmts. © 1979 by Heinrichshofen's Verlag, Wilhelmshaven, Germany. Ed. no. 1494. Used by permission of publisher.*

with M. Berlioz in Euphonia—Example 1.7a), the same dissonance is even more prominently stated; all notes in this passage have the duration of two eighth notes—a significant departure from, and a subliminal conflict against, the notated meter. The passage is characterized not only by dissonance in the metrical domain but also by pitch dissonance. Resolution in both domains occurs as the next section begins. Here, then, I began to explore the coordination of pitch and metrical dissonance, and of metrical dissonance and form.

"The second movement of the Piano Quartet is the most interesting from the standpoint of metrical dissonance. Already in the first three measures of the Minuet (Example 3.13), a 2-layer (1=quarter) formed by syncopation in the cello conflicts with the barely established triple layer to result in indirect and subliminal G3/2. Durational accents in mm. 1–3 suggest an additional 2-layer, displaced in relation to that arising from the cello syncopation, so that D2+1 emerges. In m. 5, yet a third dissonance is introduced: the figure "8th-8th-8th-8th-quarter" is imitated at the distance of a quarter note, resulting in D3+1. Measures 6-8 reiterate G3/2; the harmonic rhythm forms a 3-layer while two nonaligned 2-layers result from the slurring and the durational accents, respectively. As in mm. 1-3, the 2-layers produce D2+1. This metrically intricate opening section ends with a reference to D3+1, again produced by imitation.

After the double bar, I elaborate on or intensify individual dissonances. The lengthy passages encompassed by mm. 9–19, 34–39, and 46–57, for instance, are occupied by D3+1, produced either by dynamic and durational accents on

EXAMPLE 3.13. *Metrical dissonance in Schumann's Piano Quartet in C Minor (1828), ed. Wolfgang Boetticher, second mvmt. © 1979 by Heinrichshofen's Verlag, Wilhelmshaven, Germany. Ed. no. 1494. Used by permission of publisher.*

the second beat or by imitation of a three-beat motivic pattern at one-quarter-note intervals. In mm. 72–74, the G3/2 dissonance weakly articulated at the beginning of the movement and at the reprise (m. 42) is presented much more powerfully, the dissonance resulting here not from mere juxtaposition of a barely established triple meter and duple groups, but rather from the superposition of strong expressions of the metrical 3-layer and an equally prominent 2-layer. These dissonances are interspersed with brief resolving passages, which, however, are very much in the minority in this primarily dissonant Minuet. Part of the reason for the prevalence of dissonance in the Minuet was my desire for contrast against Eusebius's Trio, which is entirely consonant. The two complementary sections combine to form a movement in which metrical consonance and dissonance are used, I believe, quite boldly and effectively."

When he finished, Florestan thirstily drained his glass. As he did so, his gaze happened once more to fall upon the mirror across the room. He gasped in terror when again he saw the gaunt violinist, providing demonic music for a crowd of dancing skeletons and wraiths. But now the wraiths had the faces of Hummel, Moscheles, Bach, Beethoven, and Schubert; and now he heard the sounds of the violin—the ferocious displacements from the ending of Paganini's sixteenth Caprice.[18] Before Raro was able to stop him, he hurled his glass at the mirror. As slivers of snifter and mirror rained to the floor, Eusebius started wildly out of his chair and, perceiving Florestan's frenzied state, rushed to his side.

Clara, to whom the noise had penetrated even through her practicing, burst into the room. She stared, aghast, at the broken mirror and at Robert's wild-eyed and terrified face. It took her some time to calm him and to convince him that it was time to go to bed. With great effort—for in reaction to his outburst, he soon went limp as a ragdoll—she succeeded in transporting him to his room and putting him to bed.

FOUR

Metrical Progressions and Processes

When Eusebius, unable to sleep after the recent upheaval, suggested to Florestan that they should begin another chapter of the manuscript, Florestan listlessly acquiesced. They rose, settled on their sofa, and began to read, and after a few paragraphs Florestan became as absorbed as Eusebius in the author's argument. Clara, meanwhile, was attempting to calm herself by playing Beethoven's *Emperor Concerto*, the noble tones of which provided a background for Florestan and Eusebius's reading.[1]

METRICAL PROGRESSIONS

As was mentioned earlier, within each musical work a particular metrical consonance—the primary consonance—assumes the role of the normative state for that work. This normative state, however, is generally not a *steady* state. Most works do not continuously articulate the primary consonance; the degree of perceptibility of the primary metrical layer fluctuates, and antimetrical layers fade in and out. Most musical works are, in fact, spanned by a succession of metrical consonances and dissonances—a "metrical progression."

Inspection of the metrical progression of a work can tell us a great deal about that work's rhythmic structure. Among the questions that might be answered by the analysis of a metrical progression are the following:

1. Do particular dissonances recur? If particular themes of a work contain metrical dissonances, unaltered restatements of those themes will, of course, result in the recurrence of those metrical dissonances. Recurrence is more interesting, however, where it occurs independently of the restatement of a theme.

82

When a given dissonance recurs frequently within a work, that dissonance becomes motivic in function.

2. Are particular families of dissonances active in the work? We have determined that dissonances fall into various types of families, generally on the basis of similarities in their resultant rhythms. Musical works can be based on the members of a particular family of dissonances, with the result that the metrical structure of those works is highly cohesive.

3. Are particular metrical dissonances repeatedly juxtaposed or superimposed? Again, recurrence of such associations is most interesting when it does not occur in connection with the restatement of entire passages. Recurring juxtapositions or superpositions can act as motives, as can recurring individual dissonances.

4. What proportion of the work is consonant, and what proportion is dissonant on the surface level? There is a significant difference between a work that is mostly consonant, with only a few incursions of dissonance, and one that is mostly dissonant with a few islands of consonance.

5. How much subliminal dissonance does the work contain? The answer to this question, combined with that to the preceding one, reveals the extent to which the notated meter is contradicted within the work.

6. How frequently does the metrical state change? Does it change regularly? Does the frequency of change vary during the work? Frequency of change is an important way to characterize the rhythmic volatility of a work or section.

7. To what underlying progression can the surface progression be reduced? The term "metrical dissonance" suggests that, by analogy with pitch theory, dissonance is ornamental and could be subjected to a reductive process to expose underlying consonances. 🎵

"I suppose," Eusebius mused, "that the 'reductive process' to which the author refers is something like that which Johann Philipp Kirnberger applies to opera arias in his *Kunst des reinen Satzes*."[2]

The most basic metrical consonance, that to which any metrical progression would ultimately reduce (by analogy with the background tonic triad in the pitch domain), is the primary metrical consonance. In most works, dissonances, being temporary deviations from the primary consonance, are perceived as embellishments of that consonance.[3] In fact, certain embellishment types that are common in the pitch domain have metrical analogues. A metrical progression of the type "C-D-C" (where C is the primary metrical consonance and D some metrical dissonance) is often analogous to a neighboring motion in the pitch domain and, like a neighboring motion, reduces to the framing event C. Many metrical dissonances fall into this category. 🎵

Eusebius looked up, lifted his finger to command Florestan's attention to the passage from the first movement of Beethoven's Fifth Piano Concerto that rang through the house, and said, "Chiarina is just playing an example of such a 'neighboring motion'; a sixteenth-note passage clearly expressing the primary consonance leads into a segment in which triplet eighths are grouped into twos, and in which, in addition, there is some low-level two-against-three dissonance. There follows another consonant passage in eighth notes (mm. 149–59)."

$\mathcal{S}$ome metrical progressions are more reminiscent of another pitch dissonance type, namely the passing tone: these begin with a consonance C_1 and move through some dissonance D to a different consonance C_2. The analogy to passing motion is particularly clear when D is a grouping dissonance composed of one layer contained in C_1 and one contained in C_2, so that the effect of passing gradually from C_1 to C_2 is quite audible. Such dissonances reduce first to the progression "C_1-C_2." The next level of reduction would eliminate whichever of the two consonances is not the primary one (and which is therefore subliminally dissonant against that consonance).

Although these pitch/rhythm analogies are intriguing, an attempt at rigorous reduction of the metrical progression of an entire work does not lead to interesting results.[4] There are two problems with such reductions. In the pitch domain (in pre-twentieth-century tonal music), everything reduces to the tonic triad on the highest level; below that level, however, numerous passages reduce to other consonances, with the result that middleground levels are quite interesting and varied. In the metrical domain, on the other hand, the contents of the level analogous to the middleground are predictable; there is usually only one consonance (the primary consonance), and at most, two (the primary consonance and one other), to which all events reduce.

A second problem that arises when we attempt to reduce metrical progressions in a rigorous way is the role of duration. In pitch reduction of tonal music, duration is not a factor in the determination of structural significance; even very brief events (such as a cadential dominant supporting the scale degree 2 of a fundamental line) might be extremely significant. In the reduction of progressions that are composed of units of time, on the other hand, duration could hardly be ignored. It does not seem feasible, however, to establish a set of rules for the use of duration as a criterion for structural significance. Given a progression of the type "C-D-C" in which "D" is considerably longer in duration than "C," is the reduction to "C," by analogy to neighboring motion in the pitch domain, still valid? Just how much longer than "C" must "D" be before such reduction becomes unconvincing? Presumably, different listeners would answer these questions differently.

Given these problems, I abandon the attempt to reduce metrical progressions in a systematic manner in favor of intuitive, informal reductions to an underlying basic progression that spans the given work. Possible progressions of this type are large neighboring motions of the form "C-D-C" (where the work begins in a primarily consonant fashion, becomes more dissonant, and ends with restoration of the original mainly consonant state); curtailments of such motions, namely C-D (where the work begins consonantly but becomes dissonant and ends dissonantly) and D-C (where the work begins dissonantly but ultimately resolves the dissonance); and innumerable shadings of the basic states of consonance and dissonance (for example, a state "D," composed of a variety of individual dissonances or of a variety of degrees of intensity of a single dissonance). Such informal "bird's-eye views" of a metrical progression take us to the rhythmic heart of a given work — to its most basic metrical "narrative."

METRICAL MAPS

A "map" of the surface metrical progression of a work gives a convenient overview of its metrical structure. Furthermore, the comparison of metrical maps of different works quickly brings their metrical differences and similarities into focus. There are various possible formats for such maps. For example, one might list in the left margin the cardinalities of all metrical layers operative within the work, and might draw horizontal lines, with reference to a measure grid, to indicate where within the work the various layers are active. Pairs of parallel lines would show the consonances and dissonances resulting from the interactions of the layers. A map of this type, however, becomes difficult to read when a work contains many different layers of motion. It is generally more convenient to list the labels of all metrical dissonances and all consonances other than the primary one in the left margin. Horizontal lines, laid over a measure-grid, indicate the locations of each dissonance. The distinction between weak and intense versions of dissonances may be made by drawing different types of lines; I use normal lines for intense dissonances and dotted lines for weak dissonances. Those portions of the map not spanned by lines indicate passages governed by the primary consonance. ❧

Florestan, now having regained his customary energy, suggested, "Let us attempt to construct a metrical map of a short piece — perhaps the 'Valse allemande' from *Carnaval*." Eusebius said, "We should each construct a map and then compare them. You go ahead with the 'Valse'; I shall work on 'Estrella,' a piece of similar length." He fetched pencils and two sheets of paper, and for a time they scribbled busily.

When they were both finished, they surveyed each other's diagrams (Figures 4.1a and 4.1b). Florestan remarked, "These metrical maps show that the metrical progressions of the two pieces are similar in some respects: both are occupied almost entirely by dissonance, and both begin dissonantly and end consonantly. We might say that they both play out the basic metrical narrative 'D-C.'" "On the other hand," Eusebius countered, "the diagrams show significant differences between the pieces. For example, in 'Estrella,' one dissonance, D3+1 (1=quarter), remains active throughout, and is joined in the central area of the piece by others.

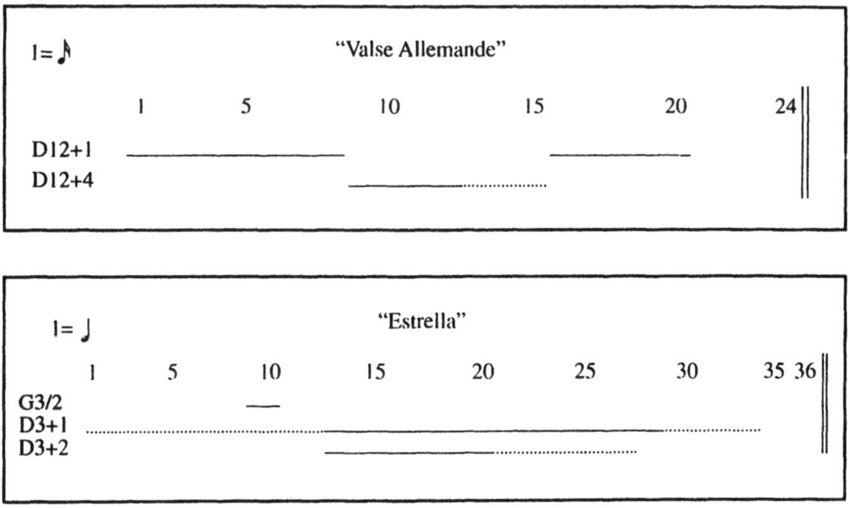

FIGURE 4.1. *Metrical maps of "Valse allemande" and "Estrella" from* Carnaval

The 'Valse' on the other hand is spanned by no single dissonance; D12+1 (1=16th) is active in the outer sections, but disappears in the middle section, where a different dissonance, D12+4, takes over. Furthermore, the metrical states change more frequently in 'Estrella'; in the 'Valse' there are three changes in metrical state (at mm. 9, 16, and 21), whereas in 'Estrella' there are five, namely at mm. 9, 11, 13, 28, and 35. If one were to count changes in intensity, there would be ten changes of state." Florestan added, "Your map suggests that a particular process underlies 'Estrella': the piece begins with weak dissonance, the dissonance is intensified, then gradually weakened and ultimately resolved." Eusebius noted, "I see that the author addresses precisely such processes in the following section." They continued their reading:

METRICAL PROCESSES

Another question that we might ask about a given metrical progression is, "Does the progression involve some sort of logic and order?" The statement that metrical progressions reduce to underlying narratives already implies that these progressions may be more than haphazard successions of metrical states. The orderliness of metrical progressions becomes even more apparent when one locates within a work particular processes affecting one or more states. Such metrical processes frequently function as shadings of the basic narratives "C-D-C," "C-D," and "D-C," resulting in subtle links between the basic states of consonance and dissonance, and even causing those states to merge gradually into each other rather than being bluntly juxtaposed. In the following sections, I investigate a number of metrical processes, categorized as follows: consonance-to-

EXAMPLE 4.1. *An abrupt consonance-dissonance motion in the "Préambule" from* Carnaval *(mm. 112–16)*

dissonance processes (abbreviated "C-D processes"), processes within a dissonant state ("D-processes"), and finally dissonance-to-consonance processes ("D-C processes").[5]

Consonance-to-Dissonance Processes

There are two possibilities for consonance-to-dissonance successions: they may be abrupt, or they may be gradual, in the sense that some foreshadowing of the dissonance may occur prior to its actual establishment. For abrupt establishment of dissonance, there are again two possibilities: 1) one or more interpretive layers that conflict with the existing consonance (usually the primary consonance) are superimposed on that consonance; or 2) the layer(s) that formed the consonance is/are abandoned, and a dissonance consisting of new layers is established. The former procedure is by far the more common one. 🎵

Eusebius interjected, "Most of our dissonant passages do illustrate the first procedure; but on occasion we have used the second, less common one. Your Préambule to the *Carnaval* contains an example, Florestan; from the primary consonance of mm. 106–13 you abruptly progress to a dissonance that does not explicitly contain the metrical 3-layer, namely D2+1 (1=quarter—Example 4.1)."

I refer to the more gradual manner of moving from consonance to dissonance by the term "preparation." This term is often associated with a particular dissonance type in the pitch domain, namely the suspension; the pitch that is to become a suspension is prepared by a prior statement of the same pitch in a consonant context. Metrical dissonances, too, may be prepared by allusions to a coming dissonance within primarily consonant passages. Metrical preparation generally takes the form of the suggestion of an antimetrical layer by just one or two pulses — not enough pulses securely to establish a layer and a metrical dissonance, but certainly enough to prepare a later appearance of the dissonance. Such preparation is found in Schumann's eleventh *Papillon*. Early in the piece (Example 4.2a), a single accent on the second eighth note of a measure hints at

EXAMPLE 4.2. *Preparation of dissonance in* Papillon *no. 11*

but does not yet establish the dissonance Dx+1 (1=8th; there is no way of identifying the cardinality of the layer at this point). This shard of dissonance,
placed at the beginning of the first section proper, relates to the later *Più lento*
section, in which D2+1 (1=8th) plays a large role; the dissonance is very strong
in mm. 32 and 41–43 (Examples 4.2b and c), and only slightly weaker (because
of the lack of dynamic accents) in the measures between those two passages. ❦

Florestan remarked, "Actually, I believe I intended the dynamic accents of m. 32
to continue throughout mm. 32–39. Perhaps I should have written them all out,
tedious though it would have been!"

The dissonance D3+1 at m. 27 of the Préambule from *Carnaval* (Example
2.7) is also prepared by earlier allusions. In mm. 7–8, Schumann begins to hint,
by dynamically stressing the second beats, at a displaced 3-layer and hence at
D3+1 (1=quarter). Several consonant measures follow, but in mm. 15–16, the
same suggestion of D3+1 returns. Again, a number of consonant measures fol-

EXAMPLE 4.3. *Preparation of dissonance in the "Préambule" from* Carnaval, *mm. 47–52*

low (mm. 17–26). In m. 27, the shifted 3-layer appears once more, and the resulting dissonance D3+1, prepared by two two-measure allusions, now lasts for no less than sixteen measures (taking the repeat sign into account). Another example of preparation occurs later in the same movement. In mm. 48, 49, 50, and 52 (Example 4.3), Schumann hints at a 2-layer, and hence at G3/2, by interspersing left-hand "oom-pah-pah's" with a few "oom-pah's." In mm. 54–61, the duple "oom-pah's" take over completely while the right hand continues to articulate a 3-layer. Sporadic, intermittent G3/2 prepares uninterrupted, continuous G3/2. 🎵

Eusebius remarked, "Our fifth *Novellette*, op. 21, contains another fine example of preparation; the opening measures prepare not one but several later dissonances. Your dynamic accents on metrically weak eighth notes in mm. 1 and 2 (Example 4.4a) foreshadow my extensive use of D2+1 (1=8th) in the relatively placid section at mm. 88–111 (Example 4.4b). Your dynamic accents on the last quarter-note beats of mm. 1 and 2 prepare the weak, yet audible D6+4 dissonances within the additional quiet interludes that I contributed to this piece—at mm. 33–35 (Example 4.4c), mm. 52–56, and mm. 205–9. (Some of these dissonances can be heard as D6–2). The third-beat accents in the opening measures also prepare your own more vociferous statement of D6+4 in mm. 153–57 (where you create the antimetrical layer with dynamic accents on the third beats)." Florestan remarked, "With the dynamic accents on the *second* beats of mm. 3 and 5, I prepare the D6+2 within your quiet second section (mm. 49–51—Example 4.4d). Finally, I hint in the first two measures at G6/4; the two V-I progressions, each occupying four eighth-note pulses, and the following two beats of F♯ harmony create a weak 4-layer. (I clarify this implicit duple grouping in the restatement of this material at m. 63, where I highlight the beginnings of the same duple groups with sforzandos.) The dissonance G6/4 is prominent within your quiet sections, namely at mm. 33–60 (Example 4.4c) and 209–19."

Florestan proceeded to mention some examples of preparation from their later works: "In the second Trio of the third movement of the First Symphony, a single third-beat dynamic accent in the strings in m. 314 hints at D3+2 (1=quarter). This dissonance comes into its own at the end of the Trio (mm. 337–42), where a succession of third-beat accents, and the initiation of harmonies on those

EXAMPLE 4.4. *Preparation of dissonance in* Novellette *op. 21 no. 5*

same beats, creates a more substantial and very prominent stretch of D3+2. (For harmonic reasons, it can also be heard as D3-1.) In the finale of the Piano Concerto op. 54, the very extensive G3/2 that we discussed earlier (mm. 188–228) is prepared by a brief hemiola a few measures before (mm. 181–85)." Eusebius added, "Another dissonance that we discussed earlier, namely the G9/6 from the end of the first movement of the Piano Trio op. 80 (Example 2.21), is similarly prepared by a few pulses of an antimetrical layer; in mm. 404–5, then again in mm. 406–8, we group the duplet eighth notes into threes by melodic contour, thus hinting at the 9-layer that will form continuous, though subliminal G9/6 in mm. 410–13."

Eusebius turned back to the manuscript and continued to read. Florestan, however, mused, "My mental and emotional 'dissonances,' like my metrical ones, sometimes arise abruptly, out of the blue. At other times, I can feel the storm clouds forming gradually within me. I know that an outburst is imminent, and I am powerless to avert it. . . ." When Eusebius began to turn the page, Florestan snapped out of his brown study, begged Eusebius to wait a moment, and quickly read what the latter had already absorbed.

Processes within Dissonant States

Metrical processes within dissonant passages may adjust a given dissonance, or transform one dissonance into another. Among the most common "D-processes" are those that adjust the intensity of a given dissonance. These may involve any of, and any combination of, the factors that distinguish weak dissonances from strong—the increasing of the continuousness and quantity of antimetrical accents; the increasing of the number of accent types that form the antimetrical layer; the addition of the particularly powerful accent types mentioned in chapter 2 (dynamic or harmonic new-event accents); the reinforcement by grouping of antimetrical layers initially delineated only by accent, or vice versa; the transference of an antimetrical layer initially announced in an inner voice to a more prominent voice, and so on. These processes may be reversed to create effects of deintensification.

A simple example of intensification is found at the beginning of Schumann's first *Papillon* (Example 4.5). In mm. 1–3, density accents within the accompaniment pattern very weakly establish an antimetrical 3-layer (1=quarter) and hence the dissonance D3+1; the metrical 3-layer emerges from chord changes and from the bass attacks. In mm. 4–6, Schumann conjoins the density accents with left-hand durational accents, so that D3+1 becomes slightly more intense. A peak of intensity is reached in the final measure of the first section, where Schumann adds a second-beat dynamic accent to the preexisting types. He maintains this maximal intensity of dissonance during the first two measures of the second section, then proceeds to deintensify the dissonance by eliminating accent types. In mm. 11–12, he drops the second-beat dynamic accents, and in mm. 13–15, the durational accents as well. (I consider the durational accents still to be present in mm. 11–12; although the second-beat notes are not sus-

EXAMPLE 4.5. *Intensification of dissonance in* Papillon *no. 1*

tained, the melody notes beginning on that beat remain in effect for the same relatively large amount of time as the sustained notes in the preceding measures.) In m. 16 Schumann surprisingly and wittily reminds us of the maximal intensity of the central measures. ❦

Florestan argued, "Are accompaniment patterns of the 'oom-pah-pah' form, with thick chords on the 'pah's,' always metrically dissonant? I do not think so." Eusebius mused, "The author does admit that such a dissonance is very weak. And although it seems unconvincing at first to consider the accompaniment pattern at the opening of our *Papillon* dissonant, I have no difficulty hearing it that way within the context of our gradual intensification process."

A more complex intensification process is found in the second section of Schumann's sixth *Novellette* (Example 4.6). Registral accents on the second beat in the uppermost voice in mm. 17 and 21, and durational accents on the same beat in the "tenor" voice in mm. 18 and 22, create a sporadic antimetrical 4-layer (1=8th), so that weak D4+2 emerges. In mm. 25–32, Schumann begins to

EXAMPLE 4.6. *Intensification of dissonance in* Novellette *op. 21 no. 6, mm. 17–40*

intensify this dissonance. The antimetrical 4-layer becomes more continuous in these measures—only one pulse is missing (in m. 28). A further intensifying factor is the involvement in mm. 25 and 29 of *three* voices rather than just one in the antimetrical durational accents. Futhermore, in mm. 25–26, 29, and 32, durational accents occur in an outer voice (as opposed to the "tenor" voice of earlier measures). Finally, in mm. 27–32, Schumann increases the number of accent types that participate in the delineation of the antimetrical layer; on the second beat of m. 27 he combines a registral accent with an accent of ornamentation, on the second beat of m. 29 a dynamic with a durational accent, on the second beat of m. 31 a registral accent with an accent of ornamentation, and on the second beat of m. 32 a durational and a harmonic new-event accent. The latter particularly prominent accent results in a peak of dissonance intensity.

As the opening music of the section reappears in m. 33, the dissonance is deintensified; multiple accents yield to single accents, and weak-beat durational accents retreat from prominent voices into an inner voice (compare mm. 32 and 33–34). The intensification-deintensification process is neatly coordinated with the ternary form of the section; the A subsections contain weak D4+2, and the B subsection intensifies this dissonance. ❦

Eusebius said, "Another fine example of intensification occurs in the piece that I named after the bringer of this manuscript — 'Vogel als Prophet.' I weakly suggest the dissonance D2+1 (1=quarter) in mm. 1–10 (Example 4.7a). The metrical layer is clearly audible in these measures, mainly because of the 'oom-pah-rest-pah' pattern in the left hand, sometimes curtailed to just 'oom-pah.' An aligned 2-layer is implied, as within any 4-layer, but I do not bring it to the surface as yet. I clearly establish an antimetrical 2-layer, however, by density and registral accents on the two weak beats of the measures; the thickest chords and frequently also the highest right-hand pitches occur on those beats. The dissonance is absent from mm. 11–12, but I bring it back with greater intensity in mm. 13–14 (Example 4.7b), where my placement of the main harmonies delineates a metrical 2-layer, and where an antimetrical 2-layer is strongly established by dynamic accents. The A section ends, as it began, with weak D2+1." Florestan continued, "In mm. 18–24, however, you take the intensification process one step further. You keep the metrical 2-layer just barely alive by durationally accenting the third beats of mm. 19, 20, 22, and 23 (in the right hand) and by the harmonic changes in m. 22. A prominent displaced 2-layer results from durational, registral, dynamic and/or harmonic new-event accents on beats 2 and 4; your frequent combination of numerous accents, including the most potent types, results in D2+1 of unprecedented intensity (Example 4.7c). The term 'Verschiebung' at m. 23 was a witty stroke of yours, Eusebius; it refers, of course, to the soft pedal, but it also means 'displacement,' which is at its most obvious here. In the final section you restore the weaker dissonance of the opening and retrace the intensification process only as far as the dynamically enhanced version corresponding to mm. 13–14." They turned to the manuscript and read:

Closely related to processes of intensification and deintensification applied to individual dissonances are those that intensify or deintensify dissonance in general within a given passage. A particular passage may become successively more or less dissonant in a variety of ways aside from the manipulation of one dissonance. Increased duration of dissonance, or increased variety of dissonance in juxtaposition or superimposition, may play a role in such generalized intensification of dissonance. A process of this type is found, for example, in the first sixty measures of the third movement of the Piano Sonata op. 11. Schu-

EXAMPLE 4.7. *Intensification of dissonance in "Vogel als Prophet" from* Waldscenen *op. 82*

mann begins the movement with short bursts of dissonance. In mm. 1–2 (Example 4.8a) and 4–6, sforzandos on third beats hint at D3+2. In the same measures, repetition of the resultant rhythm "quarter, dotted eighth, sixteenth" in conjunction with durational accents suggests a 2-layer and hence G3/2. In mm. 14–15, Schumann briefly refers to G3/2 dissonance, and in mm. 20–22 and 24–25 equally briefly presents D3+2. In mm. 27–32, Schumann allows G3/2 to occupy a much wider expanse (Example 4.8b); these measures represent an intermediate step between the initial short bursts of dissonance and the culmination of the intensification process in the first Trio. In this Trio (mm. 51–98 — Example 4.8c), Schumann not only continues the trend of durational expansion of dissonance, adhering to a dissonant state for no less than forty-eight measures, but also combines (in mm. 51–66) the two dissonances briefly stated within the first section (G3/2 and D3+2). 🐝

EXAMPLE 4.8. *Intensification of dissonance in the Piano Sonata op. 11, third mvmt.*

Florestan said, "The reverse of such generalized intensification is also found in our works. In my namesake piece from *Carnaval*, for example, the initial combination of D3+1 and D3+2 (mm. 2 and 4) is subsequently separated out; D3+2 occurs on its own in mm. 5–6, and D3+1 in m. 8. The dissection of the initial compound dissonance results in an effect of deintensification of dissonance."

Eusebius queried, "I wonder about mm. 27–32 of the third movement of op. 11 (Example 4.8b). These measures participate in an intensification process in the sense that they durationally expand upon earlier allusions to G3/2. On the other hand, the dissonance in a sense becomes less perceptible in these measures, for one of its constituent layers—the metrical layer—is not articulated." Florestan answered, "I believe the author addresses this point in the following paragraph."

℟elated to intensification/deintensification are processes that convert surface dissonance into subliminal dissonance, and vice versa. It might seem that a subliminal version of a given dissonance, lacking articulation of the metrical layers, would be weaker than a version where all layers are clearly perceptible, and that progressions from surface to subliminal, and subliminal to surface, dissonance should be regarded merely as special types of deintensification and intensification, respectively. The situation is, however, not quite so straightforward. Subliminal dissonances are indeed less intense than surface dissonances in the sense that they do not involve explicit superposition of nonaligned layers. On the other hand, they disrupt the normative metrical state in a clearly perceptible fashion, and in this sense do deserve to be considered "intense" dissonances. Because the relative degree of intensity of surface and subliminal dissonances is subject to interpretation, I prefer to designate processes that interchange subliminal and surface dissonance with terms other than intensification and deintensification. I apply the term "submerging" when a dissonance begins in a form involving explicit articulation of all constituent layers but then, by the elimination of the metrical layer, becomes a subliminal dissonance. I use the term "surfacing" for the reverse.

A submerging process is shown in Example 2.18. In mm. 45–46, the dissonance D4+1 is on the surface; the metrical 4-layer is delineated by harmonic change, the antimetrical layer by durational accents. Beginning in m. 48, however, only the antimetrical layer is clearly articulated, so that the dissonance is submerged.

The original finale of the Piano Sonata op. 22 (*Presto in G Minor*) opens with submerging and surfacing processes (Example 2.6). G3/2 is initially on the surface. The durational accents within the melodic line and a dynamic accent on the fourth sixteenth-note attack clearly express the metrical layer in mm. 1–2. An antimetrical 2-layer is suggested by a dynamic accent on the third sixteenth note and a low-point registral accent in the bass on the fifth sixteenth note. In mm. 3–4, G3/2 is submerged; the metrical 3-layer disappears while the 2-layer, now expressed by successive melodic attacks in both hands, becomes more clearly apparent. Measures 5–8 reiterate the process of mm. 1–4, as do mm. 9–12. In mm. 11–12, however (Example 2.6b), Schumann takes the submerging of G3/2 a step further by using dynamic accents to bring the antimetrical 2-layer into greater focus than ever before; the metrical layer remains unarticulated. The following cadential measures (mm. 13–14) restore the 3-layer while maintaining the 2-layer, so that G3/2 reappears on the surface. ❦

Eusebius inquired, "We earlier agreed that during subliminally dissonant passages, the performer should emphasize the otherwise suppressed metrical layer. If the performer does so, however, during works in which a given dissonance appears in both surface-level and subliminal forms, will not the distinction between those two forms of the dissonance be blurred?" Florestan responded, "The distinction, and the sense of surfacing or submerging, will indeed disappear if the performer overstresses the metrical layer. Performers should not assume that the metrical layer must be stressed in all pieces. In some of my works I desire an effect of a disjointed dialogue between different meters, rather than one of a unifying, consistently present metrical layer. Much of the opening of this *Presto in G Minor* falls into this category; I desire the performer and the listener to be hurled back and forth between states of superimposed triple and duple layers (surface-level G3/2 dissonances), states in which the duple layer dominates (subliminal G3/2), and states in which the triple layer dominates (metrical consonance). Thus, the performer should not attempt to stress the metrical layer during the subliminally dissonant passages in this piece." Eusebius said, "It would in any case be almost impossible to do so at this speed. The pianist will have his or her hands full with the stresses that you notate!"

Florestan nodded, then remarked, "I must mention a fine example of the surfacing of a displacement dissonance: the opening of my *Intermezzo* op. 4 no. 2 (see Example 8.7). In mm. 1–9, I form a displaced 6-layer by pattern repetition, by the attacks of a slow upward arpeggiation (E3-G3-B3-B3-E4) and, in mm. 3–5, by dynamic accents. I initiate the metrical 6-layer by the tonic octave in m. 1, but thereafter hardly articulate it, with the result that the displacement dissonance D6+5 (possibly heard as D6-1) is here only subliminal. In mm. 9–13, I again articulate the antimetrical 6-layer by dynamic accents, but now allow the metrical layer to be heard as well; it emerges from the entries of the left hand. Thus D6+5, at first subliminal, moves to the musical surface."

Eusebius added, "We have at times associated the processes of dissonance intensification and submerging to create an increasing sense of conflict against the notated meter across a passage or work. 'Abendmusik' from the *Bunte Blätter* op. 99 is a good example. The fanfare-like introduction establishes the primary metrical 3-layer (1=quarter) by durational accents on the downbeats. The main theme (mm. 4–12—Example 4.9a) immediately begins to challenge this layer. Durational accents in the bass fall, with two interruptions in mm. 7 and 11, on the third beats to form an antimetrical 3-layer, while durational accents in the melody confirm the metrical layer; the interaction of these two layers results in the dissonance D3+2. In mm. 6–8 and 10–11, we allude to G3/2; the metrical 3-layer is not clearly articulated in these measures, while the harmonies change at two-quarter-note intervals, creating an antimetrical duple layer and hence subliminal G3/2. In the second section (mm. 12–28—Example 4.9b), subliminal G3/2 becomes pervasive rather than intermittent. The varied repetition of the opening section in mm. 28–36 involves proliferation of the other dissonance established at the opening, namely D3+2; the antimetrical layer and the resulting dissonance here proceed without interruption (in the first section there were two gaps). We intensify the antimetrical layer and hence the subliminal dissonance G3/2 within the varied repetition of the second section (mm. 36–42), expressing the antimetrical layer not only by grouping (as in the corresponding mm. 12–28) but also by dynamic accentuation. In the new section encompassing mm. 62–86, similar to the Gb major section of your earlier piece 'Grillen' (cf. Examples 4.9c and 2.16), we revert to D3+2—here probably heard as D3-1—and submerge it by entirely suppressing the metrical 3-layer; there are no attacks on notated downbeats until the final cadence of the section. The concluding section restates

EXAMPLE 4.9. *Intensification and submerging in "Abendmusik" from* Bunte Blätter *op. 99*

the opening. Up until that return, the durational expansion of dissonances combined with increasing suppression of the metrical layer inexorably increases the sense of metrical disorientation. Against this process of metrical decay, I set occasional calls to metrical order—the 'all-ottava' utterances at the beginning and ending and at mm. 52–53 and 86–87, which counteract the disorientation by durationally accentuating the notated downbeats."

As Eusebius spoke, Florestan reflected, "The dissonance that ravages my soul occasionally comes to the surface in spite of Eusebius's 'calls to order.' But even when I appear calm and untroubled on the surface, dissonance rages within me—submerged, but nonetheless intense."

When Eusebius had concluded his remarks, he turned back to the manuscript, and Florestan, too, attempted to focus his attention on the next section:

We have so far studied D-processes that manipulate a given dissonance without changing its identity. There also exist processes that involve alteration of identity, generally from one dissonance to a related one. The simplest of these are the processes of augmentation and diminution—progressions from lower-level to higher-level, and higher-level to lower-level members, respectively, of dissonances belonging to the families "Gx/y" or "Dx+n." A passage from the

EXAMPLE 4.10. *Diminution in the Piano Sonata op. 14, first mvmt., mm. 8–14*

opening of Schumann's Piano Sonata op. 14 (Example 4.10) provides a simple illustration of augmentation and diminution of a displacement dissonance. Measures 8–11 are characterized by D8+2 (1=8th); dynamic, durational, and density accents on the second beats of these measures create a displaced 8-layer, while the metrical 8-layer emerges from durational accents (cessation of sixteenth-note activity) on the downbeats. In the immediately following measures (mm. 12–15), dynamic accents on metrically weak eighth notes result in D4+1, a diminution of the earlier dissonance. (D8+2 continues in a weaker form during the diminution.) In mm. 16–20, the process is reversed as the material of mm. 8–11 returns.[6]

In his Study op. 10 no. 2, a transcription of Paganini's Caprice op. 1 no. 6 (cf. Example 3.6), Schumann applies diminution to a dissonance prominent in Paganini's Caprice, namely G9/6 (where 1=a triplet thirty-second note). Schumann begins his transcription by emphasizing this same conflict (Example 4.11a). In mm. 1 and 3, as in Paganini's work, registral accents suggest a 9-layer. Schumann, however, adds a left-hand part in which durational accents fall on the second quarter-note beat; these accents clearly imply a 6-layer, and hence render G9/6 more apparent than at the opening of Paganini's Caprice.

In addition to intensifying Paganini's G9/6, Schumann transfers that dissonance to lower rhythmic levels; his transcription introduces the diminutions G1.5/1 and G3/2. In mm. 5–9 (Example 4.11b) and 13–15, Schumann superimposes triplet and duple sixteenth pulses, the latter pulse being the resultant of the nonaligned right-hand and left-hand eighth notes; these pulses together form G1.5/1.

EXAMPLE 4.11. *Diminution in the Study op. 10 no. 2*

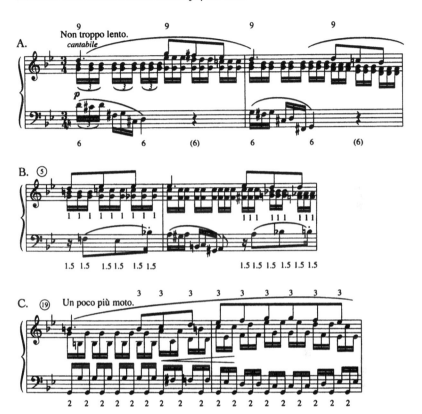

In mm. 19–26, Schumann introduces another diminution of Paganini's 9/6 conflict, namely G3/2. The duple grouping of triplet sixteenth notes is already implied in Schumann's left-hand figuration at the opening of the work, where chord members appear at two-triplet intervals. This grouping and the dissonance G3/2 become much clearer, however, at m. 19 (Example 4.11c), where a new oscillatory accompaniment pattern results in a 2-layer, while harmonic rhythm and right-hand melodic attacks continue the 3-layer. (Pianists will feel the tug-of-war between the two layers as they play the passage.) G3/2 continues in the right hand of mm. 27–35, and in mm. 27–35 Schumann combines G3/2 and G1.5/1. 🌸

Eusebius said, "We treat a displacement dissonance originating in the Paganini Caprice, namely D6+3, in a similar manner in our transcription. The dissonance appears only briefly and weakly in Paganini's work, namely in m. 8, where an antimetrical 6-layer is created by dynamic accents, and in mm. 13–15, where the same layer is suggested by slurring. We dispense with the displace-

EXAMPLE 4.12. *The final stage of a diminution process in the Piano Quintet op. 44, finale, mm. 224–26*

ment dissonance in m. 8 of our transcription, but intensify it in mm. 13–15 by accenting the beginning points of Paganini's displaced segments. We add hints at the dissonance at the beginning of the coda (mm. 46–47), where the left hand's high notes create registral accents on the metrically weak eighth notes. Diminution of D6+3 occurs at several points in our transcription: the staggered eighth-note pulses in mm. 5–9 (Example 4.11b), 13–15, and at similar places, which in conjunction with the triplet sixteenth-note pulse form the dissonance G1.5/1, create the displacement dissonance D3+1.5 in interaction with the right hand's metrically aligned eighth notes."

Florestan, again engrossed in metrical issues, added, "The Study op. 10 no. 2 illustrates that the dissonances involved in diminution are not necessarily contiguous; a diminution process may span a large area, its various stages interspersed with material not involved in the process. Another example of such an extended, intermittent diminution process is found in the finale of the Piano Quintet op. 44. At m. 21, we initiate the dissonance D8+4 (1=8th), and mm. 37–39 contain the same dissonance. A few measures later (m. 43), the diminution D4+2 appears; harmonic changes and string attacks determine the metrical 4-layer while the piano's density accents create a displaced 4-layer. (This metrical diminution arises from diminution of the entire earlier passage.) The progression 'D8+4 to D4+2' occurs again in mm. 156–84, where the material of mm. 21–49 is restated. The music at mm. 224–47 is the final stage of this diminution process (Example 4.12); the piano's agitated syncopation in eighth notes results in D2+1. The process contributes a great deal to the sense of growing excitement within the movement.

"The first movement of our First Symphony ends with a broad augmentation process applied to the dissonance D2+1 (1=8th). The horns form this dissonance in mm. 432–37 by syncopating at the eighth-note level (Example 4.13a). The strings in mm. 439–59, and the winds in mm. 447–59, syncopate at the quarter-note level, resulting in the augmentation D4+2. In mm. 464 and 468–74 (Example 4.13b), finally, the interaction of layers formed by significant harmonic change and recurrent bass attacks on the one hand, and by dynamic, durational, and registral accents on the other, results in the further augmentation D8+4. We place some reminders of an earlier stage of the process in the string parts at mm. 468–79, where quarter-note syncopations recall D4+2."

Eusebius chimed in, "Our Second Symphony is even richer in such proce-

EXAMPLE 4.13. *Augmentation in Symphony no. 1, first mvmt.*

dures. Your second movement ends with striking usages of augmentation and diminution. In mm. 357–59 you powerfully state D2+1 (1=8th) by placing dynamic accents on metrically weak eighth notes in all instruments. The first few measures of the subsequent frantic coda are consonant, but mm. 365–76 are dominated by the augmentation of the preceding dissonance, D4+2, formed again by dynamic accents on metrically weak pulses. In mm. 378–81 and 388–89, you bring back the quicker dissonance to generate momentum toward the final cadence; the antimetrical layer is now formed by accents of density, then duration, rather than by dynamic accents. In mm. 390–93, just before the final cadence, you once more state the augmented version of the dissonance by dynamically accenting the second beats."

Eusebius continued, "The third movement of the Second Symphony—one of my best slow movements—is spanned by an elaborate large-scale augmentation process. The initial accompaniment figure in the violas is syncopated at the sixteenth-note level, creating D2+1 (1=16th). In the violin melody, I immediately launch the augmentation D4+2; there is almost continuous eighth-note syncopation (durational accentuation of the second eighth note) in mm. 2–19. After a brief consonant stretch, D4+2 appears alone, formed by syncopation in the strings (mm. 26–30), but I soon reunite it with D2+1 (mm. 35–43). Another

EXAMPLE 4.14. *Tightening in the "Ländler" op. 124 no. 7*

brief consonant passage follows; thereupon, I bring back D4+2 and D2+1 and combine them with another augmentation, D8+4, created by quarter-note syncopation in the clarinets in mm. 48–53." Florestan commented, "I have always admired how you coordinated this climax of the augmentation process with climactic effects in other domains: in dynamics (*poco a poco crescendo*), register (highest pitches in the first violins), and foreground rhythm (trills). But we must finish this chapter; it is getting very late." They read:

Some D-processes apply only to displacement dissonances. I have made a distinction between tight and loose displacement dissonances — those involving frequent and infrequent contradiction of metrical layers, respectively. The motion from a given displacement dissonance to a tighter or looser relative results in processes that I call "tightening" and "loosening," respectively. Tightening involves the preservation of the displacement index while the cardinality is reduced by some integral factor. Loosening, on the other hand, involves increase of cardinality with preservation of the displacement index. These processes are related to augmentation and diminution; whereas the latter, however, are based on alteration of cardinality *and* displacement index, tightening and loosening involve alteration of the cardinality only.

Tightening is illustrated in the middle section of Schumann's "Ländler," op. 124 no. 7 (Example 4.14). In mm. 8–12, during two sequential statements of a V6/5-I progression (tonicizing V and III♯, respectively), the third beats of alternate measures are dynamically accented, resulting in D6+2 (1=quarter). In mm. 12–15, Schumann shrinks the sequential segments to a length of three beats by eliminating the neighboring embellishment of mm. 8–12. He continues to accent the beginning of each sequential segment; the resulting third-beat accents, now in *each* measure, create the tighter dissonance D3+2 (or D3-1). The 6-layers do not entirely disappear as tightening begins. Our attention, however, focuses on the 3-layers after m. 12.

A similar example is found in mm. 143–68 of the sixth *Novellette*. At m. 143, within a passage in which a 4-layer (1=quarter) is formed by harmonic changes at two-measure intervals, Schumann initiates dynamic accentuation of alternate second beats, resulting in the dissonance D4+1. Displacement by a quarter note continues after m. 151 (see Example 2.11), but the cardinalities of the obvious conflicting layers are reduced to 2, resulting in the tighter dissonance D2+1. In mm. 151–57, for example, harmonies change on each downbeat, reinforcing the metrical 2-layer, and dynamic and durational accents on each second beat create an antimetrical 2-layer. Tightening of displacement dissonance is matched by a steady increase in dynamic level, and resolution of D2+1 at m. 169 coincides with an abrupt decrease in volume. 🐝

Eusebius said, "We thoroughly explored the processes of tightening and loosening in our string quartets. I could mention many examples: the tightening near the beginning of the finale of the First Quartet (mm. 11–17) from D4+1 to D2+1 (1=quarter); from D6+2 to D3+2 (1=quarter) in mm. 49–56 of the first movement of the Second Quartet; and from D6+5 (or D6-1) to D3+2 (or D3-1; 1=8th) in mm. 1–16, 17–25, and 25–48 of the second movement of the Third Quartet. The exposition of the first movement of the First Quartet demonstrates that tightening and loosening, like augmentation and diminution, may take place over broad expanses, the dissonances involved not necessarily being absolutely contiguous. This exposition is based on an alternation between tightening and loosening, resulting (if I may say so myself) in a pleasing rise and fall of tension. The first theme area begins with D12+3 (1=8th); there are dynamic accents on weak dotted-quarter beats of alternate measures in mm. 36–49 (Example 4.15a). In mm. 52–55 (Example 4.15b), we tighten the dissonance to D6+3; the cello provides durational accents on the weak beat of each measure. Loosening (reversion to D12+3) occurs in mm. 58–63 (where the first violin's durational accents and pattern repetitions delineate a hypermetrical 12-layer, while the second violin's and cello's durational accents on weak beats of alternate measures result in a displaced 12-layer—Example 4.15c). We adhere obsessively to D12+3 in mm. 68–91, whereupon our placement of dynamic accents on all weak beats in mm. 92–95 again tightens the dissonance to D6+3 (Example 4.15d). We once again loosen the dissonance in mm. 95–98, where dynamic accents fall only on alternate weak beats. A consonant patch follows (mm. 99–116), but at the very end of the exposition, we apply the tightening and loosening processes once again to the same motivic dissonances."

Florestan recalled some instances of tightening and loosening from the symphonies: "The coda of the finale of the First Symphony illustrates that tightening may skip a step, so to speak. In mm. 265–68 (Example 4.16a) and the related

EXAMPLE 4.15. *Tightening and loosening in the exposition of the String Quartet op. 41 no. 1, first mvmt.*

mm. 275–82, the dissonance D8+5 (1=quarter) results from dynamic accents on the second quarter notes of alternate measures (that is, on the fifth attacks of eight-pulse hypermeasures). In mm. 285–88 (Example 4.16b), we create D2+1 by placing dynamic, then durational accents on second and fourth quarters. The progression from D8+5 to the tighter relative D2+1 skips over the intermediate D4+1 (which, to be sure, is embedded in D2+1). After repeating the progression 'D8+5 to D2+1' in mm. 297–312, however, we fill in the skipped step. In mm. 313–20, D8+5 returns, again produced by dynamic accents on second quarters of alternate measures. As before, D2+1 follows, but this time we place the embedded D4+1 into relief by dynamically stressing the second quarters of all measures (mm. 320–22 — Example 4.16c).

EXAMPLE 4.16. *Tightening in the coda of the finale of Symphony no. 1*

"A large part of the exposition of the finale of the Fourth Symphony is spanned by successive tightening. The melody of mm. 27–37 is characterized by descending arpeggiations in each measure. We precede the arpeggiation of every second measure with an octave leap that delays the arpeggiation by one beat and results in registral and durational accents on the second beats (Example 4.17a). These accents, reinforced by dynamic stress, interact with the hypermetrical 8-layer created by pattern repetition to form the dissonance D8+1 (1=quarter). The related theme in mm. 39–57 (Example 4.17b) is characterized by second-beat durational, registral, and/or dynamic accents in each bar (with a few exceptions), which result in the tighter dissonance D4+1. Measures 58–62 are consonant, but within their varied repetition in mm. 63–65 (Example 4.17c), we add dynamic accents on all metrically weak beats, resulting in a further tightening to D2+1. With this broad tightening process," Florestan concluded, "we attempted to imbue this exposition with a sense of heightening tension."

Eusebius remarked, "The author's D-processes are all associated in some manner with effects of increasing or decreasing of tension. In the case of intensification and deintensification, these effects are obvious. Diminution and tightening, since they involve an increase of speed and in frequency of contradiction of

EXAMPLE 4.17. *Tightening in the finale of Symphony no. 4*

metrical pulses, respectively, are appropriate when an increase of tension is desired, whereas augmentation and loosening suggest relaxation." Florestan said, "The process of submerging is more difficult to classify in terms of its degree of tension. Since in this process the metrical component of a dissonance disappears from the musical surface, resulting in a decrease in *obvious* contradiction of metrical layers, the overall effect might appear to be one of decrease of tension. On the other hand, as the author suggests, because submerging involves suppression of metrical layers, it is a particularly strong contradiction of the primary consonance. It is the latter perspective on submerging that underlies our subliminal dissonances; we expect the performer to ensure that submerged dissonances convey an effect of tension rather than relaxation."

Eusebius yawned and said, "Speaking of relaxation, I would very much like to sleep now." Florestan, however, observed that there was only one more unit in the chapter, and insisted that they should finish it before retiring.

Dissonance-to-Consonance Processes (Resolutions)

Progressions from dissonance to consonance can, following our pitch-to-rhythm analogy, be termed "resolutions."[7] Whereas in tonal music, many dissonances in the pitch domain arouse the expectation of a particular resolution even out of context, metrical dissonances do not in themselves imply specific resolutions.

EXAMPLE 4.18. *Resolution of dissonance in the "Préambule" from* Carnaval

Within a given context, however, particular resolutions may well be implied by the composer, and expected by the listener. If, for example, a 3-layer is the well-established primary metrical layer, and a 2-layer is for a time superimposed on that layer, the listener will expect the 2-layer to be abandoned and the triple consonance to be restored. When such restoration of earlier consonance occurs, there is undeniably an effect akin to that associated with resolution of pitch dissonance—a sense of satisfaction, of a devoutly wished consummation. The term "resolution," in short, seems perfectly appropriate as a designation for dissonance-to-consonance processes.

Resolution may occur abruptly, or gradually. Abruptness of resolution is always relative, never absolute, for any juxtaposition of dissonance with consonance results in an indirect dissonance between juxtaposed interpretive layers, which endures until the listener's memory of the abandoned layer fades. There is thus always a transitional phase between a metrical dissonance and a resolving consonance. Nevertheless, some dissonances resolve relatively abruptly and others only by stages.

Abrupt resolutions subdivide into two classes: those that occur by the abandonment of one (or more) of the layers of motion contained within the dissonance, and those that occur by the establishment of a consonance none of whose layers were contained within the dissonance. The latter class of resolutions is rare. Such resolution is most likely to occur when a dissonance that did not contain the primary metrical layer is followed by the primary consonance. A striking example occurs at the end of the Préambule of *Carnaval* (Example 4.18). Measures 130–34 are occupied by the displacement dissonance D2+1; the left hand's "oom-pah's" create one of the constituent 2-layers, the right hand's dynamically accented attacks form the other. At the end of the movement, as one would expect, the 2-layers drop out and the metrical 3-layer is reinstated. 🦋

Florestan pointed out, "The three final chords cannot entirely erase the 2-layers from the listener's mind. And 'Pierrot', in duple time, immediately brings them back, one of them now being the metrical layer. The other, displaced 2-layer appears in the form of *forte* exclamations at the ends of phrases and, in the middle section, in the form of syncopations."[8]

Much more common is the type of abrupt resolution arising from the abandonment of one of the layers contained within the dissonance. This type frequently occurs in the situation mentioned at the beginning of this section: a work establishes the primary consonance, the primary metrical layer is joined for a time by one or more dissonant layers, then the latter are abandoned so as to restore the primary consonance. Some of the examples from the beginning of chapter 2 illustrate such resolution. Immediately after the passage shown in Example 2.1, the displaced layer formed by dynamic accents is eliminated, so that the primary consonance remains. In Example 2.3, the antimetrical dotted-quarter layer is abandoned in mm. 3–4, again leaving behind the primary consonance.

A common ingredient of abrupt resolutions into the primary consonance is a dynamic accent that reinforces the initiation of that consonance. I refer to such accents as "corrective accents." An illustration is found in Example 2.16; Schumann highlights the end of the subliminal dissonance G3/2 and the reappearance of the metrical 3-layer by placing a dynamic accent on the downbeat of m. 71. Another example of a corrective accent is found in m. 99 of the first movement of the First Quartet (Example 4.15d). ❦

Eusebius said, "It is not necessarily the primary consonance that appears upon deletion of one of the constituent layers. In my slow movement of the Quartet op. 41 no. 2, for example, the section marked *Molto più lento* (mm. 64–76—see Example 8.33) is permeated by G3/2 (1=8th). The cello attacks clearly express a two-eighth-note layer, while the other instruments maintain the primary 3-layer by durational and dynamic accents and, to some extent, by their three-note complete neighbor groups. As the *Un poco più vivace* section begins (m. 77—see Example 8.34), the 3-layer (the primary metrical layer of the movement) disappears, and the continuing 2-layer forms a duple consonance in interaction with the eighth-note pulse." Florestan remarked, "One might think of such resolutions as 'deceptive'; the listener would expect abandonment of the antimetrical layer during resolution rather than deletion of the metrical layer."

Gradual resolution can take place in a number of ways. Many such resolutions involve D-processes that somehow prepare the impending state of consonance. A deintensification process, for example, can lead gradually from a state of dissonance to one of consonance. The dissonance shown in Example 2.2 is resolved in this manner. D6+2 (1=8th), produced by antimetrical dynamic and durational accents, endures throughout the *Tempo risoluto* variation. At the opening of the following coda (mm. 224–31—Example 4.19a), dynamic accentuation ceases, so that the antimetrical 6-layer (when it is present at all) is produced only by durational accents. This deintensification paves the way for the resolution at m. 232. Schumann maintains metrical consonance in the greater part of the coda, but concludes the movement with a review of the progression from dissonance through deintensification to consonance (Example 4.19b).

EXAMPLE 4.19. *Gradual resolution by deintensification in the String Quartet op. 41 no. 3, second mvmt.*

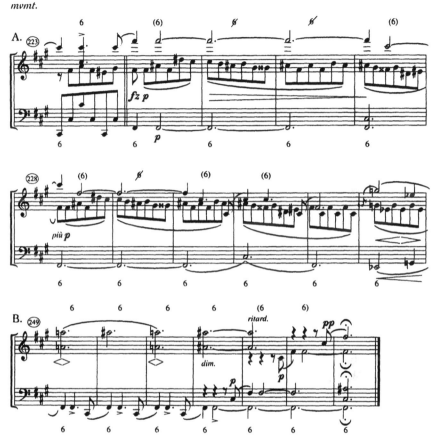

The above example involves a form of loosening as well; Schumann drops attacks of the antimetrical layer in the first seven measures of the coda (though not in the systematic fashion of other instances of loosening mentioned here). The process of loosening is another appropriate vehicle for gradual resolution. It provides an intermediate stage of "dilution" between the original dissonance and the state of resolution; some antimetrical accents are eliminated, in preparation for the elimination of all of them. Further instances of loosening leading into resolution can be found in the first movement of the First String Quartet. The progression of D6+3 to D12+3 in mm. 92–98 (Example 4.15d) leads nicely into the following consonance. The same metrical progression takes place at the beginning of the development section (mm. 129–41) and in mm. 193–207.

Resolution of compound dissonances frequently occurs by a gradual shedding of interpretive layers until only one, and thus metrical consonance (usually the primary consonance), remains. The compound dissonance shown in Example 4.8c resolves in this manner. Both constituent dissonances (D3+2 and G3/2) remain in place from m. 50 to m. 66. In the latter measure, Schumann eliminates the 2-layer by altering the bass line. A displaced 3-layer, however, remains in effect along with the metrical layer (which continues to be expressed by the recurring bouncing eighth-note idea).[9] In mm. 94 and 96–98, the antimetrical 3-layer, highlighted by dynamic accents, flares up to a peak of intensity, then fizzles out in m. 99, so that D3+2 is at least temporarily resolved. 🎔

Eusebius observed, "My second theme for the first movement of the Third String Quartet provides another fine example of gradual resolution of a compound dissonance. Deintensification also plays a role within this resolution. I begin the theme (Example 4.20a) with a blend of D2+1 (or D2-1) and D12+8 (1=8th). The former dissonance arises from the persistent nonalignment of the melody and accompaniment. If I had written the accompaniment chords as afterbeats, the dissonance would be relatively weak (as in other cases of the 'oom-pah' type of accompaniment). Since the first accompaniment chord, however, precedes the first melody note, the layer formed by the chords assumes great prominence. It sounds, in fact, like the metrical layer, and the layer formed by the melody notes sounds syncopated, or antimetrical; the result is a situation of intense dissonance. The other component of the compound dissonance, D12+8, arises from my placement of registral and durational accents on alternate second beats. The metrical 12-layer is, in fact, virtually imperceptible, with the result that D12+8 is subliminal. At m. 62 (Example 4.20b), I weaken the dissonance, expressing the antimetrical 2-layer in the viola alone rather than by chords in three instruments. This deintensification process foreshadows the complete resolution of D2+1, which occurs when I entirely eliminate the displaced 2-layer at m. 74. D12+8 remains in effect throughout my resolution of D2+1. In mm. 76–80 (Example 4.20c), rather than initiating the resolution of the remaining dissonance, I place durational and dynamic accents on all second beats, thus creating D6+2, a tighter relative of D12+8. This tightening, associated with a rising chromatic sequence, is a deliberate reversal of the relaxing trend of the passage. It is, however, a temporary reversal; immediately thereafter, I return to and complete the resolution process. During the mysterious C♯-major arpeggiation in mm. 81–83, I eliminate the displaced 6-layer and clearly express the metrical layer by durational accents. After a few more rufflings of the metrical surface, I close the exposition with secure metrical consonance." Florestan said, "This is indeed a fine, imaginative instance of an extended resolution process. And now, Eusebius, we have only one more paragraph to read!"

As I mentioned earlier, we frequently refer to the most pervasive metrical consonance of a work as "the meter." The meter in a broader sense, however, includes not only that consonance but also the various conflicts against it, and processes such as those that I have described—in fact, the entire metrical progression of the work. Meter in this sense is not a monolithic, inflexible grid, but

EXAMPLE 4.20. *Gradual resolution of compound dissonance in the String Quartet op. 41 no. 3, first mvmt.*

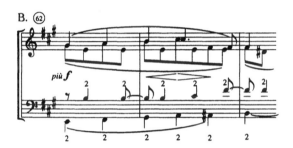

is as organic and expressive as any other component of music.[10] The moves from one metrical state to another in Schumann's music, and his adjustments of individual states, contribute greatly to the impact of his works; the resulting waves of tension and relaxation cannot fail to bear us as listeners with them, in fact to *move* us. ❧

Florestan closed the manuscript and said, "Now it is time for us to move from this sofa into our beds, and to resolve in sleep, at least temporarily, the tensions that have wrenched us this evening." They bade each other a good night and went to bed.

Intermezzo II

FIVE

Metrical Revisions

Florestan and Eusebius arose late the following morning. Clara, who was already practicing busily, had left breakfast for them on the table. They sat down and ate and drank in silence for awhile. The flow of coffee, however, was soon succeeded by a flow of conversation. Florestan's eye happened to fall on the shelves stacked with the manuscripts and sketches for their works, arranged in tidy bundles and bound volumes, and he said to his companion, "I recall your reference in Euphonia to my 'mutation' of your idea for the first Trio from the Piano Sonata op. 11. It seems to me that such revisions of metrical structure occurred frequently during our compositional travails."[1] Eusebius, thoughtfully sipping coffee, said, "They did indeed. Most of them involved your addition of metrical dissonance to passages that I had conceived in consonant form. Sometimes you inserted dissonant segments into my consonant contexts. In my early version of the original finale for the Piano Sonata op. 22 as well as in my later fair copy, the dissonance G3/2 (1=triplet 16th) that now occupies mm. 99–106 (Example 2.6c) was not present. When you revised the fair copy, you placed crosses and alphabetical labels at m. 99 and corresponding measures, and wrote the material to be inserted on similarly labeled loose pages. In an even later manuscript of the complete sonata, you included the dissonant passage at m. 99 and at several later points."[2] Florestan interjected, "I recall that we had some arguments then about whether or not to let the passage stand (the movement was rather long even without it). You crossed it out, but I, too captivated by its beauty to relinquish it, insisted on its inclusion. You finally relented, and permitted me to write 'gilt' in ink beside the passage."[3]

Eusebius went on, "I recall a similar revision in the Second String Quartet. In the completed finale, you included a four-measure passage in which all metri-

117

EXAMPLE 5.1. *String Quartet op. 41 no. 2, fourth mvmt., mm. 90–94*

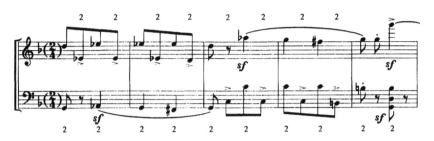

cally weak eighth notes are dynamically accented, resulting in D2+1 (1=8th; Example 5.1). In my first draft, these measures were absent."[4] As he spoke, Eusebius rose from the table, drew the folder containing the quartet sketches from the shelf, opened it to the page that he was discussing, and pointed out to Florestan that the present m. 89 was originally followed by a double bar, then by the present m. 94. As they continued their reminiscing, they constantly interrupted their breakfasts to remove another manuscript from the shelves, and the open folders and volumes gradually formed a rampart around their dishes.

Florestan observed, "More often than inserting dissonant measures into your consonant passages, I added new voices that were metrically dissonant against the existing material. My revision of mm. 25–27 of the Préambule from *Carnaval* comes to mind. In your early sketch of the passage—here it is on page 16 of our "musical diary"[5]—an emphatic, octave-doubled statement of the main motive in both hands was succeeded by two measures of soft repeated chords, then by a restatement of the motive in the left hand alone. I later followed the octave-doubled motive directly with a left-hand restatement and added to it a right-hand imitation (Example 2.7). The entry of the imitated motive on beat two of m. 27 already created D3+1, which dissonance I further intensified by dynamically accenting the beginning of the imitative entry. In the following measures (28–30, also 32–34), I added an 'oom-pah' accompaniment pattern whose pairs of quarter notes interacted with the continuing three-quarter-note motive to form G3/2. Thus, I clad your consonant passage in two types of dissonance by the addition of textural layers.

"Similar examples abound in our chamber music," Florestan continued. "In your draft of mm. 81–88 of the first movement of the Second String Quartet, you originally notated only the second violin part, which quotes the consonant opening theme in the dominant key.[6] In the fair copy I added a first violin and viola counterpoint in mm. 81–84, and open fifths simulating the drone of a bagpipe in the cello in mm. 84–87. Both the counterpoint and the drone durationally accentuate the eighth-note pulses just before the downbeats of the theme, resulting in the dissonance D6+5 (or D6-1; Example 5.2).[7] And do you remember, Eusebius, how we agonized over mm. 162–74 of the first movement of the Piano Trio op. 80—a contrapuntal spinning out of a portion of the second theme? There are three crossed-out attempts at this passage in our first draft.[8] Missing in all drafts, however, was the piano bass which, in mm. 165–70 of the final version, has dy-

EXAMPLE 5.2. *String Quartet op. 41 no. 2, first mvmt., mm. 80–88*

namic accents on the third and sixth eighth notes of the bar, resulting in D3+2 (Example 5.3). I added that voice and that dissonance in the fair copy."[9]

Eusebius, helping himself to a second roll and filling his coffee cup, said, "As the passage that I mentioned in Euphonia illustrates, you sometimes created metrical dissonance by adjusting the alignment of existing textural layers rather than by adding new ones. My first brief sketch of this first Trio from the third movement of the Sonata op. 11 shows that I originally conceived of its melody as being in accord with the notated meter; the melody's durational accents consistently fell on the notated downbeats (Example 1.6a). In your later, more detailed sketch (Example 1.6b), you shifted the melody backward to create the dissonance D3+2. You revised mm. 46–53 of the finale of the Piano Sonata op. 14—the *Concert sans orchestre*—in a similar manner. In your beautifully conceived final version (Example 5.4a), the triplet sixteenth-note figuration is composed of three voices, two moving by step and one reiterating a single pitch. The attacks of the lower and more prominent of the linear voices, each of which carries a 'new-event' accent, are not aligned with the eighth-note pulses of the two-four measures." Florestan interposed, "Furthermore, whereas most of the chords arpeggiated during the sixteenth-note figuration are passing chords, the second-to-last sixteenth note in each measure sounds like a strong harmonic arrival. The accents created by these new harmonies and those created by the melodic new-event accents that you have mentioned result in displacement dissonance on two levels." Eusebius continued, "In my rather tame early sketch for part of the passage (Example

EXAMPLE 5.3. *Piano Trio op. 80, first mvmt., mm. 165–70, piano part*

EXAMPLE 5.4A. *Piano Sonata op. 14, fourth mvmt., mm. 46–50*

5.4b), the various voices were aligned on the metrical eighth-note pulses, with no hint of dissonance.[10] Your revised version is a brilliantly colored butterfly that emerged from the humble chrysalis of my idea."

Florestan pulled the third sketchbook off the shelf and opened it to page 109, saying, "Here is a rather different and particularly interesting example of my injection of dissonance into one of your consonant ideas. In your sketch, apparently intended for violin and piano (Example 5.5a), a 2-layer (1=quarter) arose from the durational accents within the reiterated 'four-sixteenth-note, quarter-note' figure and from the dynamic accents in mm. 8–10. This layer interacted with a 4-layer produced by harmonic change to create the primary metrical consonance." As he turned to page 38 of the same sketchbook, he said, "Now look at my radical reworking of your material (Example 5.5b), which in every respect, including key, time signature, and instrumentation, much more closely resembles the ultimate destination of the passage—the second section of the *Intermezzo* op. 4 no. 5. From m. 5 of this second version onward, your 'four-sixteenth-note, quarter-note' motive, already announced in the initial measures, becomes particularly prominent. As in your earlier version, the durational accents within the motive form a 2-layer. Within my revised metrical context, however, this layer results in metrical dissonance; it conflicts with the primary metrical 3-layer, which I establish in the initial three bars by durational accents and repetition of the note D, and which I uphold in mm. 6–7 by the harmonic rhythm.[11] Thus, I created met-

EXAMPLE 5.4B. *Sketch for the same passage, Archiv der Gesellschaft der Musikfreunde in Wien, A285, p. 2, br. 7*

EXAMPLE 5.5A. *Sketch destined to be absorbed into the* Intermezzo op. 4 no. 5, *Universitäts- und Landesbibliothek Bonn (ULB Bonn), Manuscripts Division, Schumann 15 (Sketchbook III), p. 109, br. 1, mm. 5–10*

rical dissonance by importing a layer that was originally in alignment with the metrical layer into a new metrical context with which it conflicts."

Eusebius, spreading plum jam on his roll, said, "We have so far mentioned only your revisions involving the addition of new dissonance to my consonant passages. I believe, however, that most of your metrical revisions involved the manipulation of dissonances that already existed in my first versions (for not all of my initial sketches were devoid of metrical conflict!). Sometimes your manipulations took the form of altering the dissonance type that I had chosen.[12] More frequently, however, you simply enhanced the dissonances that I had already sketched."

EXAMPLE 5.5B. *Sketch for* Intermezzo op. 4 no. 5, *ULB Bonn, Manuscripts Division, Schumann 15, p. 38, br. 1–2*

EXAMPLE 5.6. *Draft of* Papillon *op. 2 no. 8, mm. 25–26, ULB Bonn, Manuscripts Division, Schumann 15 (Sketchbook III), p. 96, br. 1*

"Or," said Florestan, "that *I* had sketched. For instance, in my final revision of the 'mutated' version of the first Trio of the third movement of the Sonata op. 11, I added even more dissonance (compare Examples 1.6b and 4.8c); I made the bass hop back and forth between the tonic and dominant notes, rather than woodenly reiterating the tonic note. By pattern repetition and low-point accents, this activated bass established a 2-layer (1=quarter), which resulted in the addition of G3/2 to the existing D3+2, and in the conversion of a simple dissonance into a compound dissonance."[13] Eusebius noted, "My contribution to the final version was the elimination of the second version's inner-voice dynamic accents; I felt that listeners might find it difficult to absorb your added grouping dissonance if the displacement dissonance were too prominent."

Eusebius continued, "More often than adding layers to create compound dissonances, you merely intensified my simple dissonances, usually by adding dynamic accents.[14] Your fine-tuning of accentuation is evident even in our earliest works. In an early draft for op. 2 no. 8 (Example 5.6), I included a hint at D6+4 (1=8th) in the form of an inner-voice tie linking the third beat of m. 24 to the first of m. 25. In the final version, I eliminated this antimetrical durational accent; you, on the other hand, added dynamic accents on the third beats of mm. 24, 25, 27, 29, and 31, thereby greatly intensifying D6+4. Another early example of added accentuation is found in the ninth *Impromptu*, op. 5. I already suggested the dissonance D3+1 in my first version by writing durational and registral accents in the left hand (Example 5.7).[15] In both published versions, your added dynamic accents on the treble and bass notes played by the left hand significantly enhance the dissonance."

EXAMPLE 5.7. *Sketch for the opening of* Impromptu *op. 5 no. 9, Schumann-Haus Zwickau 4648–A1, recto, br. 4*

EXAMPLE 5.8A. *Draft of String Quartet op. 41 no. 1, first mvmt., mm. 20–23, Deutsche Staatsbibliothek zu Berlin—Preußischer Kulturbesitz, Musikabteilung mit Mendelssohn-Archiv, Mus. ms. autogr. R. Schumann 19, p. 3, br. 5–6*

Florestan, pouring some more coffee for both of them, said, "My practice of adding dynamic accents continued to be frequent in later works. Compare your draft of mm. 20–22 of the first movement of the First String Quartet (Example 5.8a) with my final version (Example 5.8b). In the former, registral accents in the first violin part (mm. 21–22) and two dynamic accents on a metrically weak sixteenth note (mm. 21 and 23) already resulted in a hint of D2+1 (1=16th). In my final version, mm. 20–22 contain numerous dynamic and some registral accents on metrically weak sixteenth notes, resulting in more intense dissonance. Similarly, in your sketch of mm. 47–51 of the finale of the Third Symphony, the weak-beat dynamic accents of my final version (Example 2.18) were lacking.[16] Whereas your consistent antimetrical durational accents already suggested D4+1 (1=quarter), my reinforcement of the durational accents by dynamic accents resulted in much stronger dissonance."

Eusebius observed, "May I remind you that occasionally it was I who intensified dissonances that existed in *your* first versions? I did so, to be sure, by removing dynamic accents rather than by adding them." In the booklet of sketches relating to the String Quartets, op. 41, he turned to the beginning of the Scherzo movement of the second quartet and said, "The original version was typical of

EXAMPLE 5.8B. *Final version of the passage*

EXAMPLE 5.9A. *Draft of String Quartet op. 41 no. 2, third mvmt., mm. 1–3, Deutsche Staatsbibliothek zu Berlin—Preußischer Kulturbesitz, Musikabteilung mit Mendelssohn-Archiv, Mus. ms. autogr. R. Schumann 19, p. 27, br. 3*

your style; you insistently contradicted the notated meter by placing density accents, harmonic new-event accents, and some dynamic stresses on the upbeats (Example 5.9a). When I copied your version out, I initially left its metrical structure unchanged, except that I transformed pairs of your three-four measures into measures of six-eight (since I felt that eighth notes better suggested the fleet-footed character of the movement). Subsequently, however, I revised the passage by crossing out all of your dynamic stresses on weak beats and adding downbeat stresses in m. 4 and in the corresponding m. 12; we agreed to publish the passage in this revised form (Example 5.9b).[17] Whereas your draft, with its offbeat stresses, *looked* strongly dissonant, I realized that the dissonance would hardly be evident to listeners. One of the layers involved in the apparent dissonance—the metrical layer—was virtually imperceptible. Most listeners would likely have heard the layer of motion resulting from the dynamic stresses as the metrical layer, and would have perceived no conflict against it. My final version incorporates features that clearly convey the metrical layer—the added downbeat stresses, and retains others that establish a displaced 6-layer—the density and harmonic new-event accents, with the result that a conflict between nonaligned layers becomes much more clearly apparent."

Florestan said, "I recall that you advocated a similar revision at the opening of the finale of the Piano Sonata op. 11. As Meister Raro pointed out yesterday, the

EXAMPLE 5.9B. *Final version of the passage, mm. 1–5*

EXAMPLE 5.10. *Piano Sonata op. 11, finale, mm. 1–4*

opening theme of this movement involves a clear duple grouping of quarter-note beats that conflicts with the notated three-four meter (Example 5.10). In my early version of the opening, virtually identical to the final version in terms of pitches and durations, I had emphasized the 2-layer by placing dynamic accents on the first and third beats of the first measure, a tenuto marking on the second beat of m. 2, and similar tenuto markings in mm. 4 and 6.[18] I did not realize at first that since this was the opening of a movement and the notated meter had in no way been established, this version, in spite of its appearance, did not sound dissonant, but gave the impression of undisturbed duple meter (with a larger triple grouping). Your elimination of the dynamic accents in the final version gave the notated three-four meter a fighting chance of becoming audible; the pianist, not told to accent the attacks of the duple layer, was now at liberty to give some subtle accentuation to the notated downbeats so as to render audible the conflict between the metrical 3-layer and the built-in 2-layer. But please refresh my memory, Eusebius: why did you not excise the corresponding accents during the restatements of the opening theme in mm. 49–57, 190–205, 238–46, and 381–96?" Eusebius responded, "I felt that at these later points, the listener would have sufficiently grasped the notated triple meter, would be able to maintain it during the theme, and, in spite of the accents, would perceive the dissonance G3/2 rather than duple consonance."

Florestan, wiping some jam from his hand, said, "Your revisions, Eusebius, notwithstanding the two movements that we have just discussed, generally resulted not in intensification but in deletion or deintensification of dissonance. At times you persuaded me to eliminate dissonant passages entirely. The fourth piece in our first edition of the *Impromptus* op. 5, for example, contained much displacement dissonance. When we prepared the second edition, you recommended the elimination of this variation and its replacement with a metrically consonant one of livelier character. Similarly, I planned to include in the slow movement of the Piano Sonata op. 14 a variation in six-eight time in which the second eighth notes of numerous groups of three were dynamically accented, creating D3+1 (Example 5.11). On your advice, I omitted this intensely dissonant variation." Eusebius responded, "I still think I advised you well. Displacement dissonance was already prevalent in several of the other variations, and also permeated the remaining movements of the work. I felt that some relief from this conflict would be appropriate."[19]

EXAMPLE 5.11. *Sketch for a variation intended for the slow mvmt. of the Piano Sonata op. 14, ULB Bonn, Manuscripts Division, Schumann 2, p. 3, br. 4, mm. 5–7*

Eusebius continued, "More frequently than I eliminated entire dissonant sections, I modified accentuation so as to weaken your dissonances. The manuscript of the *Davidsbündlertänze*, for instance, shows that you originally intended the middle section of no. 13 to be dissonant; under a right-hand part identical to the present one, you initially notated a syncopated bass line.[20] I crossed out this line and pasted the present nonsyncopated bass over it. My elimination of antimetrical durational accents resulted in a virtually consonant middle section."

Florestan said, "You revised my original conclusion for the *Papillons* (corresponding to mm. 63–92 of the finale) in a similar manner. You recall that the left-hand statement of the horn-call-like opening theme yielded in this early version to a chromatic progression in contrary motion, moving in steady quarter notes. My strategy within this progression was to replace an increasing number of the quarter-note pulses with silence—a strategy that I was also employing within the melody. After four measures of unbroken quarter-note motion, I suppressed the downbeats of four successive measures, then eliminated every second quarter-note attack (Example 5.12). The suppression of downbeats resulted in weak D3+2 (since durational accents occurred on the third beats), and the duple layer formed by the elimination of alternate quarters conflicted with the underlying primary metrical 3-layer to create G3/2." Eusebius observed, "In my final version, I retained your weak D3+2 (mm. 74–88), but dispensed with the more striking G3/2, so that dissonance in the passage is markedly less strong."[21]

He continued, "You have mentioned your addition of G3/2 to the passage that we eventually used as mm. 20–26 of the *Intermezzo* op. 4 no. 5 (see Example

EXAMPLE 5.12. *Sketch for the conclusion of* Papillons, *ULB Bonn, Manuscripts Division, Schumann 15 (Sketchbook III), p. 53, br. 1–2*

EXAMPLE 5.13. Intermezzo *op. 4 no. 5, mm. 20–26*

5.5). But I later reshaped the passage once again, eliminating the dissonance (Example 5.13). I excised a dynamic accent and a tie across the bar line—that is, an antimetrical durational accent—that contributed to the establishment of this dissonance (compare m. 3 of Example 5.5b and m. 25 of Example 5.13). After the cadence in m. 26, I dispensed with the imitation of the 'four-sixteenth-note, quarter-note' motive, thereby eliminating durational accents on alternate beats that had also participated in the formation of G3/2."

Florestan remarked, "In connection with op. 4 no. 5, you have mentioned the removal of a dynamic accent. I believe that you most frequently accomplished the weakening of my metrical dissonances by this method." Eusebius agreed, saying, "Striking examples of my removal of dynamic accents are found in the tenth *Papillon*. In your earliest version of the third section (Example 5.14a)—so early as to be in the 'wrong' key—you had only very weakly expressed the primary met-

EXAMPLE 5.14A. *Early sketch for* Papillon *op. 2, no. 10, mm. 25–29, ULB Bonn, Manuscripts Division, Schumann 15 (Sketchbook III), p. 88, br. 4–5*

EXAMPLE 5.14B. *Later sketch for the passage, ULB Bonn, Manuscripts Division, Schumann 15, p. 53, br. 4–5*

EXAMPLE 5.15. *Piano Quintet op. 44, first mvmt., reconstruction of the subsequently revised opening measures of the recapitulation (mm. 207–10), ULB Bonn, Manuscripts Division, Schumann 5, p. 13, br. 1*

rical 3-layer by registral accents resulting from the high points and low points within the left-hand accompaniment pattern. Your melodic new-event accents as well as occasional dynamic accents on third beats resulted in a prominent displaced 3-layer and hence in strong D3+2 (or D3-1). In my later version in the same sketchbook (Example 5.14b), in the 'correct' key of C major, I almost eliminated the dissonance by doing away with all antimetrical dynamic and new-event accentuation. The durational accents on the third beats (within the accompaniment pattern) kept the dissonance alive, but only as a shadow of its former self." Florestan pointed out, "Your weaker dissonance actually sounds much more like D3+2 than D3-1; with the disappearance of my anticipatory ties, there is no longer a sense of 'backward' displacement." Eusebius went on, "In our final version of this passage (Example 2.8), we stood by the elimination of the original syncopation but, with my approval, you reinstated and in fact multiplied the antimetrical dynamic stresses. The dissonance became considerably more intense than in the second version, but, because of the absence of melodic syncopation, remained weaker than in the first."

Florestan said, "I must mention one more of your deintensifying revisions." He opened the fair copy of the first movement of the Piano Quintet op. 44 to the beginning of the recapitulation. "Here, Eusebius, you see that I originally intended the recapitulation to begin with strong metrical dissonance (Example 5.15). I gave the right hand of the piano part an eighth note accompaniment pattern—a continuation of the pattern from the end of the development section. In the first two bars of the recapitulation, this counterpoint included new-event harmonic, registral (high point) and dynamic accents on the eighth notes just before the metrically accented points, resulting in the dissonance D4+3 (or D4-1; 1=8th). In the third and fourth measures of the recapitulation, I changed the right-hand pattern, retaining the steady eighth note rhythm but placing dynamically accented double notes, anticipating the following harmonies, on metrically weak eighth notes. The dynamic, new-event harmonic and density accents carried by these double notes resulted in a prominent antimetrical 2-layer, and in a tightening of the dissonance of the preceding two measures from D4+3 to D2+1 (or D4-1 to D2-1)." Eusebius interposed, "The manuscript clearly shows my revision of the passage; I crossed out (in red ink) all of the piano's metrically weak eighth notes and most of the antimetrical accents from m. 207 onward. (The retained antimetrical accents are inactive because the notes to which they pertain are deleted.) I rewrote the dynamic accents on the somewhat revised half note chords in red ink so that the metrical layer remained very clear; the antimetrical layer, however, was removed." Florestan added, "I did persuade you to leave one vestige of the dissonance in place, namely the sforzando on the last eighth note of m. 206, which highlights the beginning of the recapitulation."[22]

The door opened, and Clara walked into the room. When she saw the jampot in precarious proximity to the beautifully bound manuscript of the Piano Quintet, and a coffee cup perched on the open third sketchbook, she threw up her hands in horror and shrieked, "Robert! How can you eat and drink amidst your manuscripts! Do you not realize how much value these documents will have for later generations? Put them away immediately!" Eusebius said, "Now, Chiarina, do not excite yourself. The manuscripts are unharmed. Florestan and I have been consulting them while we have ruminated about our frequent revisions of metrical structure. Pray have a seat and let us show you some of the interesting examples that we have recalled."

Although his strange manner of speaking pained her, her interest in the subject was aroused and she joined him at the table. Eusebius tenderly put his arm about her and said, "First it is necessary to share with you what we have recently learned about metrical conflict." He explained to her the various types of metrical dissonance and the labels associated with them, and the processes within which these metrical states can be employed. She listened raptly, delighted by the lucidity of his exposition and captivated by the material. Florestan proceeded to show her some examples of metrical revision. She soon interrupted him, saying, "I would be very interested to hear for what reasons you made these changes."

Florestan mused, "Some of these revisions lie in the distant past; nevertheless, I believe we can recall the reasons for most of them. Sometimes the reason was internal to the given passage. My first sketch for the third section of the tenth *Papillon* (Example 5.14a) was frankly rather ugly; the displaced melodic attacks resulted in unpleasant dissonances against the accompaniment pattern."[23] After briefly surveying the sketch, Clara pointed out, "There are also concealed parallel octaves in the first two measures of the sketch, where the succession 'B-C♯' is duplicated, with displacement, in the outer voices." Florestan grimaced and said, "You are right. Eusebius's revision eliminated these problems. On the other hand, some passages conceived by Eusebius were originally rather bland, and my additions of metrical dissonance provided a pleasing pungency. This was the case, for example, in the development section of the first movement of the Piano Trio op. 80. The passage at m. 165 consisted, in Eusebius's original version (forgive me, my friend), of rather pedestrian imitation. My added displacement dissonance, created by offbeat accents in the piano part, rendered the passage vastly more distinctive (Example 5.3). Sometimes I added or intensified dissonance in order to avoid monotony within the recurrence of an earlier passage. In m. 25 of the eighth *Papillon*, for example, my third-beat accents at the second appearance of the Db-major theme (which were not present in Eusebius's first sketch — Example 5.6) lend the restatement a sense of novelty."

Eusebius said, "The explanations for most of our metrical revisions, however, are to be found not within the given passages alone but within their contexts. Some of the revisions arose from our consideration of the function of a passage within the form. For example, I persuaded Florestan to eliminate the displacement dissonance at the beginning of the recapitulation of the first movement Piano Quintet op. 44 (Example 5.15) because I felt that the tensions of the development section should here be resolved." Clara interjected, "Some of the revisions that you have shown me occur near the ends of works or movement. Did you perhaps feel that metrical dissonance might detract from an effect of closure?" Eusebius responded, "Yes; I eliminated the duple groups of quarter notes in Florestan's original ending for the *Papillons*, for instance (Example 5.12), precisely for that reason. Further examples of my enhancing of closure by the deintensification of dissonance are found in the *Davidsbündlertänze*, for example, in the coda of the sixth piece. The manuscript had dynamic accents on the fifth eighth notes of mm. 87–88 and 91–96, resulting in strong D6+4 (1=8th). I eliminated these accents between the manuscript and the first edition. At the end of the thirteenth *Davidsbündlertanz*, my deletion of the dynamic accents on the syncopated notes in the right hand weakened the dissonance and allowed the final metrically consonant chords to fulfill their resolving function in a more satisfying fashion."[24]

Florestan drained his cup, rose from his chair, and took Chiarina's arm, saying, "I need some fresh air; let us go for a walk. We can continue our discussion as we do so." Although she felt that she should return to her practicing, she agreed to come along. They put the various manuscripts back onto the shelves, donned their coats and hats, and left the house. It was a cool but fine day, and Florestan suggested that they make for the Rhine (he found himself irresistibly drawn toward the river in those days). As they walked, he picked up the thread of their conversation, observing, "A number of our metrical revisions were motivated by our desire to clarify the form, either by intensifying contrast between sections or by highlighting formal boundaries. The dissonant measures that I inserted at the beginnings of restatements of the second theme in the original finale for op. 22 (Example 2.6c), for instance, help to articulate this important formal boundary. The revisions of the third section of the tenth *Papillon* illustrate the enhancement of sectional contrast. I conceived the highly dissonant first version, you remember, as the opening of a piece (Example 5.14a).[25] By the time Eusebius wrote his virtually consonant second version (Example 5.14b), we were at the stage of searching for an appropriate larger context for the passage. When we moved this second version into its ultimate location, that is, after two metrically consonant sections, we immediately realized that its very weak dissonance provided insufficient contrast to the foregoing material, and we agreed to restore some of the original dissonance."

As they walked onto the bridge not far from their house, Clara inquired, "Would your extensive revision of the second episode of the second movement of the Piano Quintet have arisen from similar considerations? The first episode already involved the pervasive grouping dissonance of triplet quarter notes (in the piano) against groups of four eighth notes (in the strings), and the dissonance in your first version of the second episode was very similar. Your decision to base the second episode on a contrasting dissonance type (D4+1 at the quarter-note level) was a wise one. In the final version of the movement, each section has a distinct metrical character." Florestan agreed with Clara's assessment of this revision, and Eusebius added, "Another instance of metrical revision that enhanced the contrast between sections was my elimination of displacement dissonance from the middle section of the thirteenth *Davidsbündlertanz*; since the outer sections contained a fair amount of such dissonance, I decided that respite from that dissonance in the middle section would be desirable."

As they stopped on the bridge and gazed down at the mighty Rhine, swollen by the winter rains, Eusebius continued, "A number of our revisions were intended to create relationships to other passages rather than to create contrasts. Since we wrote many of the early piano pieces by gluing together existing fragments, it was important to create some links between the various fragments, and metrical revision was one means to that end.[26] The tenth *Papillon* illustrates this reason for revision in addition to the other reasons that we have mentioned. In the process of eliminating the unpleasant features of the first version, I had rendered the original dissonance virtually imperceptible, and had thus removed a significant connection between this passage and other *Papillons* that feature D3+2." Clara interjected, "You mean the fourth (mm. 19–22), the sixth (mm. 32–33) and the eighth (mm. 24–31)." Eusebius nodded and continued, "Florestan's reinstatement of the dissonance in the final revision was motivated in part by the desire to restore this connection." Florestan said, "My addition of third-beat dynamic accents in the eighth *Papillon* (Example 5.6), of course, also contributed to the network of connections between the movements."

Clara said, "You showed me how you added D3+1 to mm. 27–34 of the Préambule to *Carnaval*. Surely you did so in part because you wished to create a clear link to the first section, where this dissonance is foreshadowed at two points by accents on the second beats (mm. 7–8 and 15–16)." Florestan and Eusebius agreed, and the former added, "The G3/2 formed at m. 28 by my new accompaniment pattern, on the other hand, created links with later passages (mm. 48–62 and 99–109) in which 'oom-pah' accompaniments similarly form G3/2." Eusebius continued, "Florestan's addition of displacement to the idea at m. 46 of the finale of the op. 14 Sonata (Example 5.4) not only rendered the passage intriguingly beautiful, but resulted in a relationship to the opening theme of the movement where similar, though more intense, displacement dissonance occurs.[27] And to mention once more the first Trio from the third movement of op. 11, Florestan's addition of D3+2 and G3/2 to that originally consonant passage resulted in clear connections to the first section of the movement, where both dissonances already occur."

Clara now urged that they should return home. As they turned to leave the bridge, she asked, "Were any of your metrical revisions motivated by a desire to create the kinds of metrical processes that you mentioned to me earlier?" Florestan responded, "Yes, I recall several such examples. One revision that resulted in a process, albeit of small scale, was that in the introduction of the First String Quartet (Example 5.8). The opening motive of the completed introduction already contains a registral accent on the third sixteenth-note pulse of the measure. In later measures there are similar but successively stronger accents; the intervals by which the highest note is approached increase in size (from a minor second in m. 1 to a fourth in m. 3 to an octave in m. 11), resulting in ever more perceptible D8+2 (1=16th). At m. 9, my dynamic accent on the third sixteenth note further contributes to the intensification process. In m. 10, the strongest registral accent occurs on the third sixteenth note of the second beat; taken together with the similar accent on the third sixteenth note of the following measure, this accent results in a tightening of D8+2 to D4+2. The sforzandos in mm. 20–22 (Example 5.8), which I added in the fair copy, create D2+1.[28] This dissonance, besides being a diminution of the earlier D4+2, completes a process of successive reduction of cardinality. The proliferation of dynamic accents, furthermore, completes the intensification process initiated at the beginning of the introduction."

During his remarks, they had noticed an acquaintance—Julius Tausch, Robert's successor as conductor of the Düsseldorf Musikverein—walking quickly toward them.[29] They would gladly have avoided him, but, aside from leaping off the bridge, there was no possibility of doing so. Tausch came up to them and said, "Herr Doktor Schumann, Frau Schumann, how glad I am to meet you!" Without the slightest acknowledgment of Herr Tausch's presence, Eusebius continued the discussion of metrical revisions, while Florestan with difficulty restrained himself from hurling into Tausch's smiling face the vituperative epithets that boiled up within him, and while Clara stood there tight-lipped and flushed with embarrassment. Herr Tausch spoke softly to her during Robert's disquisition: "*I have just called at your home to invite you to our house this afternoon.* An-other instance of small-scale process achieved by a series of revisions (**you scheming scoundrel!**) is found in the first *Papillon* (see Example 4.5). *Several members of the Verein will be there, and we shall have chamber music and tea!* The inter-mediate stages of the processes of intensification and deintensification (**you hyp-ocritical hound!**) were not present in our first two versions of the piece. In both, the inner-voice durational accents of mm. 4–6 were absent. *Come if you can—both of you.* In the first version, moreover, the second beats of mm. 9–12 were all dy-namically accented. The gradual additions and deletions of accents that render the metrical process in the final version so elegant were not fully worked out until our fair copy of the work (**you snivelling sycophant!**)."[30]

When Robert finished, Clara thanked Herr Tausch with all the grace that she could muster and accepted his invitation. With a sidelong glance at the now silent figure next to her, he raised his hat in farewell and strode swiftly back into the town. Following more slowly, Clara and Robert returned to their house and walked upstairs, where Clara, after embracing him, ran tearfully from the room.

Florestan and Eusebius sat down once more at the table, and the former said, "I remember some interesting examples of revisions that resulted in metrical

EXAMPLE 5.16. *Metrical dissonance in the "Fandango" draft, Archiv der Gesellschaft der Musik-freunde in Wien, Ms. autogr. R. Schumann A283*

processes of larger scale. One of these occurred during the composition of our Piano Sonata op. 11." Fetching and opening a manuscript that was labeled 'Fandango,' he continued, "We began this draft, destined to become the opening of the exposition of the first movement, with the dissonance D4+2 (1=16th—Example 5.16a).[31] In the first sixteen measures (corresponding to the present mm. 54–70), we consistently displaced the bass and/or inner voices by two sixteenth notes with respect to the melody (whose durational accents corroborate the metrical layer). We abandoned the dissonance in mm. 17–42 of the draft (most of the third through sixth staves), where the motivic rhythm, its long durations still coordinated with the metrical beats, took over the entire texture."

Eusebius pointed to mm. 43–46 (corresponding to the present mm. 106–9), and said, "In this climactic passage, syncopation in an inner voice, dynamic accents on the final eighth notes of measures and left-hand new-event accents on the second eighth notes together resulted in a return of the initial D4+2 (Example 5.16b). In the continuation of this section (the last two bars on page 1), the dissonance was maintained by a syncopated inner-voice melody. The following section (mm. 52–62—the first two staves of page 2) reverted to the obsessive, metrically consonant opening rhythm (cf. mm. 123–39 of the final version). Thereupon we gradually phased out this rhythm, first relegating it to the bass alone (on the third staff of page 2), then abandoning it entirely as we initiated a second theme in steady eighth notes (corresponding to mm. 140–74 of the final version)." Florestan said, "Metrical dissonance appeared only once more within the draft, namely at mm. 64–68 (the first five measures on the third staff of page 2), where quarter note syncopation in the upper voices resulted in D8+4, an augmentation of the initial D4+2. The 'Fandango' draft, in short, began with a

EXAMPLE 5.17. *Metrical dissonance in the exposition of the Piano Sonata op. 11, first mvmt.*

prominent metrical dissonance and returned to it occasionally, but did not develop it in any coherent manner."[32]

Eusebius observed, "How different was the published exposition, completed four years later! Here you added many more statements of the initial dissonance. In mm. 76–86 (the second of three F♯-minor statements of the opening theme), you created, by dynamic accents and by registral accents resulting from the left hand's excursions into high altitudes, the dissonance D16+10 (1=16th), a loose relative of D4+2 (Example 5.17a)."[33] Florestan interposed, "The dynamic accents with which you reinforce the meter at mm. 89–92 in the final version are not present in the draft. I suppose you felt them to be necessary only after I had added the metrical dissonance in the immediately preceding measures." Eusebius nodded, and continued, "In mm. 94–106 (the third F♯-minor statement and its afterphrase—a passage that in the draft consisted of reiterations of the metrically consonant motivic rhythm), you added a great deal of D4+2. In mm. 94–95, the dissonance arises from new dynamic accents (Example 5.17b), and in mm. 99–106 from antimetrical slurs and harmonic new-event accents. (In the latter passage, the dissonance could be heard as D4-2.) Finally, you added inner-voice syncopation and hence D4+2 within the second theme in A major (mm. 150–51 of the final version). In the completed exposition, then, D4+2 is much more significant as a unifying feature."

Florestan added, "Furthermore, whereas in the draft there were no intermediate stages between the initial D4+2 (Example 5.16a) and the more intense statement of mm. 43–46 (Example 5.16b), we engage D4+2 in a process of gradual intensification in the final version. Significantly, you slightly weaken the first appearance of D4+2 in comparison to the beginning of the draft, thus crouching the better to spring; at the opening of the exposition (mm. 54–57—cf. Examples 5.17c and 5.16a), you conceal the displaced layer in inner voices, rather than immediately placing it in a prominent outer voice. The migration of the displaced layer to an outer voice in m. 56 already creates an effect of intensification. In mm. 62 and 66, we offer subtle hints at the manner in which D4+2 is to be further intensified: in the former measure, we initiate a new harmony (B minor, replacing B major) on the second eighth note, and in the latter, we place a dynamic accent on the same eighth note in the bass. Neither hint is present in the draft."

Eusebius gleefully observed, "The significance of these hints begins to emerge at mm. 94–95, where we intensify D4+2 by dynamic accentuation. In mm. 106–18, the climactic region of the exposition (corresponding to mm. 43–46 of the sketch—Example 5.16b), we state D4+2 in an equally intense manner. We create it here by a blend of the techniques hinted at in mm. 62 and 66: new-event harmonic accents appear on the second eighth-note pulses, and dynamic accents on the fourth eighth-note pulses of each measure. In mm. 110–13, we again form D4+2 by antimetrical dynamic and new-event harmonic accents; the dynamic accents are your addition to the corresponding draft measures."

Florestan remarked, "The gradual intensification of D4+2 is only one component of a general, not exclusively metrical intensification process that spans the first forty-five measures of our completed exposition. Another important element in the process is the rise in register across the aforementioned three statements of the opening theme: the first statement (Example 5.17c) remains quite low, the second one (mm. 74–92—Example 5.17a) begins to champ at the registral bit with its momentary left-hand leaps into a higher register, and the treble part of the third statement (mm. 94–98—Example 5.17b) is an octave higher than that of the first. This gradual registral rise is lacking in the draft, in which the left hand does not reach over the right, and in which even the third statement remains within its original low register. In the completed exposition, an increase in dynamic level in mm. 85 through 94 adds to the overall effect of intensification; this crescendo, too, is missing in the draft. A generally static character was acceptable for a little fandango, but we felt that in a sonata exposition a greater sense of controlled process was necessary. By means of judicious metrical revision as well as by the addition of the other features that I have mentioned, we accomplished the transformation of a character piece into a dramatic sonata exposition."

Eusebius rose and brought another manuscript to the table. As he turned to its first page, he said, "Another work that comes to mind in connection with re-

EXAMPLE 5.18. *Metrical dissonance in the "Exercice" (draft for the* Toccata *op. 7), the Robert Owen Lehman Collection, on deposit in the Pierpont Morgan Library*

vision for the sake of large-scale metrical process is our *Toccata* op. 7. My first version of this work from 1830, entitled 'Exercice,' was in many ways quite different from the published *Toccata*, completed in 1832.[34] For example, my notation was originally predominantly in eighth notes rather than sixteenths.[35] There are significant harmonic differences between the versions as well; the key of ♭III, for example, reached at m. 14 in the final version, was already attained at m. 8 in my 'Exercice.' The sonata-allegro form of the work became much clearer in the published version; my first version already contained a section in the dominant, but the contrasting theme that highlights the dominant area in the final version was barely suggested."[36]

Florestan took over: "In addition, I made many changes in the treatment of metrical dissonance. Your first version already contained many of the displacement dissonances that are significant in the final version. Allusions to D8+2 (1=8th) in the form of accents on the third sixteenth- or eighth-note pulse appeared in mm. 1, 29 (Example 5.18a) and 59 (Example 5.18b); in m. 1 the antimetrical accent is registral, and in the other two measures, it is dynamic. At the very end of the development section, you suggested D8+2 by placing registral accents on those same pulses in a few consecutive measures (Example 5.18c). D8+7 (1=16th, which corresponds to the eighth-note pulse used on the other pages of the 'Exercice') occurred at mm. 11–14, where the last left-hand sixteenth note of each measure was tied over the bar line, resulting in a series of durational accents. You suggested D4+1 (1=8th) by the slurring at mm. 29–30 of the exposition (see Example 5.18a), and at various other points by left-hand durational accents. Another 4-displacement, D4+2 (1=16th), appeared at mm. 17–22 of the exposition, where the displaced layer resulted from registral accents, then more briefly at mm. 54–55 (1=8th), where the displacement was created by dynamic accents (Example 5.18d). D4+3 (1=16th) appeared briefly in m. 15, created by ties from the fourth to the first sixteenth in two groups (Example 5.18e). You broached D2+1 (1=8th), finally, with antimetrical slurs at various points, for instance, in mm. 27–28 (Example 5.18f) and 48–50. All of your dissonances occurred only relatively briefly, most of them weakly, and—forgive me for saying so—with little semblance of order."

Florestan continued, "In the final version, I enhanced all of these dissonances, using them as a means for unification, and as distinguishing features for individual sections. My elevation of D8+2 (1=16th) to motivic significance is already initiated in the opening measures of the second version. I establish the dissonance by placing durational accents on the second eighth notes of the two introductory measures (Example 5.19a). In the first theme area (mm. 3–24), the bass continues these durational accents on second eighth notes (Example 5.19b) while harmonic changes reinforce the metrical 8-layer; I thus maintain D8+2 throughout that section, with interruptions only in mm. 18 and 20. D8+2 returns at the dominant harmony that heralds the second theme area (mm. 42–43). Large portions of the development section are occupied by the same dissonance (mm. 100–110, 121–39), as is the first portion of the recapitulation (mm. 149–72)." Eusebius said, "You coordinate most of the appearances of the disso-

EXAMPLE 5.19. *Metrical dissonance in the final version of the* Toccata *op. 7*

EXAMPLE 5.19. (*continued*)

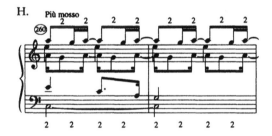

nance with significant formal junctures: the opening, the cadence leading into the second theme, the opening of the development section, and the opening of the recapitulation. The comparison with my sporadic and haphazard statements of D8+2 in the first version is striking indeed."

Florestan continued, "I similarly advance the status of D4+3 in the revised version. I first hint at it in mm. 61–62, where slurs initiate groups on the final sixteenth notes of two successive beats (Example 5.19c). At mm. 69–71 (Example 5.19d) and 75–79, I state the dissonance somewhat more strongly, creating it by durational accentuation rather than mere grouping. (At these points, the dissonance could be heard as D4-1.) D4+3 reaches the height of its prominence at the end of my version. In mm. 229–37 (Example 5.19e), the melodic framework (C-D for three measures, then E-F for one measure, all repeated an octave higher) articulates the metrical 4-layer. Significant harmonic changes, however, occur on the fourth sixteenth notes of mm. 229–30, on the fourth and final sixteenth notes in m. 231, and on the fourth sixteenth of m. 232, resulting first in intermittent, then constant D4+3 (or D4-1). The same is true of mm. 233–37. In mm. 237–42, then at greater length in mm. 250–55 and 260–80, I create the antimetrical 4-layer of D4+3 (or D4-1) by durational accents in the highest voice and by harmonic changes.

"Another dissonance that appears much more frequently in my final version is D2+1. I allude to it in mm. 38, 40, and 112, then allow it to pervade the coda of the work (mm. 213–81). In mm. 213–37 (Example 5.19f), the significant melodic notes (the chord tones) consistently articulate the metrical 2-layer, but harmonic changes and density accents occur on the intervening sixteenth-note pulses." Eusebius interjected, "You recall that in my sketch of the passage in the musical diary, the density accents and harmonic changes reinforced the metrical 2-layer, so that the passage was virtually consonant."[37] Florestan went on, "At m. 237, I submerge D2+1 (and D4+3); nothing supports the notated meter except the notation!"

Eusebius interrupted, "Did you intend the pianist to articulate the notated meter in this passage?" Florestan responded, "This is another of those exceptional situations where I would not advise the pianist to do so. I doubt that it is possible for human hands to bring out both metrical and antimetrical layers during this frantic passage. I would suggest that the pianist abandon the metrical layer until m. 250, and generate the tension of the passage by physical attitude, by the high speed, and by the indirect dissonances that occur at the points of abandonment and reinstatement of the metrical layer." He continued, "At m. 250 both of the conflicting 2-layers are operative; the uppermost two voices state significant members of the prevailing D harmony (A and D) at eighth-note intervals, while the attacks in the lowest voice in the right hand establish a displaced 2-layer. The culmination of my development of D2+1 occurs at mm. 256–59 (Example 5.19g), where the vehement chordal attacks of the left and right hands create metrical and antimetrical 2-layers, respectively."

Eusebius inquired, "Do these chords not simply merge into a series of accented sixteenth-note pulses, so that the effect of dissonance is minimal?" Florestan said, "The registral space between the two chordal layers prevents them, at least at first, from merging into a single pulse. By the end of the passage, to be sure, the hands are very close together, and the dissonance becomes weak. But this deintensification is precisely what I desired here; it paves the way for the murmurous mm. 260–80 (Example 5.19h). You obviously had a hand in these measures, Eusebius, for D2+1 here assumes a relatively serene guise. As in m. 250, the uppermost two voices articulate the metrical 2-layer by stating significant members of the prevailing harmony (E and G) at eighth-note intervals; this layer is reinforced by the 'tenor' statement of the second theme. The attacks in the lowest voice in the right hand, meanwhile, establish a displaced 2-layer. D2+1 is fully resolved only by the final cadential chords in quarter notes (mm. 281–83)." Eusebius observed, "Your treatment of D2+1 again demonstrates the elevation of a dissonance that I used only briefly in my first version to a pervasive and highly significant role."

He continued, "Even more remarkable than the proliferation of certain dissonances, and hence the intensification of dissonance in many passages, is the increased involvement in your second version of dissonances in logical processes. The dissonances in my first version—I admit it freely—are like players in a team without a captain; they mill about without a plan of action. In your version, the players are organized and made to work together. First, I notice in your *Toccata* an overall progression from displacements of large cardinalities to displacements of small cardinalities. Just over half of the work (mm. 1–172) is dominated by 8-displacements. After m. 172, you abandon them, shifting to 4-displacements and finally to the 2-displacement (sometimes with larger displacements superimposed). This large progression is nicely foreshadowed by the first portion of your metrical progression (D8+2 to D4+1 to D2+1 in mm. 1–40). At times, the progression from a larger to a smaller displacement involves a more specific process, for example, diminution (the progression from D8+2 to D4+1 at m. 25) or tightening (the progressions from D4+3 to D2+1 in mm. 25–38, from D8+7 to D4+3 in mm. 67–71 and 72–79, and from D8+2 to D4+2 in mm. 121–48 and 149–80).

"You also subject individual dissonances to interesting processes," Eusebius went on. "For example, as you mentioned earlier, you abandon the pervasive dissonance D8+2 briefly at two points within the first theme (mm. 18 and 20). These interruptions neatly presage your longer departure from D8+2 in m. 25. The expansive treatment of D2+1 in the coda is briefly foreshadowed in mm. 38 and 40, where the uppermost voice states displaced eighth-note pulses. The long passage dominated by D2+1 at mm. 213–80 contains some subtle processes which prevent it from becoming monotonous. The antimetrical 2-layer is at first not absolutely constant. In mm. 213–28, dominant-tonic progressions at the ends of all measures strongly assert the metrical layer (Example 5.19f). It is difficult to imagine the antimetrical 2-layer continuing through these progressions; the tonics on the downbeats are so clearly the more strongly accented of the two chords. At m. 229 (Example 5.19e), you deemphasize the downbeat tonics, subsuming them within sustained dominant notes. D2+1 thus remains uninterrupted, in contrast to mm. 213–38. In the central portion of the coda, you gradually add further metrical colors to D2+1: intermittent, then constant D4+3 beginning in m. 229, and D8+3 in mm. 237–41. (One might just as well say that by adding accents at particular points, you gradually render explicit certain displacements already implicit within D2+1.) None of these processes is present in my first version. You in effect turned my 'Exercice' in piano technique into a thoroughgoing study in displacement dissonance."

Florestan smiled smugly, then rose and said, "Shall we continue our reading of the Prophet Bird's manuscript?" Eusebius agreed with alacrity. After putting the "Fandango" and "Exercice" documents away, they mounted the stairs to the top floor of the house, Eusebius's light treads and Florestan's heavy footfalls forming the dissonance D2+1.

SIX

Interactions of Metrical Dissonance
with Pitch Structure, Form, and
Extramusical Elements

Florestan and Eusebius settled on their sofa, opened the manuscript, and read:

The upper portion of Figure 6.1 shows the metrical structure of Schumann's transcription, or rather recomposition, of Paganini's Caprice op. 1 no. 6 (published as the second of the *Concert Etudes* op. 10). At the very top of the figure, I have summarized the formal and harmonic events of the composition; the remainder of the figure is a metrical map of the type described in chapter 4. The figure makes clear that meter and pitch interact in interesting ways in Schumann's piece. Significant large-scale harmonic events coincide with metrical resolutions; the beginning of the retransitional dominant prolongation (m. 36) coincides with the resolution of G3/2 and D6+1.5, and as the dominant moves to the recapitulatory tonic, the remaining dissonance, G1.5/1, is resolved as well. The process of harmonic stabilization and resolution that heralds the end of the study is beautifully matched by a gradual casting off of veils of metrical dissonance. Harmonic events of smaller scale are no less carefully coordinated with metrical states. For example, Schumann associates each of three sequential passages within the central section with a unique dissonant state: the first (mm. 19–26) with the combination of G9/6 and G3/2, the second (mm. 27–31) with the continuation of those dissonances along with intermittent G1.5/1 and D3+1.5, the third (mm. 32–35) with a blend of G3/2, G1.5/1, and D6+1.5. The sense of increasing instability and tension produced by the progressive curtailment of the sequential cells (shown by the slurs at the top of the figure) is enhanced by an overall increase in amount of metrical dissonance in mm. 19–35.

The coordination between metrical structure and form in the transcription

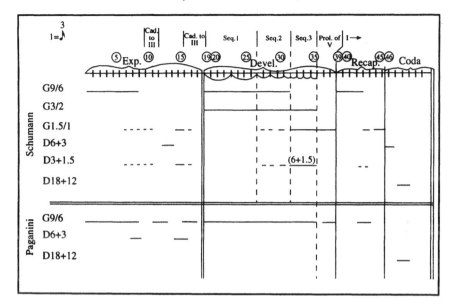

FIGURE 6.1. *Comparison of interactions of metrical structure, form, and pitch structure in Schumann's Study op. 10 no. 2 and Paganini's Caprice op. 1 no. 6*

is no less remarkable than that between metrical structure and harmony. Schumann ends the first section (mm. 1–18) by resolving all dissonances. He reinitiates G9/6 and also establishes the new diminution, G3/2, at the beginning of the second section (m. 19). He resolves G1.5/1 precisely at the point of recapitulation (m. 39) and marks the beginning of the coda (m. 46) with the same resolving gesture.

Such concern for coordination between metrical structure and pitch and form is evident in many of Schumann's other works. In the first part of this chapter, I offer further examples of the interaction between form and meter, and between pitch and meter. The second part of the chapter begins with a discussion of relationships between metrical structure and text in Schumann's vocal works. This discussion provides a springboard into some speculations on possible meanings of metrical dissonance in Schumann's instrumental music.

INTERACTIONS OF METRICAL DISSONANCE WITH FORM AND PITCH STRUCTURE

Among the ways in which Schumann associates metrical states and form is the highlighting of a formal boundary by a change in metrical state.[1] Resolution of metrical dissonance, for example, frequently coincides with the close of a formal unit, be it a low-level unit such as a phrase or a period, or a higher-level unit such as a thematic section of a sonata form. "Eusebius" from *Carnaval* provides a simple example of the former situation. The second and third measures of the

EXAMPLE 6.1. *"Grillen" from* Phantasiestücke, *mm. 1–8*

first two phrases (mm. 2–3 and 6–7) contain the low-level dissonance of septuplets against quarter notes. In the final measures of these phrases, however,
Schumann dispenses with the dissonance, replacing the right-hand septuplets
with normal eighth notes. The first eight-measure phrase of "Grillen" from the
Phantasiestücke (Example 6.1) begins with metrical consonance, but in m. 3 a
suggestion of dissonance (D3+2, 1=quarter) appears in the form of a dynamic accent on the third beat. The phrase becomes more dissonant as it proceeds; in
mm. 5–6, dynamic and durational accents on the second beats result in intense
D3+1. No dissonance, however, disturbs the succeeding cadential measures; as
in "Eusebius," Schumann associates the close of a formal unit with resolution of
dissonance. In the first piece from *Kreisleriana*, the initial displacement dissonance D2+1 (1=8th), created by the nonalignment of right-hand arpeggiated
harmonies and left-hand attacks and, in mm. 11–12, by dynamic accents on metrically weak eighth notes, is brought up short at the strongest cadences, where
the two hands come together (for instance, at mm. 7–8—Example 6.2). 🌸

Eusebius said, "At the final cadence of the agitated first section (mm.
21–24), we allot more time to the state of consonance than at m. 8, as if to suggest
that the section ending with which it is associated is a more significant formal
boundary than the earlier one." He continued, "A good example of similar coordination is found at the end of the second theme of the first movement of op. 80

EXAMPLE 6.2. Kreisleriana *op. 16 no. 1, mm. 7–8*

EXAMPLE 6.3. *Piano Trio op. 80, first mvmt., mm. 78–86 (piano part only)*

(mm. 78–85—Example 6.3). In mm. 78–81, we produce D6+3 (1=8th) by very powerful accents, namely new-event harmonic accents in conjunction with durational and sometimes dynamic accents. In mm. 82–84, the measures leading into the final cadence of the second theme, we significantly deintensify the dissonance. The accents that form the dissonance become much weaker than in the preceding measures; in m. 83, there is a dynamic accent in just one voice (the cello) and a density accent in m. 84, as opposed to the earlier full-texture dynamic and harmonic new-event accents. Immediately after the cadence, we reintensify the dissonance, thus setting off the cadence with weaker dissonance." Florestan added, "The coordination with pitch structure is interesting here as well; the final phrase of the second theme is quite heavily chromatic during the metrically dissonant portion, but as the dissonance is weakened, the harmony becomes diatonic (mm. 83–85). It is this sense of simultaneous relaxation in three domains that renders our cadence so beautiful."

Eusebius continued, "There are plenty of additional examples of coordination between phrase ends and metrical resolution in our works. In the finale of the Sonata op. 11, the first theme (see Example 5.10) is permeated by subliminal G3/2 (1=quarter), but temporary resolutions of the metrical dissonance occur at the two main cadences of the theme (at mm. 8 and 16). In the first movement of the First String Quartet, we associate important cadences at the end of the exposition (m. 137a) and the recapitulation (m. 334) with resolution of D6+3 (1=8th). At the end of the fourth movement of that quartet, resolutions of metrical dissonance—of low-level three-against-four dissonance plus D8+4 (1=8th), and D8+4 alone, respectively—coincide perfectly with phrase ends (mm. 294–98 and 310–14). I see that the author comments further on this movement." They read:

At times, Schumann employs a particular dissonance as a "marker" at formal dividing points. In the finale of the First String Quartet, D8+4 (1=8th) performs such a function. This dissonance, created by antimetrical dynamic accents, first appears at the end of the exposition (mm. 71–72). Allusions to D8+4 open the development section (mm. 77 and 81), and at m. 148—just before the somewhat confusing recapitulation begins—D8+4 appears once again. The occurrence at m. 200, corresponding to that of m. 71, heralds the delayed return of the opening theme at m. 213. 🎵

EXAMPLE 6.4. Papillon *op. 2 no. 11, mm. 1–3*

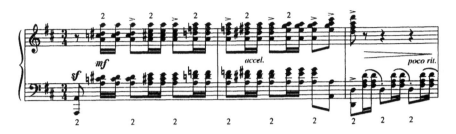

Eusebius pointed out, "None of these statements of D8+4 was present in my first draft of the movement.[2] You inserted them later, to aid listeners in orienting themselves within the unusual form and tonal structure of this finale, in which the second theme group is recapitulated in F major before the first group returns in A minor."

Instead of highlighting formal boundaries by particular metrical events, Schumann sometimes associates an entire section with a particular metrical state, thereby setting the given section apart from its context and clarifying the form. There are many examples in the piano works. The *Papillon* op. 2 no. 11, for instance, begins with a brief introductory passage, which leads into the main body of the piece in m. 3 (Example 6.4). The introduction is permeated by D2+1; dynamic and durational accents convey the metrical 2-layer while harmonic new-event accents create an antimetrical 2-layer (1=8th). At the end of the introduction, the latter 2-layer disappears, resulting in a state of consonance (except for the references to D2+1 shown in Example 4.2). The introduction is thus clearly set apart from the beginning of the main portion of the piece.

A larger-scale instance of the association of an introductory passage with metrical dissonance is found at the opening of the Fourth Symphony (Example 6.5a). There is some conflict against the metrical 6-layer (1=8th) at the outset; the initial dominant note occurs on the upbeat, and when Schumann emphatically jerks the wandering harmony back to the dominant in m. 5, he does so on

EXAMPLE 6.5A. *Symphony no. 4, first mvmt., mm. 1–5*

EXAMPLE 6.5B. *Sketch for a fugue subject, Deutsche Staatsbibliothek zu Berlin — Preußischer Kulturbesitz, Musikabteilung mit Mendelssohn-Archiv, Mus. ms. autogr. R. Schumann 36, no. 10, recto, st. 5*

the second beat. Most of the dissonance, however, occurs at lower levels. In many measures of the introduction there is a conflict between 2- and 3-layers. In mm. 1–3, for example, the eighth-note pulse is grouped not only notationally but also by harmonic events, into threes; the 3-layer is set into motion by a chord change after the first three eighth notes, and the listener tends to maintain that layer in subsequent measures.

Eusebius interjected, "Do you remember a fugue subject in D minor that you sketched in 1845 — a subject very similar to the opening of the Fourth Symphony (Example 6.5b)? In that sketch, you more obviously realized the potential for triple grouping of the eighth notes; you couched the theme in three-eight time, with a note stating that six-eight is an alternate metrical possibility."

Later measures of the symphony's introduction render the 3-layer even more prominent; in mm. 13–14 and 18, for example, large leaps between the third and fourth eighth notes in the first violin part clearly demarcate two triple groups per measure, and articulation changes in most instruments halfway through each of mm. 18, 19, and 20 have the same effect. The metrical 2-layer, on the other hand, is articulated by harmonic change in mm. 4–5 (see Example 6.5a) and by the voice exchanges between the first violin and bass parts in m. 21. This layer is also implied by dynamic accentuation of the third quarter-note beat in mm. 2–3, 6–9, and 11–12, and by the surface-level attacks of the outermost voices in mm. 7–10.

At m. 22, where the surge toward the actual exposition begins, Schumann drops the 3-layer while clearly expressing the metrical 2-layer with bass neighboring motion. In m. 25, he imposes a 4-layer upon the 2-layer (i.e., he alters the meter from three-four to two-four) and begins to increase the tempo. These changes, combined with the elimination of the 3-layer, herald the exposition of the movement, which is based on the consonance 4/2. The metrical resolution at the boundary of introduction and exposition contributes significantly to the sense of "getting down to business" that is appropriate for this point of the form.

Schumann employs distinctive metrical states for many formal situations other than introductions. In many of his short ternary forms, he enhances contrast in the middle section by allotting to it a metrical state significantly different from that of the outer sections. In the "Scherzino," op. 124 no. 3, a piece written around the time of the *Papillons*, the outer sections are consonant, whereas the middle section is dominated by G3/2 (1=16th). In "Wichtige Begebenheit" from the *Kinderscenen*, the outer sections contain subtle grouping dissonance; most of the attacks of an underlying stepwise descent in the melody take place at two-quarter-note intervals, resulting in a 2-layer (1=quarter) that conflicts with the subliminal metrical 3-layer. In the middle section in the subdominant key (mm. 8–16), however, the 2-layer disappears and the downbeats receive durational and dynamic accents, so that metrical consonance reigns. The outer sections of the first piece of the *Kreisleriana*, as was mentioned above, are rich in displacement dissonance. The middle section, however, is virtually consonant; only a few stabs of accentuation on the third sixteenth notes of triple groups ruffle the placid metrical surface. ❦

Florestan remarked, "Our distinguishing of sections by means of metrical structure is not restricted to works in ternary form. In 'Grillen,' which is in rondo form, we assigned a different metrical progression to each of the three different sections. The A sections (mm. 1–16, 44–60, 96–112, and 140–56—see Example 6.1) twice move through the metrical progression 'consonance—D3+1 (1=quarter)—consonance.' The B sections (mm. 16–44 and 112–40) begin with D12+11, or D12-1 (produced by dynamic accents on every fourth upbeat), and move to the tighter dissonance D3+2 at the first double bar and back to the original D12+11 at the second double bar. We perfectly coordinate the tightening and loosening procedure with the subsections of the B section. In my C section (mm. 60–96), I tighten the initial D6+5 (or D6-1) to D3+2 (or D3-1), then loosen to D6+5 again (at the subsection boundaries—mm. 72 and 80, respectively). In addition, I throw in the dramatic incursions of subliminal G3/2 that we discussed yesterday" (Example 2.16).

Eusebius said, "We use metrical dissonance in a similar manner to set off the sections of our later larger forms. In many of our sonata forms, we assign clearly distinguishable metrical states to particular thematic areas. In the first movements of the First and Second String Quartets, displacement dissonances in the closing themes effectively distinguish those sections from the preceding consonant material." Florestan interposed, "These dissonances were absent from, or very weak, in your first drafts; I added them in part because I wished to set apart the closing themes."[3] Eusebius continued, "Another relevant example is the second theme of the first movement of the Third String Quartet, which is permeated by a combination of two displacement dissonances as yet unused in the movement (Example 4.20). In the second theme of the opening movement of the Third Symphony, we follow the opposite procedure; in contrast to the first theme, which is dominated by G6/4 (1=8th), the second theme area (mm. 95–165) is almost entirely metrically consonant (with the exception of the last few measures)."

Florestan pointed out, "As we discussed this morning, metrical dissonance can serve not only to separate sections from each other, but also to create links between sections, be they adjacent or nonadjacent. We often allow a metrical dissonance established in one section to reappear in an entirely different guise in a later contrasting section, so that the dissonance provides a subtle but audible link to the earlier section. In our conversations about metrical revision, we mentioned a number of works in which we employed metrical dissonance as a link between sections. Additional examples include the *Intermezzo* op. 4 no. 5, the first two sections of which are connected by their usage of D6+2 (1=8th; cf. Examples 8.9a and 5.13), and 'Vogel als Prophet' in which the thinly textured A section and the fuller, chorale-like B section are linked by D2+1 (see Example 4.7)." Eusebius added, "In some works, we employ related rather than identical states to provide a connection between contrasting sections. In the sixth *Novellette*, you vociferously announce the dissonance D2+1 (1=8th) in the first section (mm. 9–12), and I take up its augmentation, D4+2, in my calmer second section (see Example 4.6)."

The door opened and Clara's head appeared. "Robert," she urged, "it is time to leave for the Tausches!" When she encountered his abstracted gaze, she knew that she would be going alone that day. She came to him, kissed his brow, and rushed off. Florestan and Eusebius continued their reading.

A number of the above remarks with regard to form have already broached the subject of coordination between metrical and pitch structure. When metrical dissonance is associated with a formal dividing point, it is likely also to be linked with a significant harmonic event (a cadence). The relationship between metrical dissonance and pitch, furthermore, has already been addressed in prior chapters, where it became obvious that pitch structure has a significant impact on the establishment of layers of motion. Here, I investigate some additional possibilities for the interplay of metrical structure and pitch structure.

The analysis of Schumann's study in Figure 6.1 illustrates one way in which pitch and metrical structure can interact. In mm. 19–35, a passage that is tonally unstable is metrically dissonant (i.e. unstable) throughout; thus, metrical dissonance is coordinated with an analogous pitch state. Schumann associates tonal and metrical instability in numerous works. In the first *Papillon* (Example 4.5), the unstable, sequential measures that initiate the second half are associated with strong D3+1. As the sequence makes its way back toward the tonic, the dissonance is weakened and resolved. Measures 9–12 of the fifth *Papillon* illustrate a similar pitch/meter coordination; an unstable, sequential section is associated with displacement dissonance, the dissonance being resolved as harmonic stability, in the form of the tonic, reappears. ❦

Florestan recalled, "Pitch and meter were not originally thus coordinated in the fifth *Papillon*; in our first version, metrical dissonance appeared at the point where the sequence ended (m. 12).[4] The achievement of coordination between metrical structure and other musical aspects is certainly another common motivation for our metrical revisions."

Numerous pitch states other than instability can be considered analogous to metrical dissonance and can therefore logically be coordinated with the latter state. Pitch dissonance is the most obvious of these. Metrical dissonance and pitch dissonance are frequently associated in Schumann's music, with the result that effects of tension generated individually by the two classes of dissonance are magnified. Suspensions and retardations, both involving displacement dissonance in conjunction with pitch dissonance, are simple examples of such coordination. Some of Schumann's combinations of displacement dissonance with pitch dissonance, such as the first of the *Impromptus* op. 5 and the fourth *Davidsbündlertanz*, consist primarily of straightforward suspensions or retardations. Other associations of displacement and pitch dissonance are related to the suspension idea in the sense that they project potentially congruent harmonic planes that have been shifted out of alignment—for example, the passage at mm. 9–14 of the finale of the Piano Sonata op. 14 and the opening of the first piece of *Kreisleriana*.

Fascinating though they are, the above passages cannot be regarded as deliberate coordinations of dissonance in two domains, for within suspensions or retardations, pitch and metrical dissonance are by definition inseparable. We look now at a few instances of coordination of dissonance in the two parameters that are not based on suspension or retardation and that therefore suggest a conscious effort on Schumann's part to synchronize events within the domains of pitch and meter.

The third section of the tenth *Papillon* (see Example 2.8) follows two sections that are virtually consonant both with respect to pitch (aside from dominant seventh chords and momentary passing notes) and meter. Within the third section, Schumann associates D3+2 with some harsh pitch dissonance (especially in mm. 34–36, not shown in Example 2.8). In the displacement-ridden opening theme of the first movement of the Piano Sonata op. 14 (Example 4.10), numerous outer-voice sevenths and ninths coincide with the accents that produce the displacement dissonance. The following metrically consonant sections, on the other hand (mm. 22–26, 26–38, 38–46), are significantly more consonant with respect to intervallic structure as well; the outer voices of mm. 26–38, for example, move primarily in tenths.

Intermezzo II from the second piece of *Kreisleriana* illustrates a well-crafted coordination of intensification of pitch and metrical dissonance. The Intermezzo is in rounded binary form. The A section begins with D6+2 (1=quarter—mm. 91–95), then presents the tighter dissonance D3+2 (mm. 95–96), the antimetrical layer arising mostly from durational accents in the bass. The final measures of the section (mm. 97–99) are metrically virtually consonant. The metrically dissonant measures contain occasional prominent pitch dissonances (the A/B♭ clash in m. 93 and the G/F in m. 95), whereas the metrically consonant final measures are entirely consonant in terms of pitch. Most of the B section is permeated by intense D3+1 in addition to weaker D3+2; D3+1 is initiated by the dynamic accent on the second beat of m. 99 and is maintained by similar accents in mm. 100–106, and D3+2 arises from durational accents on third beats (Ex-

EXAMPLE 6.6. Kreisleriana *no. 2, mm. 104–11*

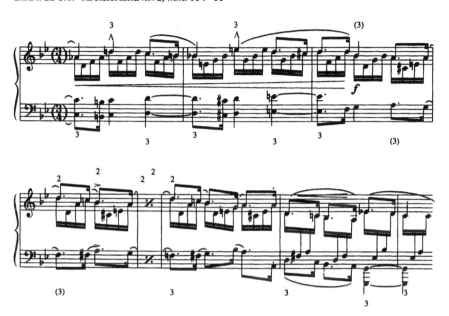

ample 6.6). In mm. 107–8, Schumann abandons all of the 3-layers and establishes two conflicting 2-layers, one by regularly reiterating D minor harmony, the other by dynamic accents. These 2-layers create indirect and subliminal G3/2 as well as D2+1. Because D3+1 is the diminution of the A section's D6+2 and hence involves more frequent contradiction of metrical pulses; because dissonances are created to a greater extent by dynamic accents; and because the metrical layer is strongly contradicted by subliminal dissonance (in mm. 107–8), the B section is metrically much more intensely dissonant than the A section. Exactly the same is true of pitch dissonance; the outer voices in mm. 101–8 obsessively state sevenths and ninths. In mm. 107–8, where contradiction of the primary metrical layer reaches an apex, pitch dissonance is particularly violent as well; both measures contain parallel ninths. In the final two measures of the B section (mm.109–10), all metrical dissonance is resolved. Simultaneously, the outer voices begin to state consonant intervals and, in m. 110, merge into a single octave-doubled voice![5] 🐦

Florestan muttered, "An interesting example, to be sure! We do not, however, always coordinate intervallic and metrical dissonance in this manner. In the first movement of the *Faschingsschwank*, for instance, some of the passages that are metrically most dissonant are completely consonant in terms of pitch, such as the subliminally dissonant passage in mm. 87–126 (Example 2.14). The same is true of the displaced passage comprising mm. 340–56 of that movement (Example 8.24c); the chords in this passage, with the exception of those built on F♯ in

EXAMPLE 6.7. Faschingsschwank aus Wien, *first mvmt., mm. 357–62*

mm. 342–43, are either consonant or relatively mildly dissonant (dominant and diminished sevenths)." Eusebius countered, "In the following section, however (mm. 356–62 — Example 6.7), you do associate the continuing displacement dissonance with strikingly dissonant chords." Florestan said, "You are right, but I wished to indicate that the association of pitch and metrical dissonance does not always take the most obvious form." They continued their reading.

A Schenkerian perspective suggests additional interesting ways to associate metrical dissonance with an analogous pitch state. In the eleventh *Papillon*, the relinquishing of the primary tone on the middleground level—a yielding of middleground melodic stability to instability—is associated with metrical dissonance. The primary tone A is embellished on the middleground level until m. 10 by repeated downward octave coupling. At the end of m. 10, a middleground linear progression, already foreshadowed on the foreground during the first beat, is initiated. Precisely at the point where the primary tone is dislodged, Schumann brings the indirect metrical dissonances G3/2 and G4/3 into play by interjecting a measure of common time. ❧

Florestan impatiently remarked, "I do not understand most of the terminology in the paragraph that we just read." Eusebius agreed, "I, too, do not understand it completely. It seems to me, however, that this 'Schenkerian' theory has to do with layers or levels in the domain of pitch." They read on:

In the "Ländler," op. 124 no. 7, Schumann associates an unstable melodic event of another kind, namely interruption, with metrical dissonance. The primary tone is F♯. In the first section, two linear progressions (F♯-E-D) prolong the primary tone. After the double bar (see Example 4.14), the background descends to the second scale degree, which is then prolonged by octave coupling until the return of the opening in m. 16. The prolongation of scale degree 2, unstable in terms of the background level, is coordinated with displacement dissonance. As the primary tone returns, the dissonance resolves.

The fifteenth piece from op. 124 (see Example 7.3) involves a more unusual type of instability in the pitch domain: Schumann leaves the fundamental line incomplete. The primary tone is scale degree 5 (E♭), and descents as far as scale degree 3 (C) occur a number of times (mm. 1–4, 5–8, and in the final phrase). The line, however, never reaches full repose on the tonic. Schumann parallels this large-scale melodic instability by allowing the metrical dissonance D3+2 (or D3-1), which is active through most of the piece, to remain unresolved at the end.

Early nineteenth-century composers sometimes organize passages and even entire works around a rivalry between two keys.[6] The analogy between such a tonal conflict and conflict between two or more layers of motion is obvious, and Schumann does occasionally coordinate these analogous states. The fifth *Intermezzo* from op. 4 no. 5 provides an example. (Portions of this work are shown in Examples 5.13, 8.9, and 8.10.) The governing tonal conflict between the keys of F major and D minor is exposed during the initial section (mm. 1–19), which begins in F major but at m. 13 moves into D minor. A similar shift from F to D takes place within each recurrence of the opening music. Further manifestations of the F/D conflict are found in the second section. In mm. 32–34, a rising root progression by fifths connects the contending tonics (D to F), whereupon the music returns to D minor. Whereas the first ending remains in the latter key and leads to its dominant, the second leads to the dominant of F. The section at mm. 37–45 (see Example 8.9b) contributes to the D/F conflict by prominently presenting references to the enharmonically equivalent dyads C/C♯ and C/D♭, the former suggesting the key of D, the latter suggesting and indeed leading into the key of F.[7] The "Alternativo" section arrives powerfully on V of D minor (m. 135), but V of F is immediately set against it as the opening music returns. The key of D minor ultimately wins the tonal battle.

An important component of the tonal conflict is the rivalry between two contenders for primary tone status, one per key. The apparent primary tone at the beginning is C, that tone being solidly established by an upward octave coupling in mm. 2–6. In mm. 13–20, C moves to C♯. Since C♯ is the enharmonic equivalent of the D♭ that acts as an upper neighbor to C within the F-major portion of the opening theme, the large C to C♯ motion in mm. 13–20 not only contributes to the modulation to D minor, but in a broader sense encapsulates the overall D/F conflict. In mm. 20–36, the C♯ resolves to D, but above that D the new primary tone F appears (mm. 21–26 and 30–32). This tone, like the initial C, is coupled upward (mm. 21–30); Schumann's similar treatment of F and C corroborates the apparent equality of these two primary tones. It is F that assumes ultimate primacy; the final descent of the piece emanates from this pitch (mm. 204–5). In a strict Schenkerian sense, then, F is the true primary tone of the work.

How does Schumann coordinate metrical conflict with the conflict between the tonics of F and D? First, it is obvious that the piece exhibits a large amount of metrical dissonance; in broad terms, we can state that Schumann has chosen to suffuse a piece governed by tonal conflict with conflict in the metrical domain as well. But there are more specific pitch/meter coordinations as well. For example, striking metrical dissonances highlight significant points within the D/F

conflict. Strong displacement dissonance at m. 21 (see Example 5.13) is coordinated with the first appearance of the final key and the actual primary tone F.
The passage comprising mm. 32–36, in which Schumann so clearly traverses a
path from one tonic to the other, is permeated by subliminal G3/2. In mm.
37–38 (see Example 8.9b), intense D2+1 (or D2−1) highlights the C/C♯ and
C/D♭ dyads that embody the D/F conflict.

The contending primary tones, too, are highlighted by metrical means. At
the opening, Schumann contributes to the pretense that C is the primary tone
by presenting it in a metrically stable manner; he places it on the downbeats of
mm. 2, 4, 10, and 12. The true primary tone, F, on the other hand, is metrically
displaced at its first arrival at mm. 21–24. Schumann subtly foreshadows, by
metrical means, the outcome of the battle of the primary tones; he lets the "primary tone" C migrate onto an accented third beat at m. 6, whereas the true primary tone F migrates from its initial displaced position onto a downbeat at
m. 32. ❦

"Well, Florestan," said Eusebius, "were you aware of all of that?" Florestan
responded, "To be honest, I never thought about these matters in such detail. I
did, however, sense that we were creating interesting parallelisms between tonal
and metrical conflict in this piece."

In the preceding paragraphs, we have seen several examples of Schumann's use of metrical dissonance in order to highlight a significant point within
a tonal conflict. Such highlighting is by no means restricted to situations of
tonal conflict; metrical dissonance can emphasize any significant pitch-related
event.[8] In the *Intermezzo* op. 4 no. 5, metrical dissonance draws attention not
only to important moments within the F/D conflict, but also to events not directly involved in that conflict. For example, the melodic line of the B♭-major
"Alternativo" section is characterized by an upward-striving motion—a reaching-
over, in Schenkerian terms—the ultimate aim of which is to couple D4 to D7.
The first wave of the reaching-over begins with the D4 in m. 69 and attains B4
at mm. 79–82 before dropping back to D4. The second wave retraces the same
path (to m. 100), but a third wave moves beyond B4 as far as B♭5 (mm.
101–13). A final wave breaks through the latter barrier at m. 131 and reaches
D7 at m. 132. Each of the three registral crests is allied with metrical dissonance
(which, since the "Alternativo" is otherwise virtually consonant, stands out
clearly from the context). The arrival at B4 in mm. 79–82 is highlighted by
D3+1 (inner-voice durational accents) and D3+2 (dynamic accent in m. 82).
The approach to B♭5 (see Example 8.9c) features a compound dissonance composed of G3/2, D6+2, and D6+5. Both the ascent to the final registral peak and
the recession from it are associated with particularly intense metrical dissonance, the ascent with G3/2 (mm. 129–31—see Example 8.10b), the descent
with the augmentation G6/4 (1=8th).

Schumann sometimes coordinates not only analogous states, but also analogous processes, in the domains of pitch and meter. We have already touched upon this matter in connection with earlier examples in this chapter; we have noted, for instance, the simultaneous intensification of pitch and metrical dissonance in the second piece of *Kreisleriana*, the simultaneous resolution of dissonances, and the coincidence of significant large-scale harmonic resolutions (cadences) with resolutions of metrical dissonances. I mention only two more examples of process coordination here.

A metrical process that occasionally coincides with a parallel pitch process is preparation. One pitch process that is analogous to metrical preparation is the preparation of modulatory goals by single prominent pitches. Schumann sometimes links such a process with the preparation by one or two antimetrical pulses of a coming metrical dissonance. In "Grillen," for example, the first hint at metrical dissonance—the dynamic accent on the third beat in m. 3 (see Example 6.1)—prepares D3+2, a metrical dissonance to be featured prominently in the G♭ major section (especially mm. 72–80). Interestingly, the harmony to which the preparatory accent in m. 3 is affixed is V7 of G♭, which prepares the later prolongation of G♭.

In "Vogel als Prophet," Schumann employs gradual intensification of metrical dissonance in conjunction with the equally gradual seeping of a particular pitch, namely E♭, into deeper levels of structure. The metrical process—intensification of D2+1—was traced in an earlier chapter (see Example 4.7). The corresponding pitch process begins in mm. 1–3, where D2+1 is weak. Here, E♭ acts as a lowly neighbor-note (enharmonically respelled to D♯ in m. 3). A few measures later, E♭ is promoted to membership in two significant harmonies; it becomes the seventh within a prolonged dominant harmony (mm. 8–10), then the third of a C minor triad that acts as a cadential goal (m. 12). These steps in the promotion of E♭ occur just before a passage in which D2+1 is greatly intensified—mm. 13–14. The final step in the pitch process occurs at the end of the B section, that is, during the section that is metrically most intensely dissonant; E♭ here attains its highest status: that of the root of the main modulatory goal of the work (mm. 24–25).[9] 🐝

Florestan said, "A most interesting example! I can think of even more ways in which we coordinated pitch structure with metrical consonance and dissonance. One of these has to do with harmonic parentheses—passages that briefly deviate from the main harmonic argument. We have at times coordinated such parentheses with 'metrical parentheses'—with metrical states that deviate temporarily from the prevailing state. An example occurs in the first movement of the Third String Quartet (mm. 81–84—see Example 4.20c). From m. 76 onward, near the end of your metrically dissonant second theme, you arouse the expectation of a cadence to E major. Instead of providing this cadence, however, you move ever farther away from the expected E major triad, first elaborating the closely related C♯ minor triad (mm. 76–80), then surprisingly landing on C♯ major harmony. The C♯ major passage sounds parenthetical not only because it is so remote from the expected goal of E major, but because you use an ethereal high register, a low dynamic level, and a slower tempo. During this harmonic parenthesis, you resolve the dissonance D6+2 which had prevailed at the end of the second theme. When the harmonic progression regains its bearings in m. 84 (where it arrives at a six-four chord embellishing the E major triad), the dissonance D6+2 returns; the second beats of mm. 84 and 85 are emphasized by a durational and a registral accent, respectively."

Florestan went on, "At times we associated passages that were related in terms of pitch structure with the same metrical dissonance. The *Intermezzo* op. 4 no. 5 furnishes some good examples. We have just read that mm. 1–4 (Example 8.9a) and 37 (Example 8.9b) feature the enharmonically equivalent dyads C/D♭ and C/C♯, respectively. This pitch relationship between the two passages is paralleled by a metrical one: both passages are associated with the metrical dissonance D2+1. The dissonance is, to be sure, much stronger in the latter passage. Both mm. 33–35 and mm. 109–11 (Example 8.9c) involve the rising progression by fourths, G-C-F; the bass states it in the former passage, and the melody in the second. Both passages are also characterized by G3/2, a dissonance that is otherwise rare in the piece." They turned back to the manuscript, and read:

The lower portion of Figure 6.1 shows the metrical structure of the Paganini Caprice on which Schumann based his study. Comparison of the two parts of the figure reveals that in Paganini's work there is much less coordination of metrical dissonance with formal and harmonic structure. The dissonances do resolve at the most significant cadence points in the first section, at the recapitulation and at the very end of the work, and the point where the metrical conflict is most obvious (mm. 32–35) coincides with the harmonically unstable passage preceding the retransitional dominant. Schumann, however, sets up many more, and much more sophisticated correspondences between form, pitch structure, and meter. ❦

Florestan remarked, "I knew by the time I composed this study that I would not be able to emulate Paganini as a virtuoso. It was some solace to me that I was able not only to emulate but to outdo him as a composer, specifically as an ingenious and resourceful manipulator of metrical dissonance."

Eusebius, who had looked ahead to the next section of the manuscript, said, "I am pleased that the author is granting some attention to our vocal works (which so far have hardly been mentioned)." They continued to read with renewed interest.

METRICAL DISSONANCE AND TEXT

Having studied interactions of metrical structure with other musical features in Schumann's works, we now turn to an investigation of associations between metrical states and extramusical features. I begin by considering the ways in which metrical states are linked with text in Schumann's vocal works. I restrict my investigation to his songs, which are by far the richest source of metrical dissonance within his vocal oeuvre. By studying Schumann's use of metrical dissonance in the *Lieder*, we may not only discover the ways in which metrical dissonance relates to text in specific songs, but also begin to understand the meanings that this device carries in his instrumental works. 🐝

Florestan said, "The author indicates that our choral works contain less metrical conflict than our *Lieder*. He is right, and there is a good reason why this is so. I have conducted choirs,[10] and I know that choristers, many of whom are not professional musicians, have difficulty with rhythmic complexities. In our choral music, I therefore curbed my penchant for metrical intricacies." Eusebius added, "It seems to me that, in general, you indulged your metrical fancy most freely in our piano music and in our chamber works. In our symphonies, your metrical dissonances are slightly less numerous, and slightly less bold." Florestan said, "Yes; I have always felt that passages of metrical conflict were more likely to be performed properly by soloists and small ensembles than by large groups." They continued their reading:

S̲chumann's songs, though they contain more metrical dissonance than his larger vocal genres, are a less fruitful source of metrical dissonance than the instrumental works; not only does metrical dissonance appear less frequently in the songs, but it generally appears more briefly and in a more limited number of forms. Schumann may have felt that complex metrical superpositions would distract the listener from the text. Furthermore, involvement of the vocal part in a dissonance could have posed problems of declamation; the necessity of adhering to the poetic accentuation precluded the freedom with which antimetrical layers can be established in instrumental music. (Significantly, Schumann generally avoids declamation problems by using metrical dissonance within untexted portions of songs, or by placing antimetrical layers within the piano part; we shall, to be sure, encounter a few exceptions.) The metrical dissonances that do exist in Schumann's songs, however, are well worth investigating, particularly in terms of their relation to poetic content. In the following paragraphs I investigate various textual factors that may have impelled Schumann to bring metrical dissonance into play.

At a climactic moment of the ballad "Die Löwenbraut," the lion feels slighted because his beloved mistress is about to desert him in favor of a husband, and he makes his displeasure known in no uncertain terms with bloodcurdling roars. The thick, accented chords in the interlude after the words "Er im Zorn den Ausgang wehrt" ("in his fury he prevents egress"), displaced by a sixteenth note with respect to the half-note beats (Example 6.8), are surely intended to imitate the unpredictable fluctuations in sound that are characteristic of a lion's roar. Pitch dissonance and low register collaborate with metrical dissonance to achieve the desired effect. Considering that Schumann probably never heard a lion's roar, this

EXAMPLE 6.8. *The roars of the lion in "Die Löwenbraut" op. 31 no. 1*

is not a bad imitation! Schumann's song output contains numerous similar instances of the attempt to mimic with metrical dissonance particular sounds or actions mentioned in the poem. In "Warte, warte, wilder Schiffsmann" (Example 6.9), Schumann abruptly displaces the vocal line by a quarter note when the text mentions the action of shuddering. Displacement dissonance at a quick tempo evokes the regular oscillations of a shiver. Furthermore, the deliberate contradiction of textual accentuation caused by the vocal displacement suggests the uncontrolled diction associated with shuddering.[11] ❦

Florestan offered a few more examples of metrical mimicry: "In 'Lied eines Schmiedes' (op. 90 no. 1), our superposition of two nonaligned, accented half note layers suggests the blacksmith's hammer blows and their echoes. In 'Die wandelnde Glocke' (op. 79 no. 17), a similar metrical dissonance evokes the oscillations of a tolling bell. In the orchestral introduction of the third ballade from *Vom Pagen und der Königstochter*, op. 140—a duet between the queen and a merman—the low strings, clarinets, horns, and tympani articulate the metrical layer (the dotted quarter-note beats of twelve-eight time). The violins, flutes, and oboes, however, state a displaced layer, resulting in the dissonance D3+2 (1=8th). This dissonance suggests the lapping of the waves to which the opening of the text alludes."

EXAMPLE 6.9. *The shudder in "Warte, warte, wilder Schiffsmann" op. 24 no. 6*

EXAMPLE 6.10. *The answer to the riddle in "Räthsel" op. 25 no. 16*

"Räthsel" (Riddle), op. 25 no. 16 (Example 6.10), illustrates a different text-related function of metrical dissonance in song, namely that of marker or highlighter for especially significant portions of the text. The answer to the poet's riddle—the letter H—is supplied at the very end of the poem, not in the text but in musical notation: Schumann not only ends the vocal line on the note B (H in German) but, even more dramatically, reiterates syncopated B's in the piano part immediately after the parenthetical question "was ist's?" (What is it?). Syncopation has hardly occurred in the song thus far. ✿

Eusebius interjected, "There is a single syncopated B during the piano interlude after the word 'Philosophie'—a hint at the solution of the riddle that was absent from our first version."[12]

This displacement dissonance, then, stands out from the context and strongly marks for consciousness this crucial point in the song. The listener would surely solve the riddle during that striking series of metrically displaced B's! ✿

Florestan observed, "Yes, assuming that the listener understands German, has perfect pitch, and that the song is being performed at the notated pitch level!"

Another good example of the highlighting of particularly significant text by metrical dissonance is found in "Waldesgespräch" (op. 39 no. 3). The turning point of the text is the moment at which the protagonist recognizes that the lovely maiden with whom he has been dallying is the evil enchantress Lorelei. Schumann associates this point with a dramatic superposition of the displacement dissonances D3+1 and D3+2 (1=quarter; Example 6.11). The former dissonance, created throughout the man's E-major music by syncopation in the upper voice of the left hand, is formed at "Gott steh' mir bei" by a durational ac-

EXAMPLE 6.11. *The turning point in "Waldesgespräch" op. 39 no. 3*

cent on the second beat of the voice part (at "bei") and by the piano's imitation
of the voice's dotted motive at the distance of one quarter note. Schumann also,
however, places a dynamic accent on the third beat of the measure. The latter
accent and the resulting superposition of a new dissonance upon the existing
one highlights the moment of truth. ❦

Eusebius remarked, "Our use of D3+2 at this point also reflects the forcible re-
orientation within the man's psyche brought about by his sudden awareness of
the true significance of the encounter. By adhering to D3+2 during the final statement of the man's E-major music in the postlude, where the left-hand ties begin
on the third rather than the second beat, we suggest that the man's life has been
permanently and chillingly changed by his encounter with the Lorelei." Florestan
added, "The shift in the music associated with the protagonist from D3+1 to
D3+2 was not part of our initial strategy; we originally employed D3+2 at the
opening as well as in the postlude."[13]

In some of Schumann's songs, conflicting layers of motion appear to de-
note different levels or dimensions of some textual attribute, for example, of reality (the apparent versus the actual), or of time. In "Zwielicht," op. 39 no. 10,
displacement dissonance is concentrated within one stanza, that which pes-
simistically mentions the potential treachery of friends; no doubt Schumann
meant the two layers to suggest the apparent and the true nature of the
"friend." ❦

Florestan pointed out, "Some of the displacement dissonances in our opera *Genoveva* have a similar meaning. Displacement frequently coincides with words or
events that highlight Golo's treachery. His entry into Genoveva's chamber near
the beginning of Act 2, for example, is accompanied by syncopated quarter-note
chords. We associate his blatant vilifications of Genoveva before Drago with
D4+2 and D2+1 (1=quarter). A very dramatic displacement dissonance occurs

just after Siegfried's naive assertion that Golo was always loyal to him; here, a chromatically descending progression in the orchestra is festooned with dynamic accents on weak beats."

The text of "Es treibt mich hin, es treibt mich her" (op. 24 no. 2) alludes to the slow, unruffled flow of clock time and to the poet's eagerness for a rendezvous with his beloved. Schumann initiates allusions to D3+2 (or D3-1) during a reference to the languid passing of time (at "behaglich träge" and "gähnend") and intensifies this dissonance with dynamic accents in the postlude. The metrical layer might well represent the ineluctable progress of clock time, while the displaced layer, anticipating the notated downbeats, suggests the expectant lover's desire to move time forward.

By far the most common function of metrical dissonance in Schumann's songs, however, is the reflection of emotional or psychological states, particularly those of a violent nature; the dissonance in these cases suggests the loss of control associated with such states. The emotional states may be of a positive character. In "Es treibt mich hin," metrical displacement, besides representing two times, suggests the lover's excitement. Continuous low-level displacement in the third song of *Dichterliebe* ("Die Rose, die Lilie") has a similar function. In the first song of Schumann's little-known Justinus Kerner cycle, op. 35 ("Lust der Sturmnacht"), continuous displacement by a sixteenth note and occasional accentuation of the final two sixteenth-note pulses of a measure contribute significantly to the representation of a lover's exhilaration and exultation; the consistent use of low-level displacement dissonance results in a sense of excitement, and the jabs of weak-beat accentuation suggest the spurts of adrenalin associated with being happily in love. 🌿

Eusebius added, "In *Genoveva*, we sometimes associate the unsavory joys of the villains with displacement dissonance. We suggest Golo's excitement just before kissing Genoveva by eighth-note syncopation in the strings. Similarly, in the finale of Act 1, Golo's passion and Margaretha's gleeful anticipation of her revenge on Siegfried are both associated with D2+1 (1=quarter), created by dynamic accentuation of both weak beats of common-time measures."

Schumann employs metrical dissonance more frequently in connection with negative states. Example 6.12 shows an association between displacement dissonance and insanity; just as Heine's poem refers to "Wahnsinn" (madness), the piano launches into low-level displacement dissonance—an appropriate representation of a mind going awry.[14]

In a number of the passages mentioned above, metrical dissonance is associated with poetic passages that are rife with tension, the lion's roar, the shudder, and the moment of truth in "Waldesgespräch" being obvious examples. Since metrical dissonance is a tensional combination of conflicting or non-

EXAMPLE 6.12. *The setting of "Wahnsinn" in "Schöne Wiege" op. 24 no. 5*

aligned pulse groupings, its association with emotional conflicts and tensions mentioned in a text is appropriate. The resolution of a metrical conflict, on the other hand, can aptly represent the resolution of textual conflicts, or sensations of relaxation in general. Such usages of metrical consonance and dissonance are very common in Schumann's songs. A simple but lovely example is found near the end of "Mondnacht" (op. 39 no. 5). During the words "als flöge sie nach," the vocal line and the piano bass project a 2-layer (1=8th) against the continuing 3-layer of the right-hand part. The resolution of the resulting metrical dissonance precisely at the word "Haus" elicits an appropriate sensation of "homecoming"—of settling into a safe and familiar place. ❦

Eusebius noted, "The syncopation in voice and bass that makes this effect of relaxation possible was an afterthought; I added it to my inked manuscript in pencil."[15]

In *Dichterliebe*, Schumann deploys displacement dissonance over a wide musical expanse in order to reflect the increasing tension within the protagonist. The first songs of the cycle, in which the poet's love affair seems to be progressing smoothly, contain virtually no metrical dissonance. Later songs, in which it becomes increasingly clear that the affair has gone sour, involve frequent use of displacement by one eighth or sixteenth note. In the tenth song ("Hör' ich das Liedchen klingen"), D4+1 (1=16th) is prominent throughout (Example 6.13a). The dissonance is tightened to D2+1 in the postlude. The eleventh song ("Ein Jüngling liebt ein Mädchen") also exhibits D4+1 (1=8th—Example 6.13b) and the same tightening.[16] In the last song of the cycle, Schumann appropriately coordinates a prominent resolution of D2+1 (1=8th) with textual references to the end of the poet's tormented love. The throbbing syncopated chords that underlie the question "Do you know why the coffin is so large and heavy?" yield to metrically aligned music in the last line, during which the text states that the poet has buried his love and pain. ❦

EXAMPLE 6.13. *Metrical dissonance in* Dichterliebe *op. 48*

Eusebius added, "Our resolution of D6+1 in the seventh measure of the postlude is also meant to suggest the end of the poet's inner turmoil."

Florestan said, "There are numerous similar examples. In 'In der Fremde' (op. 39 no. 1), we suggest by pervasive displacement dissonance, created by dynamic and density accents on the metrically weak beats as well as by quarter-note syncopation, the disquiet of the protagonist and her dissatisfaction with her environment.[17] As she ponders the peace that will soon come to her in death ('Wie bald, ach wie bald kommt die stille Zeit'), we resolve the dissonance. During the first statement of the phrase 'da ruhe ich auch,' the dissonance reappears, suggesting a final spasm of unrest, but we again resolve it during the repetition of the phrase.[18] In 'Stiller Vorwurf' (op. 77 no. 4), the anonymous poet recalls the pain that his beloved caused him; we set this portion of the poem with frequent D4+2 and some D2+1 (1=8th), frequently creating the former dissonance by placing piano chords on the weak beats of measures (Example 6.14a). At the end, where the poet states that he cannot help forgiving the woman, we present piano chords on the strong beats, thus resolving D4+2 (Example 6.14b)." Eusebius countered, "D2+1, however, is still in effect at this point; the word 'kann' appears one eighth note later than expected, suggesting that some residual pain or anger remains in the poet's heart."

Florestan said, "D2+1 does resolve before the song concludes. Occasionally, when textual conflicts are unresolved at the end of a poem, we conclude our settings with unresolved metrical dissonance. The Lenau song 'Der schwere Abend' (op. 90 no. 6), is a good illustration. The text deals with the parting of unhappy lovers on a sultry, starless night. The final line, in which the poet wishes that he

EXAMPLE 6.14. *Metrical dissonance and resolution in "Stiller Vorwurf" op. 77 no. 4*

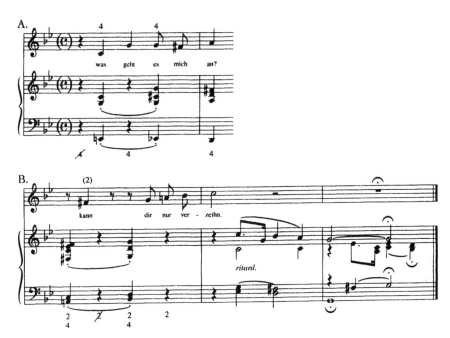

and his beloved were dead, does not relieve the prevailing tension. Throughout the song, we express the poetic tensions with grouping dissonance; quarter note duplets in the voice conflict with the piano's three quarters per measure. Brief allusions to displacement dissonance (D3+1 and D3+2, 1=quarter) during piano interludes, suggesting flashes of lightning, add to the tension (mm. 8, 28, 48). We expand upon D3+2 in the piano postlude (Example 6.15), where we place durational, then harmonic new-event accents on the third beats rather than on downbeats. (Where harmonies are initiated on the third beats, the dissonance can be heard as D3-1.) The final chord of the song does fall on a downbeat, but that single chord does little to counteract the displacement of the earlier ones. Metrical dissonance hangs over the end of the song like the brooding clouds mentioned in Lenau's text."

Eusebius remarked, "'Der schwere Abend' brings up another kind of relationship between metrical dissonance and text—a relationship that has to do not with poetic content but with poetic meter. When we initiated our text-setting activity by reading the poem, its metrical irregularities inevitably caught our attention, and in some cases influenced the anomalies in the musical meter. In 'Der schwere Abend,' the only irregularity occurs in the penultimate line ('wünscht ich bekümmert beiden'), which disrupts the straightforward iambic meter of the remainder of the poem. Now a succession of iambs suggests a duple grouping of pulses, while a dactyl like 'wünscht ich be-' suggests a triplet, taking the time of one duple group. (Other rhythmic settings of these poetic feet are, of course, pos-

EXAMPLE 6.15. *Metrical dissonance at the end of "Der schwere Abend" op. 90 no. 6*

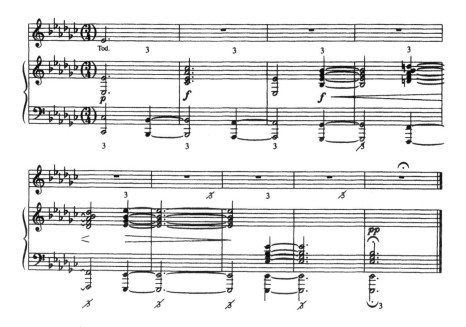

sible, but the ones I mentioned are the most obvious.) The suggestion within a text
of such indirect two-against-three dissonances might well have influenced our de-
cisions with regard to metrical dissonance in the musical setting, all questions of
poetic content aside. In the case of 'Der schwere Abend,' the poem contains the
seed of our pervasive grouping dissonance." Florestan said, "Your remarks also
apply to another of our Lenau songs, 'Meine Rose' (op. 90 no. 2). The content of
the text does not justify our pervasive metrical dissonance. The poem contains,
however, three 'triplets' amidst its many duple groups: 'reich ich den,' 'still meine,'
and 'Könnt ich dann.' These irregularities in the poem influenced our decision to
saturate the setting with G3/2 (1=8th). I see that the author is about to discuss 'Es
leuchtet meine Liebe,' one of the songs that we excised from *Dichterliebe*, which
also illustrates my point. Its text, like most of Heine's poems, is primarily iambic,
but there are numerous triplet disruptions; they increase in frequency as the poem
progresses—two in the first stanza, three in the second and third, four in the
fourth. We even expand upon Heine's disruptions in the fourth stanza by repeating one of the irregular lines ('es stolpert der Riese nach Haus'). The two-against-
three dissonance of the music, then, grows out of the meter of the poem." Eusebius
observed, "In this case, however, the content of the poem also suggests metrical
dissonance, as I am sure the author will mention." They read:

To summarize the ideas presented thus far in this chapter, I present a metrical analysis of Schumann's setting of Heine's "Es leuchtet meine Liebe" (op. 127

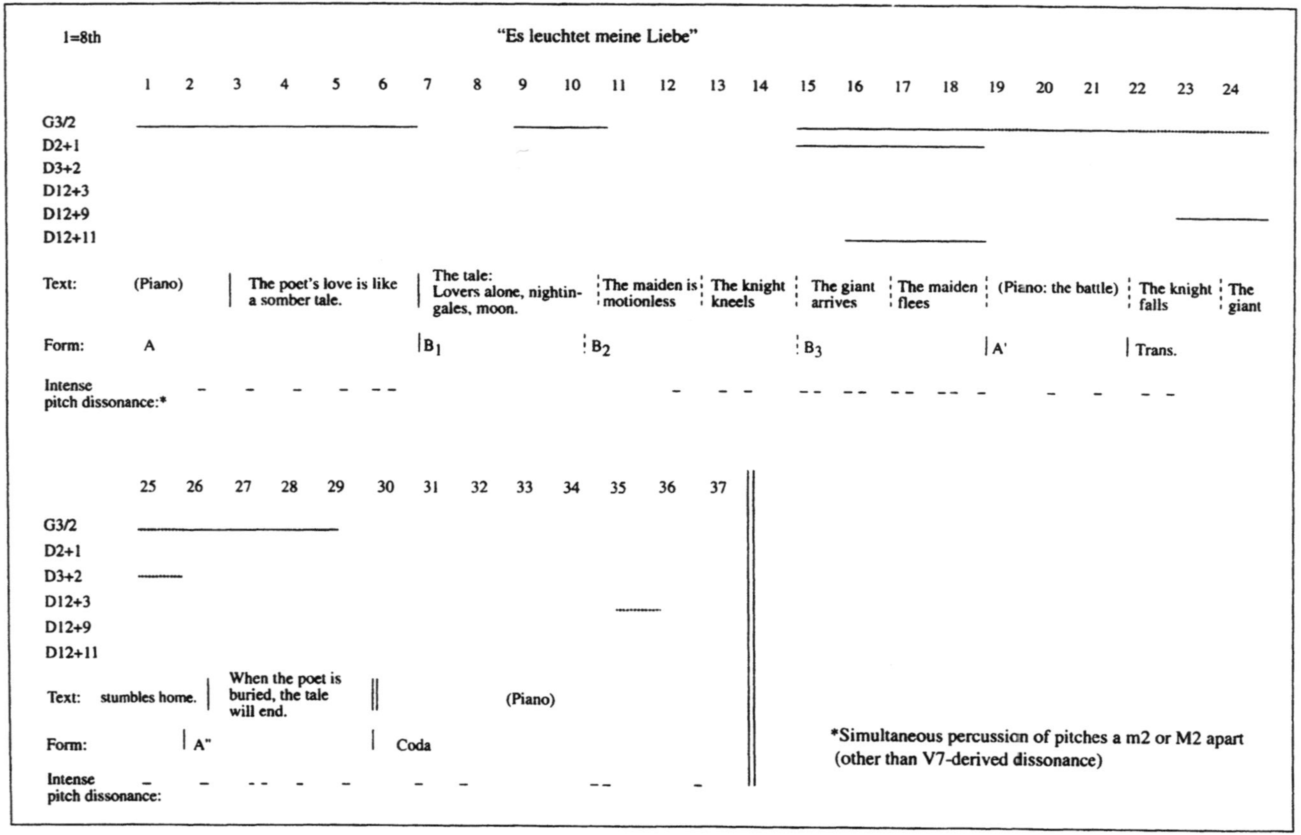

"Es leuchtet meine Liebe"

1 = 8th

1 2 3 4 5 6 7 8 9 10 11 12 13 14 15 16 17 18 19 20 21 22 23 24

G3/2
D2+1
D3+2
D12+3
D12+9
D12+11

Text: (Piano) | The poet's love is like | The tale: | The maiden is | The knight | The giant | The maiden | (Piano: the battle) | The knight | The
a somber tale. | Lovers alone, nightin- | motionless | kneels | arrives | flees | | falls | giant
gales, moon.

Form: A | B₁ | B₂ | B₃ | A' | Trans.

Intense
pitch dissonance:*

25 26 27 28 29 30 31 32 33 34 35 36 37

G3/2
D2+1
D3+2
D12+3
D12+9
D12+11

Text: stumbles home. | When the poet is | (Piano)
buried, the tale
will end.

Form: A" | Coda

Intense
pitch dissonance:

*Simultaneous percussion of pitches a m2 or M2 apart
(other than V7-derived dissonance)

FIGURE 6.2. *Interaction of metrical structure, form, pitch structure, and text in "Es leuchtet meine Liebe"*

no. 3). Heine's poem "Es leuchtet meine Liebe" opens with an analogy between the poet's love and a tragic and somber fairy tale, then shifts abruptly to the narration of just such a tale. The tale begins innocuously enough: two lovers walk silently in a magical garden, surrounded by the nightingale's song and by shimmering moonlight. The knight kneels down before his beloved, who stands still as a statue. This nocturnal tableau is rudely disrupted as the "giant of the wilderness" appears.[19] The maiden flees, and the knight and the giant engage in an affray (which is not explicitly mentioned in the poem, but is brought to life in Schumann's setting by a stormy piano interlude). The grim fairy tale concludes with the knight falling bleeding to the ground and the giant stumbling homeward. In the final line, the two planes of the poem—the poet's discussion of his love, and the fairy tale—merge; the poet's statement that the tale will be over when he is buried suggests that he is himself the wounded knight of the fairy tale.

Figure 6.2 shows the metrical and formal structure of the song, as well as one aspect of pitch structure—the locations of intense pitch dissonance. It is obvious from the figure that changes in metrical state contribute to clarification of form. Resolution of metrical dissonance occurs at the beginning of the B section (m. 7). The return of the A section in the subdominant key (m. 19) is marked by the resolution of two dissonances. In a transitional passage (mm. 22–25), G3/2 is weakened, to be restored to its former intensity precisely at the point where the goal of the passage, the A section in the tonic, is reached. The coda (mm. 30–38) begins with resolution of dissonance and remains virtually consonant throughout.

The figure also reveals that metrical dissonance is coordinated with pitch dissonance. Those passages characterized by the strongest pitch dissonances (semitone dissonances, sometimes taking the form of clusters) are precisely those in which metrical dissonance is most pervasive (mm. 1–6, 15–18, and 26–29). In mm. 7–14 and 30–38, where, with few exceptions, pitch dissonances are restricted to the mildest ones (dominant and diminished seventh chords), metrical dissonance is hardly in evidence.

Both form and pitch structure clearly correspond to the poetic form and content. The A sections in the tonic are coordinated with the external narrative—the poet's remarks about his love—while the B section sets the fairy tale that allegorically represents the circumstances of that love. Intensity of pitch dissonance changes at poetic dividing points. Since both pitch structure and form, then, are influenced by the text, the observation that metrical dissonance is coordinated with pitch structure and form indirectly implies that metrical dissonance is coordinated with the text.

But the coordination of metrical structure and text is more directly in evidence as well. The most prominent of the several dissonances, G3/2 (1=8th), is clearly intended as a musical symbol for the evil giant (who, in turn, personifies the conflicts that bedevil the poet's love). This dissonance is established at the very beginning (Example 6.16a). The pianist will likely emphasize every third eighth-note pulse in the right hand, in accordance with Schumann's time signature, thus immediately establishing the metrical 3-layer. From m. 2 on-

EXAMPLE 6.16. *Metrical dissonance in "Es leuchtet meine Liebe" op. 127 no. 3*

EXAMPLE 6.16. (*continued*)

ward, the left-hand part of the piano introduction more obviously articulates the 3-layer. A conflicting 2-layer is expressed, however, by the grouping of the right-hand chords—by the recurrent patterns "consonance-dissonance" and "tonic-dominant." When the voice enters, its durational accents (which coincide with poetic accents) join the piano bass in articulating the 3-layer, while the 2-layer continues in the right hand.

The association of metrical dissonance with the textual conflict becomes very clear at mm. 15–18, where the evil giant rears his ugly head (Example 6.16b). Metrical consonance, which has reigned since m. 11, is appropriately replaced with G3/2 at this point. While the voice part continues to articulate the metrical 3-layer, the piano expresses two 2-layers in mm. 15–18. One of these is formed by implied accents on the first notes of the slurred groups (which can be played and heard as appoggiaturas and their resolutions), and by the simultaneous syncopated repeated notes played by the right hand (E♭, F, and finally G). The other 2-layer, shown by the upper 2's in the example, arises from subsurface new-event accents on the second bass notes of the slurred groups, which together form a rising stepwise ascent through a fifth in each measure. The nonaligned 2-layers result in D2+1 in addition to G3/2. The sforzandos on the final eighth notes in mm. 16–18 create yet another dissonance (D12+11, or D12-1). The sudden pileup of dissonances in mm. 15–18 effectively mirrors the shattering of the lovers' nocturnal idyll by the entrance of the giant. ❦

Eusebius remarked, "Your mm. 15–18 are somewhat similar to my mm. 9–10; the two passages both make use of slurred duple groups. Since your measures contain so much additional metrical dissonance, however, they give the impression of a distortion rather than a mere restatement of mine. This effect of metrical distortion contributes to the musical depiction of disruption of the earlier idyllic state."

In the fortissimo piano interlude in mm. 19–21, the struggle between the knight and the giant is musically suggested by a continuation of G3/2. (The other two components of the compound dissonance are abandoned after their function of dramatizing the giant's entrance is served.) Although the 2-layer takes over the entire texture in m. 19, G3/2 remains in effect subliminally. In mm. 20–21, while the 2-layer continues to be expressed by grouping in the right hand, the piano bass clearly asserts the metrical 3-layer by accentuation of dotted quarter-note beats. The dissonance G3/2 is maintained during the narration of the succumbing of the knight (mm. 22–23) and, albeit weakly, as the victorious giant stumbles home (mm. 23–26); in the piano part of mm. 23–25, recurrence of individual pitches (F♯ in mm. 23–24 and D in m. 25) suggests a 2-layer while textual accents and contour repetition articulate the metrical 3-layer (Example 6.16c). The giant's stumbling is further suggested in m. 25 by another subtle dissonance; the descending diatonic framework of the passage is deployed in such a way that two of its members, the C natural and B flat, appear on the third eighth notes of metrical groups, resulting in a hint at D3+2. ❦

Florestan looked up and said, "I recall that when Chiarina played the piano part of this song, she placed subtle stresses on the F♯'s and D's that form the 2-layer, so that the stumbling of the giant became more audible. I found this enhancement of a dissonance that is hardly evident in the score very appropriate. Lucky the singer who has a pianist like Chiarina at his or her side!" Eusebius agreed, then remarked, "We had better finish the chapter. It is growing quite dark!"

The dissonance G3/2 continues and in fact becomes more intense as the opening material returns in m. 26 and as the text comes to a close; the subtle displacement dissonance of m. 25, however, resolves in m. 26 as the giant makes his exit. The partial resolution in m. 26 is not the only example of text-inspired resolution in the song; there are two significant resolutions of the main dissonance, G3/2. Schumann eliminates the 2-layer, and hence the dissonance, during most of the first part of the fairy tale (mm. 7–14). This resolution corresponds to a temporary reduction in poetic tension. The first part of the fairy tale appears quite idyllic; it does not yet possess the "sad and somber" quality announced at the beginning of the poem. G3/2 appears briefly at mm. 9–10—perhaps as a subtle indication that the peace of the initial portion of the fairy tale is illusory—but consonance then reigns again until m. 14. More significant, Schumann resolves G3/2 at the end of the song; he abandons the accompaniment pattern based on chords grouped in pairs, and writes new material, characterized by ominous rising octaves, that clearly expresses the metrical 3-layer. With this permanent resolution of metrical dissonance, Schumann reflects the content of the final line, "When I am buried, the tale will end" (that is, the conflicts surrounding the protagonist's love will be resolved, definitively though not happily, by his death).

In sum, in "Es leuchtet meine Liebe" Schumann effectively coordinates states of metrical dissonance and their resolutions with pitch structure and form. Furthermore, his metrical dissonances beautifully evoke particular aspects of the text. The song contains examples of many of the types of connections between metrical state and text that were mentioned earlier: the use of particular metrical states to mimic an action mentioned in the text (the giant's stumbling in m. 25), to highlight a crucial point in the poem (the appearance of the giant at m. 14), and to represent a textual conflict and its resolution.

MEANINGS OF METRICAL DISSONANCE
IN INSTRUMENTAL MUSIC

The very frequent occurrence of metrical dissonance in his music, demonstrated by the large number of examples cited in this and earlier chapters, might lead one to conclude that Schumann delights in this state for its own sake—that the effect of metrical dissonance appealed to him just as certain chord types or certain rhythms might appeal to other composers. Our investigations of metrical processes, however, suggest that his interest in metrical conflict arises from something more than aesthetic preference. The fact that he does not merely treat metrical dissonances as exciting coloristic effects, but rather develops them in a variety of ways, makes clear that he is interested in the exploration of the potential of these states as musical ideas. (Of course, his selection of these particular ideas confirms that he did enjoy them as "colors" as well.)

For Schumann, however, metrical dissonances are more than musical colors and ideas. Our study of metrical dissonance in Schumann's songs suggests that they carried particular extramusical meanings for him—meanings, in fact, that were deeply relevant to his life and his personality. Dietrich Fischer-Dieskau suggests, for example, that when setting "Es leuchtet meine Liebe," Schumann identified himself with the poet (and the knight), Clara with the maiden, and Wieck with the giant. He surmises that Schumann may also have been thinking of Wieck as he set "Die Löwenbraut"; like the lion, Wieck, about to lose his precious daughter to an interloper, became vicious in his jealousy and disappointment.[20] If Schumann related these poems to the conflicts within his own life, then the fact that he prominently or pervasively employed metrical dissonance when setting them suggests that he consciously or subconsciously linked that device with his personal conflicts. It is not far-fetched to assume that in Schumann's instrumental music, too, metrical dissonances frequently represent the conflicts that he was working through in his life.

Schumann was, even more than most artists, riven by internal conflicts and faced with external ones. Among the internal conflicts are the famous Florestan-Eusebius duality; the conflict between the poet and the musician; the conflict between Biedermeier and Bohemian (which could be generalized to "normal versus abnormal"); the conflict between the objective self and the subjective self; and so on. Among Schumann's external conflicts were the struggle against the Philistines of the musical world in which he engaged through the *Neue Zeitschrift*; and the famous protracted battle with Wieck, which also brought with it painful tensions in Schumann's relationship with Clara.[21]

These manifold dualities and conflicts inevitably impinged on Schumann's music in a variety of ways: in the dialectic between the esoteric and the accessible that animates the works of the late 1840s,[22] in the manifold juxtapositions of Eusebian and Florestanian sections, but surely also in the frequent use of metrical dissonance. The metrical layers within a particular dissonance are apt symbols for normality, for order, for the objective self, and for the Eusebian side of Schumann, whereas antimetrical layers suggest the abnormal, the irregular and the disorderly, the subjective self, or the Florestanian side.

We can never, of course, be certain precisely what Schumann might have "meant" by particular instances of instrumental metrical dissonance. We shall not be far off the mark, however, if we interpret them as representing inner or outer conflict, and their resolutions as expressing a desire to come to terms with conflict—for as Dieter Schnebel points out, in his music, unlike in his life, Schumann was able to resolve all conflicts if he so wished.[23] 🦇

Florestan mused, "Thus ends the chapter. The author is certainly on the right track when he emphasizes the connection between metrical dissonance and the various conflicts in our lives. Some of our instrumental metrical dissonances, however, have connotations other than conflict. With displacement dissonances at a very fast tempo, we sometimes express fear, panic, and breathlessness, for example, in the finale of the Piano Sonata op. 14,[24] and in the *Scherzo in F minor* excised from that same work. Some of our dissonances are humorous in intent; the unexpected association of disparate elements that underlies metrical conflicts certainly has comic potential. The subliminally dissonant passage beginning at m. 188 of the finale of our Piano Concerto is one of my humorous examples. It is certainly a good joke on the conductor, who is forced to wave his arms in accordance with a meter that has very little to do with the music that the performers are playing!"[25]

Eusebius smiled, then went on, "I have occasionally employed metrical dissonance in a manner that suggests neither conflict, panic, nor comedy, but rather evokes a suspended, dreamlike, hovering state. Do you recall the little 'Impromptu' that I dashed off in 1838, and that we recently included in our *Albumblätter* op. 124 (Example 6.17)? In this piece I superimposed three layers of motion, none of which possesses obvious primacy. The 2-layer (1=8th) that is purportedly the metrical layer is in fact the least strongly articulated in the music.

EXAMPLE 6.17. *"Impromptu" op. 124 no. 9, mm. 1–4 and 8–12*

It is difficult for listeners to come to a convincing metrical interpretation for this piece; they will likely find themselves hovering deliciously and dreamily between meters."[26] Florestan nodded and added, "These dreamlike pieces of yours perhaps come closer to liberating music from the 'tyranny of meter' than my more violent and impassioned dissonant passages."

Eusebius haltingly continued, "Sometimes the metrical dissonances in our instrumental works symbolize insanity. Moritz Hauptmann, as I pointed out in *Euphonia*, associates meter—that is, metrical consonance—with health. What better means than metrical dissonance to represent ill health—a mind gone awry—than metrical dissonance? Insanity is a theme that has recurred in our lives and in our music. Have we not always feared it? Have we not often felt its shadow fall upon us?"[27] Florestan nodded slowly and responded, "In 1840, when the struggle with Wieck loomed large on our horizon, I equated the giant in 'Es leuchtet meine Liebe' with him. But now I identify the giant with the infinitely more frightening black cloud that hovers over us, that stretches its misty tentacles out for us, that threatens to engulf us. . . ." They sat in brooding silence in the gathering dusk of the winter afternoon. Their room was now lit only by the moon, which filtered through the shrub-enshrouded windows.

The door opened and Clara entered. "Robert, you were sorely missed at the Tausches," she lied. He gazed at her and murmured, "When I am dead, the tale will be ended." She came to him, stood before him, and embraced him. He leaned his head against her breast, and thus they remained, motionless, in the shimmering moonlight.

Intermezzo III

SEVEN

Performing Metrical Dissonances

On a rainy morning in April 1854, Clara Schumann sat down at Robert's desk. A wave of depression seized her as her eye fell on his effects — the inkwell and pen from which had flowed such a wealth of music, the well-thumbed copy of *Flegeljahre*, the well-organized folders of his manuscripts. . . . With a sigh, she picked up his pen, took a sheet of paper from one of the drawers, and began to answer a letter from her former student and friend Martha von Sabinin, which had arrived early in February and had lain on the desk unanswered ever since.[1]

She wrote:

Dear Martha,

I must apologize for my long delay in responding to your letter, which arrived at a very bad time — indeed the worst time. My poor Robert's health came to a crisis in February. He had demanded for some time to be consigned to an institution, but I postponed that dire step until the dreadful day when he attempted to end his life. I have not seen him since he was taken away to Dr. Richarz's asylum at Endenich, and do not know when I shall be permitted to do so. He is very ill.

Only now that the horrid flurry of activity associated with his removal is past am I again capable of attending to my correspondence. I particularly welcome the opportunity to respond to your query about the execution of passages containing metrical conflict; my response will enable me to think about Robert's music and thereby to feel close to him.

Robert was fascinated with metrical conflict—in fact, he spoke at length to me on this subject shortly before the catastrophe—and conflicted passages occupy a prominent position in his works. You have, therefore, focused on one of the most profound problems that faces performers of his music. There are two broad issues that you must consider in preparing yourself to play such passages: first, metrical conflicts and their resolutions must be conveyed to the listener in the clearest possible fashion; and second, not only the letter but also the spirit of conflicted passages must be communicated. I can offer you a few suggestions about each of these issues. My remarks refer specifically to Robert's piano music, but they are to a large extent also relevant to works for other instruments.

In order to play metrically conflicted passages properly, you must know precisely where they begin and where they end. Hence, you must take the time to analyze with some care the work that you are preparing. Many metrical conflicts are obvious from Robert's scores; visual signals such as recurring accents at points of the measure other than the downbeat, or ties and beams that persistently cut across measure and beat boundaries, will alert you to the existence of a conflict against the meter. Other conflicts are more concealed because they are built into the melody and harmony of the work; these reveal themselves only after careful listening.

You must discover not only where the conflicted passages are, but also how they are constructed, that is, you must search out the various layers of which they are composed. The following exercises will clarify for you the nature of the components involved in a given conflict, and will at the same time train your fingers to negotiate them. If the passage involves the superposition of unequal layers—superimposed triple and duple layers are particularly common in Robert's music—begin by playing the layers separately, using the fingering that you will need to use in the end. Then combine the layers while attempting to preserve their individual character. In Robert's piano music, each hand generally plays one layer; in such cases this exercise is not difficult to perform. Sometimes, however, Robert assigns more than one layer to one hand, as in the Trio of the *Scherzo in F Minor* (see Example 8.18a), and in the first Trio from the Scherzo of the Piano Sonata op. 11 (see Example 4.8c). At other times, a given layer might be formed by a combination of events in both hands rather than being localized within one hand. At the opening of the *Presto in G Minor*, for instance (which was the original finale for the Piano Sonata op. 22), a duple layer results from the succession Bb-C-D in the left hand, each note occupying two sixteenth-note pulses, but also from the dynamic accent on the third sixteenth-note pulse in the right hand (see Example 2.6a). The separate practicing of layers becomes more difficult when layers are scattered across the texture (and across the two hands) in this manner, but it will clarify for you the role of each finger in conveying the metrical conflict within the passage. In passages containing three different layers, playing the layers in pairs is a useful exercise as well. Playing all layers together will be much less difficult after these preliminary steps.

EXAMPLE 7.1. *Metrical realignment of the opening of the finale of the Piano Sonata op. 14*

Where conflicts result from equivalent but nonaligned layers—a second type of conflict that frequently occurs in Robert's works—it is helpful to reshape the conflicted passage by aligning the layers. Play the passage in the revised form, and observe how its sound and its effect are altered. For example, at the opening of the finale of the Sonata op. 14 (Example 7.1), increase the duration of the notes marked sforzando to eighth notes and place them on the beats. Similarly, at the opening of *Kreisleriana* move the bass octaves and chords back one eighth-note pulse (Example 7.2). After playing your revised version, play the actual passage again. This procedure will bring the character of the passage as Robert wrote it into focus for you.

Once you have discovered the metrical conflicts in a work, and completed the preliminary familiarization exercises, you must consider how to render the conflicting layers audible. The meter of anything that you play, and particularly of any conflicted passage that you play, is to a large extent *in your hands*. The placement of weight or stress, and the amount of stress that you allot to individual notes or chords in such passages, will to a large extent determine how the listener perceives the meter. You must decide, then, which layer or layers you need to "bring out" by stress. Robert generally associates his "antimetrical" layers with accents of various kinds; hence it is rarely necessary for the performer to stress these layers. Doing so might, in fact, render the conflict inaudible. It is frequently necessary, on the other hand, to apply subtle stresses to the metrical layers, particularly to the notated downbeats, when they are contradicted. Sometimes, the downbeats are sufficiently accented within the music, by virtue of register, density, harmonic change, etc., and thus require no

EXAMPLE 7.2. *Metrical realignment of the opening of* Kreisleriana

EXAMPLE 7.3. *"Walzer" op. 124 no. 15, mm. 1–4*

extra effort on the part of the performer. For example, in mm. 14–16 of the Scherzo from op. 11, a passage in which a duple layer conflicts with the metrical triple layer, harmonic changes take place on the downbeats so that the metrical layer is perfectly audible without any additional emphasis. In the initial theme of the finale of the same sonata, on the other hand (Example 5.10), at the beginning of the Scherzo movements of the Second String Quartet (Example 5.9b) and of the Piano Quintet, and in similar passages in which the metrical layer is musically highlighted in no obvious way, I would suggest a very slight stressing of the notated downbeats. Since in these passages all accents within the score contradict those downbeats, only such subtle stress on the downbeats will render audible the conflict that Robert's notation suggests. (I recall that Robert spoke about having eliminated antimetrical accents from certain passages so as to leave room for the performer to articulate the notated meter.)[2]

The stresses on downbeats must always be subtle; *strong* stressing of all downbeats would be intolerable! And there are cases where downbeat stress would be entirely inappropriate. Among these are the *Scherzo in F Minor*, which was originally part of Robert's *Concert sans orchestre* (the Piano Sonata op. 14), and the aforementioned *Presto in G Minor*. Both works are based on a constant and rapid alternation between passages that support, and passages that contradict, the notated meter. The breathless excitement within these works stems precisely from this alternation; they would lose much of their effectiveness if the performer rendered the metrical layer audible at all times. It would at any rate be virtually impossible, given the breakneck speed of these two works, for a pianist to convey the antimetrical aspects of Robert's notation (accents and beams) while also providing subtle downbeat stresses.

In some of Robert's works, the stressing of downbeats is impossible for another reason: the notated downbeats are entirely suppressed for many successive measures, in the sense that no attack is associated with them. Among such passages are the initial and final sections of the "Walzer," op. 124 no. 15 (Example 7.3), and mm. 86–101 of the first movement of the *Faschingsschwank aus Wien* (Example 7.4a). In such passages, beats other than the notated downbeats easily usurp the role of downbeats, in which case an effect of metrical alignment or "consonance" arises. This must not be allowed to happen! If

EXAMPLE 7.4A. Faschingsschwank aus Wien, *first mvmt., mm. 86–88*

Robert had desired such an effect, he could easily have written the passages in an aligned manner. I am convinced that he chose the more complex notation because he wished the performer somehow to make audible the conflict that was optically evident within the score. I know that Robert worked very hard to achieve the clearest possible visual representation of the sounds that he heard in his mind or conjured up at the keyboard, and all of us will do well to trust his notation. In connection with metrical issues, this means especially that we should not ignore his time signatures and bar lines, even if they are contradicted by *all* aspects of the music.

How can such optical conflicts be communicated? In symphonic music, conductors assume a particular significance during such passages, for they display the notated meter to the audience and hence render the conflict in the score visually if not aurally perceptible. (The famous passage from the finale of the Piano Concerto is a good example!) Communicating such conflicts in nonconducted music is somewhat more difficult, but not impossible. First, it is important that you continue to *feel* the notated downbeats, even if you cannot articulate them. Doing so will create a sense of tension and frustration within you, which is bound to be transferred to the audience.[3] A slight pressing downward during suppressed downbeats, though it will have no audible result, might assist you in feeling the downbeats. Second, the notes and chords that articulate the antimetrical layer must not be overstressed; overstressing would very quickly lead the listener to hear those notes and chords as downbeats (particularly since they are already highlighted by various musical means.) Third, certain physical signals can be employed to convey conflicts within passages in which only antimetrical layers are articulated. I have, for example, heard chamber musicians and soloists inhale sharply but softly on some (not all!) suppressed downbeats. As long as such breaths do not become overly obtrusive, I find them quite appropriate. A slight leaning forward during fully displaced passages might also suggest tension; leaning back and perceptibly relaxing would be appropriate at the points where the displacement is resolved. But I should not like to prescribe specific gestures; you must do what comes naturally to you. Performance would be a sorry business if all players moved in precisely the same manner at given points of a work!

EXAMPLE 7.4B. *The effect of delay at m. 86 of* Faschingsschwank aus Wien, *first mvmt.*

A final remark regarding such fully displaced passages: it is important to avoid delay at their inceptions. Displacement depends upon *placement*, that is, on the positioning of accents in relation to the established metrical framework. If one waits even a moment too long when embarking on a displaced passage, the displacement becomes distorted; the constituent layers (metrical and antimetrical) may even become confused, the displaced layer sounding like a continuation of an established metrical layer. Here, for example, is how the aforementioned portion of the *Faschingsschwank* would sound if the pianist were to delay its beginning (Example 7.4b); the chords assume the function of downbeats, which is antithetical to the score.

Entirely different technical problems are posed by the execution of passages containing more than two conflicting layers (which are quite common in Robert's works). Such passages, not particularly problematic in ensemble music, become quite difficult when they are written for piano. Pianists will, however, after suitable practice, be able to articulate clearly the numerous layers in Robert's passages of this type.[4] Robert knew very well what he could and what he could not demand of fellow pianists. Close inspection of his many-layered passages generally reveals that he has facilitated the pianist's task in particular ways. First, as I mentioned, he writes many layers clearly into the music, for example, by manipulating density, register, and duration. These layers take care of themselves; one need not worry about "bringing them out" by added stresses, and can thus concentrate on those layers that do require reinforcement. (The pianist must, of course, determine which layers do, and which do not, require stressing.) Second, when Robert wishes one hand to articulate two layers, he generally separates those layers by register, so that they are played, respectively, by the "lower" and "upper" parts of the hand. For example, in the aforementioned passage from the first Trio of the Scherzo from op. 11 (Example 4.8c), two registrally distinct nonaligned triple layers are conveyed by the "lower" and "upper" parts of the right hand (the "lower" being the thumb and index finger, the "upper" being the remaining fingers). The same is true of the Trio of the *Scherzo in F minor* (Example 8.18), where Robert assigns the metrical sextuple layer to the fifth finger of the left hand, the metrical triple layer to its "upper" fingers, and two registrally separated duple layers to the corresponding parts of the right hand. Any accomplished pianist will be adept at such "split-hand" playing, which is a basic keyboard technique.

A piece that illustrates the pianistic challenges of multiple metrical layers is the charming "Impromptu," op. 124 no. 9. It is important to recognize that this piece is written in the style of a string quartet (Robert wrote it in 1838, when he was beginning to explore the string quartet medium.)[5] In the A sections (mm. 1–8, 12–20, 24–32—see Example 6.17a), a melodic motive is imitated between the three "upper strings." Those "instruments" not stating the motive accompany it with reiterated syncopated pitches (the "cello" does so throughout these sections). In the harmonically more mobile B sections (mm. 8–12 and 20–24—see Example 6.17b), statements of the motive in the "viola" and "second violin" are answered by outward-moving scale passages culminating in registral and dynamic peaks.

This harmonically and formally uncomplicated piece is metrically of great complexity; the score suggests at least four metrical layers. The metrical sextuple layer (1=the eighth note) is not only implied by the bar lines but is articulated by Robert's dynamic accents on downbeats. The syncopations in the accompanying voices create an antimetrical duple layer. A triple layer emerges from registral and durational accents within the opening motive, and is reinforced by registral and dynamic accents at the aforementioned peaks within the B sections. Finally, the three-four time signature suggests a duple layer aligned with the metrical sextuple layer.

It might seem that two human hands could not possibly convey all of these layers. But as I suggested earlier, it is not necessary to invest effort into bringing all of them out. The sextuple layer will be audible if the dynamic accents in the A sections are observed. The nonaligned duple layer, too, cannot fail to become audible, as the syncopated attacks that create it continue almost uninterrupted throughout the piece. The triple layer will emerge from registral and durational accents. The only layer, in fact, that the performer must actively reinforce is the metrical duple layer, which will otherwise be completely overshadowed by the antimetrical duple and triple layers. Again, the meter is in your hands. If you stress those notes of the opening motive that are already accented by register and duration, the piece will sound as if it is in six-eight time (with a conflicting duple layer provided by the syncopated notes). If you overemphasize the syncopated notes, they will sound like downbeats of a conflicted three-four meter (the three-eighth-note layer generating the conflict). Neither of these manners of performance would do justice to Robert's notation. Only a subtle stressing of the quarter-note beats of his notated three-four meter will permit that meter—the result of the interaction of the sextuple layer and an aligned duple layer—to become audible.

Such stressing need not be maintained consistently throughout the piece. It is vitally important at the beginning, so that the listener is "trained" to hear Robert's meter. Later in the piece, however, other layers could be highlighted. As in so many of his works, Robert allows us to play, and the listener to hear, his most striking and lovely passages more than once. You have the opportunity, then, to shape the meter differently when a passage returns —to allow the listener to hear it from a new perspective. You could, for instance, give primacy to the metrical duple layer at the opening by applying subtle stresses on alternate notes of the motivic statements from the first note of m. 1 onward. At m. 12, where the opening music returns, you could give slightly more weight to the triple layer, thus making the listener wonder whether the piece might not be in six-eight time after all. In the final A section, the initial manner of execution should return, so that the meter that Robert notated retains the greatest overall prominence. The result of such a flexible performance would be a certain amount of confusion for the listener. In some works, confusion should create a sense of tension and frustration. In this "Impromptu," however, the confusion should be delightfully intriguing rather than oppressive.[6]

I move on to my second major point. It is not enough to convey the letter of metrical conflicts; you must also attempt to penetrate and to communicate their spirit, that is, their meaning. To a certain extent I have already addressed this issue by referring to tension and relaxation, confusion and ambiguity. Metrical conflict almost invariably results in an increase in tension within the music, and that is an important aspect of its meaning. Such conflict can arouse a sensation of almost physical discomfort in the performer and listener, partly because of the coming apart or going awry of layers of motion that were previously aligned, partly because of the ambiguity and confusion that it generates. Metrical realignment, on the other hand, creates a sense of relaxation, of security, of homecoming. Learn to feel the waves of tension and relaxation that Robert creates so skillfully in his works. Listen for subtle hints at coming tensions, in the form of isolated accents that contradict the meter; for the full fruition of the foreshadowed tensions; and, finally, for their dispersal. If you feel these waves, your listeners will likely feel them as well. Again, I must stress the importance of analysis; if you do not know where the metrical conflicts are, from the smallest hints to the broadest conflicted expanses, you will not be able to feel and to convey the tension that appertains to them. You might wish to prepare a diagram of the metrical structure, a kind of "metrical map," as an aid in tracing the curves of tension and relaxation.

You might find it easier to perform metrical conflicts in a meaningful manner if you allow the rise and fall of tension associated with them to suggest to you a specific narrative, an image, or an emotional state (or a succession of these). Robert certainly associated metrical conflict with particular emotional or mental states, as is amply demonstrated in his songs. In his instrumental music, too, we should think about what he might have intended to convey by individual conflicted passages. You cannot, even I cannot know precisely what meaning a given metrical conflict had for Robert, and we might well arrive at interpretations that diverge from his own. No matter; a performance that convincingly suggests a certain narrative, image, or emotional state, even if they differ from those that the composer had in mind, will always be more moving and compelling than a cold, detached performance.

The "Impromptu" that I mentioned earlier, with its continuous and complex, yet languid motion, suggests to me the following image: a bough suspended in a stream, its many leaves waving gently in the current. Robert told me that he used to spend hours staring at such boughs while lying on the riverbanks around Zwickau. Although I have no idea whether he had this image in mind when writing the piece, the image helps me to achieve the "tender execution" that Robert demands, and prevents the metrical confusion from generating a tension that is certainly inappropriate.

The images and narratives that Robert's more Florestanian conflicted passages suggest to me are quite different. Lately, understandably, the narratives that occur to me often have to do with Robert's present state. I give you one example: the finale of the Piano Sonata op. 14. The initial theme suggests to me the discourse of an individual on the verge of a breakdown. He painfully, breathlessly attempts to whisper into the ear of his beloved the thoughts that chase each other at breakneck speed through his mind. At m. 6, he cries out in frustration and pauses to catch his breath, then continues his incoherent murmurings. At m. 15 (where the metrical layer begins to assert itself), the beloved attempts to quiet him, and succeeds to a certain extent; the poor man's babble does not cease, but becomes less agonized and breathless.

Most of the rest of the movement alternates between states of pronounced and more subdued panic (in metrical terms, states of very obvious and less obvious displacement). One moment stands out for me as a very special one. Measures 176–77, which lie between a restatement of the frustrated outcry first heard at m. 6 and a resumption of the mad, misaligned, murmuring sixteenth notes, are in themselves entirely without metrical conflict; the two hands suddenly line up and collaborate in an almost comically simple cadential gesture. These measures are like a gleam of good humor shining through brooding clouds of despair. Such moments in Robert's music remind me so much of him as he has been during the last few years. In the midst of some disquieting, even terrifying monologue, he blurts out a remark reminiscent of the old, healthy Robert—some ingratiating, witty epigram that, however, elicits not laughter but tears. So it is with this passage.

The conclusion of the movement represents to me the overcoming, at least temporarily, of madness and terror. The offbeat accents disappear at the final cadence (mm. 350–51), and the final measures involve coordinated arpeggiation in the two hands, a gesture unprecedented in the movement. The shift to the major mode, of course, contributes significantly to the new, more positive emotional state.

That is my story for this finale. I would not wish to impose it on anybody else; some other narrative might work equally well. I cannot imagine, however, that one could play this movement without having in mind an image relating to feverish, frenetic mental or physical activity.

Writing this letter has, as I anticipated, enabled me to feel close to him who is far away. And the remembering of his music has given me hope that perhaps his mind shall, like the meter at the end of op. 14, return to a healthy state. I hope that all is well with you, and I look forward to remaining in communication with you.

    With many friendly greetings,
    Clara Schumann 🌑

EIGHT

Carnaval des analyses

When the caretaker left, Florestan flung the tray of food that he had brought out of the window, narrowly missing one of the gardeners, then stared, trembling, at the woods and fields of Endenich. There had just been a rather violent confrontation with the caretaker, whose attempts to calm him, assisted by Eusebius, had been without avail. Florestan was silent now only because his prolonged screaming had exhausted his vocal cords. Shrieks continued to bubble up within him, and when Eusebius came up behind him and put his hand on his shoulder, one of them burst from him as a hoarse moan. Eusebius drew him away from the window with a pitying sigh and succeeded in settling him on the sofa. He sat down beside him and drew his attention to the manuscript that he held in his hand. "Look, Florestan, what I have found at the bottom of my trunk!" he said. "There is still one chapter that we have not read. It promises to be diverting; its title and subtitles allude to several of our compositions." Florestan made no response, but sat quietly as Eusebius began to read to him.[1]

"VALSE FRANÇAISE" (HECTOR BERLIOZ, "UN BAL," FROM *SYMPHONIE FANTASTIQUE*)

The music of Hector Berlioz is by no means as replete with metrical dissonance as that of Schumann. Whereas Jacques Barzun ranks Berlioz as one of the great rhythmic innovators of the nineteenth century, the novelty of his rhythms seems to be based more on irregularity, both at low and high levels, rather than on the interaction of nonaligned regular layers of motion.[2] Nevertheless, Berlioz was capable of employing such interactions with great finesse. The beginning of "Scène aux champs" from the *Symphonie fantastique* (which Schumann cites in his famous review of that work) is a good example.[3] The movement begins with the displacement dissonance D3+1 (1=8th); most of the durational, registral, and dynamic accents in the initial woodwind dialogue are one eighth note removed from the notated strong beats. This dissonance is not perceptible at first because the metrical layers are not yet established. Durational accents in mm. 2, 4, 6, 8, and 9, however, begin to suggest the metrical 3-layer. The entry of the violas on the downbeat of m. 11, very soft though it is, contributes its mite to the establishment of the metrical 3- and 6-layers. Thereafter, new-event harmonic and dynamic accents in the violas reinforce the metrical 6-layer, while dynamic accents in the woodwinds continue the antimetrical 3-layer. The initial subliminal dissonance thus gradually surfaces as the initial section of the movement unfolds. The dissonance resolves as the next section begins in m. 20, to be recalled only by occasional durational and dynamic accents on the second eighth notes of measures (for example in mm. 22 and 35).

The metrical structure of the second movement of the *Symphonie fantastique* is also worth investigating. A short summary addressing the questions listed in chapter 2 is followed by a discussion of the most salient metrical features and processes of the movement. (It is impossible to mention all interesting metrical features.) The same format is used for all analyses of complete works within this chapter.

Summary

1. Main recurring dissonances: G6/4, D6+2, and D6+4 (1=16th).
2. Families of dissonances operative in the movement: "G6/4."
3. Recurring juxtapositions or superpositions: G6/4 and the diminution G1/.67.
4. Proportion of primarily consonant and primarily dissonant passages: mostly consonant with brief incursions of dissonance, especially at cadences and in the coda.
5. Amount of subliminal dissonance: there are numerous instances of subliminal G6/4, brief enough that the metrical 6-layer can be maintained by the listener.
6. Frequency of change of metrical state: generally infrequent change, with greater frequency in the coda (for added excitement).
7. Basic metrical narrative: preparation of two main dissonances in the introduction followed by their development.

It is the latter point that I wish to discuss at some length. The movement opens in a metrical haze (Example 8.1a). The barely audible initial tremolo is noncommittal with regard to meter, and the following cello and bass arpeggiation continues the metrical ambiguity. Whereas Berlioz's placement of the first two statements of the tonic note within the arpeggiation supports the notated meter, the dynamic and registral accent on C in m. 4 suggests two distinct dissonances against the metrical 6-layer (1=16th). The hint at the displacement dissonance D6+2 is obvious. In addition, the accentuation of C hints at a partitioning of the arpeggiation into pairs of eighth notes, and hence at a 4-layer and

EXAMPLE 8.1. *G6/4 in "Un bal" from Berlioz's* Symphonie fantastique

G6/4. The same hints recur in mm. 7–8, 13–14, and, more weakly because of the lack of a sforzando, in mm. 17–18.

Within the final cadence of the introduction (mm. 30–31 — Example 8.1b), G6/4 assumes greater prominence: the arpeggios of the second harp divide into pairs of triplets on the basis of pattern repetition, creating a 4-layer, while the metrical 6-layer is articulated by the solid chords of the first harp.

Later in the movement, Berlioz maintains the association of G6/4 with cadential passages. At mm. 78–84 (Example 8.1c), where a cadential dominant is prolonged, the first violins' sixteenth notes are grouped into fours by contour, the leaps functioning as dividers. Dynamic accents in the winds, meanwhile, continue the metrical 6-layer. During the cadential portion of the central *idée fixe* statement (mm. 152–55), the melodic new-event accents in the flutes and clarinets create a 4-layer while the 6-layer is subliminally maintained. A similar subliminal dissonance is found at the prolonged dominant immediately preceding the return of the A section (mm. 171–73). The coda, an expanded cadence to

EXAMPLE 8.2. *G3/2 in "Un bal"*

the movement as a whole, opens with G6/4 (mm. 256–63 — Example 8.1d); the violins establish a 4-layer by durational accents (eighth notes) and by pattern repetition, while the metrical 6-layer continues subliminally. At the climactic cadential six-four chord at mm. 298–301, Berlioz creates a link to an earlier very similar event, namely to mm. 30–31 (Example 8.1b), by again giving repeated groups of six triplet sixteenths (forming a 4-layer in terms of the nontriplet sixteenth-note unit) to the harps. The flutes reinforce that layer with a repeating four-sixteenth-note pattern. Meanwhile, the 6-layer is subliminally maintained in mm. 298–99 and, in mm. 300–301, explicitly expressed by new-event melodic accents in the strings. One more cadential passage involving G6/4 initiates the rush toward the conclusion (mm. 320–25); the metrical layer is again subliminal, and the 4-layer results from new-event melodic and harmonic accents in the flute, oboe, first violin, harp, cello, and bass parts.[4]

Aside from these literal usages of the grouping dissonance suggested during the introduction, Berlioz uses two diminutions. The diminution G3/2 occurs particularly frequently. The main theme of the movement, whose accompaniment delineates a 2-layer, hints intermittently at a 3-layer; in the first violin part in mm. 40–41, 45, 49 (and in corresponding later measures), the measure's six sixteenth notes divide on the basis of melodic contour into two groups of three. The 3-layer is particularly clear in the precadential measures (45 and 53) because a relatively large central leap (a fourth) creates a registral accent on the fourth sixteenth note, and because a three-sixteenth-note chromatic neighbor-note pattern is repeated. During the coda, Berlioz expands upon the specific instances of G3/2 that are characteristic of the opening theme. In the melody of mm. 288–90 and 293, for instance (Example 8.2), he repeatedly uses reiterated neighboring figures separated by leaps to create a 3-layer, while the accompaniment persists in its eighth-note "oom-pah-pah" pattern. Similar passages are found in mm. 340–42 and 348–50; slurred three-note figures separated by leaps establish a 3-layer in the melodic voices, while the accompanying voices (harps) articulate the metrical 2-layer. These allusions to specific versions of G3/2 from the main theme contribute immensely to the coda's success as a summary of the movement.

Further diminution of G6/4 (G1/.67) occurs in the second harp part at mm. 30–31 (Example 8.1b), between the first violins and all other instruments at m. 61, between the harp and the strings during the restatement of the main theme at mm. 183–86, and intermittently, then steadily during the coda (from m. 258

EXAMPLE 8.3. *G6/4 and its double diminution in "Un bal" (mm. 298–99)*

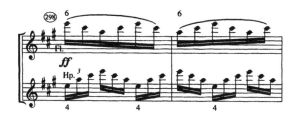

onward). The combination during the cadence at mm. 298–301 of G6/4 with its double diminution contributes significantly to the excitement of the moment (Example 8.3).

The displacement dissonance suggested during the initial measures of the movement, D6+2, begins to play a role in mm. 107–13, where density accents (harp and string chords) occur intermittently on the second eighth notes of measures. The antimetrical 6-layer arises from curtailment of a metrically aligned "oom-pah-pah" pattern, split in mm. 94–105 among the strings, harps, and winds, respectively. Deletion of the winds' final "pah" after m. 105 turns the second-beat "pah" of the harps into a durational accent. At mm. 233–45 and 248–51, Berlioz employs D6+2 during a statement of the opening theme, albeit relatively weakly: registral accents and, in m. 245, a dynamic accent in the string parts emphasize the second beats.[5] More intense statements of D6+2 occur within the coda; in mm. 265–68 (Example 8.4a) and the corresponding mm. 281–84, there are dynamic and/or density accents on the second beats, while the harmonic rhythm and durational accents maintain the metrical layer.

EXAMPLE 8.4. *D6+2 in the coda of "Un bal"*

A.

B.

In mm. 331–33 (Example 8.4b), dynamic accents again appear on the second beats, while downbeat statements of the principal harmony of the passage (16) enable the metrical layer to remain in effect. Thus is this fine "Valse française" permeated by the metrical dissonances introduced at its opening. ❦

Florestan, much calmer now, said, albeit still hoarsely, "Hector was a remarkable composer. It was good to see him in Euphonia." Eusebius agreed, then said, "I see that the next section of the chapter discusses one of our early works, the *Intermezzi* op. 4." He read:

"MÈTRES DANSANTS" (ROBERT SCHUMANN, *INTERMEZZI* OP. 4)

Summary

1. Main recurring dissonances: D6+2 and G6/4 (1=8th).
2. Families of dissonances operative in the work: D6—all members; Dx+2 (D12+2, D6+2, D3+2); "G6/4."
3. Recurring juxtapositions or superpositions: D6+2 and D2+1; D6+2 and G6/4.
4. Proportion of primarily consonant and primarily dissonant passages: mostly dissonant with brief incursions of consonance, except in no. 4, where the opposite is true.
5. Amount of subliminal dissonance: much subliminal G6/4.
6. Frequency of change of metrical state: frequent change in no. 1 (every 4–6 measures); less frequent in nos. 2–4; quite frequent in nos. 5–6 (though not as frequent as in no. 1).
7. Basic metrical narrative: no single narrative, but many interesting subplots. D6+2 undergoes many adventures, sometimes in the company of G6/4 or D2+1. G6/4 is subjected to several diminutions. Ever closer associations between the two basic classes of dissonance culminate at striking passages at mm. 109 and 129 in the fifth intermezzo, and mm. 113–14 in the sixth.

If we look up the term "intermezzo" in any reputable musical dictionary, we find that "nineteenth-century piano piece" is the most recent of its various meanings. In the seventeenth century, an intermezzo (or intermedio) was a musicodramatic entertainment involving masks and dancing that took place between the acts of a larger production, and in the eighteenth century, intermezzi were comical plays. Whereas it is not certain that Schumann was familiar with these early meanings of the term, his *Intermezzi* op. 4 have, with respect to metrical structure, something of the atmosphere of a theatrical spectacle featuring a colorful array of metrical "characters." The main *dramatis personae* are introduced early in the cycle and subsequently undergo a variety of adventures, alone or in interaction with other characters.

The metrical protagonist of the *Intermezzi* is D6+2 (1=8th); he appears more

EXAMPLE 8.5. *D6+2 in Robert Schumann's* Intermezzo *op. 4 no. 1*

frequently than any other player, in a wide variety of guises. In mm. 3–6 of the first intermezzo (Example 8.5a), D6+2 introduces himself in the role of a pedantic old schoolmaster, speaking in stentorian tones. He declaims in the same vein in mm. 17–18, 37–40, and corresponding later measures. In mm. 14–15 (Example 8.5b), 43–48, and 57–60, he reveals a gentler aspect of his character (the antimetrical layer is created by durational rather than dynamic accents, and the "schoolmasterly" imitation is abandoned).

Throughout this intermezzo, related characters cluster round D6+2 and at times push him into the background. Among these are his little cousin D2+1 (mm. 12—Example 8.6a, and 45–48—Example 8.6b); his brothers D6+3 (in the passage in Example 8.6b, D6+3 definitely overshadows D6+2) and D6+4 (mm. 24–26);[6] and his loose relative D12+2 (mm. 27–32 and corresponding later measures, where dynamic accents appear on second beats of alternate measures). A mysterious, masked stranger also appears briefly, namely sublim- inal G6/4 (in mm. 20–23—Example 8.6c—the metrical layer is submerged and dynamic accents occur on alternate beats, the latter accentuation resulting from a stretto treatment of the motive first associated with D6+2, shown in Example 8.5a). The close juxtaposition of G6/4 and D6+2 in mm. 17–21 foreshadows later even closer interactions of the two characters. A daughter of G6/4, namely G3/2, makes a brief entrance with D6+2 (and D6+3) in mm. 45–48 (Example 8.6b); the dynamic accents on the fourth eighth-note pulse result in a hint at a 3-layer and hence at G3/2. This passage presages a more intimate association of D6+2 and G3/2 in a later intermezzo.

The second intermezzo provides a complete change of scene (a new meter and a faster tempo). Two new metrical characters replace those of the first in- termezzo and romp around on the rearranged stage, namely D3+2 and his loose cousin D6+5. The former is present in mm. 2–3 (Example 8.7), 18, etc. The lat- ter is generally a faithful companion of D3+2 but also makes some independent

EXAMPLE 8.6. *"Minor characters" in op. 4 no. 1*

EXAMPLE 8.7. *D3+2 and D6+5 in op. 4 no. 2*

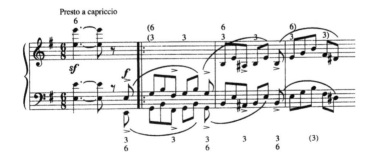

EXAMPLE 8.8. *G6/4 in op. 4 no. 3*

appearances (in mm. 4–5, 9–12, etc.). These new characters are related to those of the first piece; D6+5 is yet another sibling, and D3+2 a tight cousin of the protagonist D6+2.[7] The characters abruptly disappear as the scene changes (at the two-four section superscribed "Meine Ruh ist hin"). Here, D4+1 timidly shows himself (created by density accents in mm. 64–67 and related measures), and his tight cousin D2+1, who had already appeared during the first intermezzo, makes a brief appearance as well (mm. 97–100). As the initial stage-set of this intermezzo is restored (*Tempo I*), D2+1 exits, and D6+5 and D3+2 boisterously return at m. 105 and remain on stage almost constantly until they betake themselves off just before the end.

In the third intermezzo Schumann brings back the initial metrical scene (three-four time). The characters of the first piece also return, and some of them are developed in interesting ways. The mysterious G6/4, for example, throws off his mask and, now clearly recognizable, plays a major role within the A sections, as in mm. 1–15 (see Example 8.8), 19–24, 27–34, and 49–56. The 4-layer frequently arises from repetition of a rhythmic pattern, and at times from dynamic accents (mm. 7–9) and slurring (mm. 13–15), whereas the metrical 6-layer is established by significant harmonic changes (for example, tonic-dominant alternation in mm. 3–6). D12+8, a loose cousin of the protagonist D6+2, makes a brief appearance in this section (mm. 4–6), and D6+2 himself, revealing a new jovial side of his character, is on stage throughout mm. 11–48, where dynamic accents frequently occur on second beats. As was mentioned, G6/4 is also present in much of this section; these two characters, who had a brief encounter near the opening of the first intermezzo, now form a closer liaison. In mm. 35–48, D12+4, a loose relative of D6+2's brother D6+4, heralds the latter character's personal appearance within the "Alternativo" (note the antimetrical slurs and dynamic accents in mm. 57–64).

The metrical scene of the fourth intermezzo is very similar to that of the second (twelve-eight rather than six-eight meter). Its outer sections do not carry the metrical drama forward; much of the intermezzo is a pastoral song that stands outside the main metrical action.[8] In the central section, however (mm. 8–10 — Example 2.1), there appears D3+1.5, son of D6+3 (one of the minor characters of the first intermezzo), in the company of G1.5/1, grandson of G6/4 (isolation of three-sixteenth-note groups within the aforementioned

EXAMPLE 8.9. *Metrical dissonance in op. 4 no. 5*

D3+1.5 results in a superposition of two- and three-sixteenth-note groups, and hence in a double diminution of G6/4).

The fifth intermezzo, reverting to the scene of the first and third intermezzi, more significantly advances the metrical action, numerous familiar characters being associated in new ways. D2+1, D6+2, and D6+4 engage in dance ensembles in mm. 6–8 (Example 8.9a), 50–52, and 141–43, and D6+2 and D2+1 each dance *pas seuls* at various points—D6+2 in mm. 20–25, 65–66,[9] and later corresponding measures (Example 5.13); D2+1, with particular energy, in mm. 37–40 (Example 8.9b) and the corresponding mm. 174–77.

At mm. 109–12, there is another close encounter between the G and D clans. The former clan is represented by G3/2, daughter of G6/4. This frolicsome maiden dances vigorously across the stage in masked (subliminal) form in mm. 32–34, and coyly begins to remove her mask within the "Alternativo"

EXAMPLE 8.10. *D6+1 and other dissonances in op. 4 no. 5*

melody (which includes a weakly stated 3-layer as well as a clear 2-layer—mm. 70–76). At m. 109 (Example 8.9c), she fully reveals her identity (the 3-layer is clearly expressed in the dotted-quarter durations of the rising inner-voice melody) and dances briefly with the protagonist D6+2 and his brother D6+5. But when her father, G6/4, appears at mm. 116–18 (he is masked—the 4-layer is expressed by harmonic pattern repetition while the 6-layer is not articulated), D6+2 and D6+5 scurry off and G3/2, too, demurely begins to retreat (G3/2 is again weak in mm. 119–26).

Moments later, however, G3/2 reappears in the arms of another of D6+2's brothers, namely D6+1. D6+1, the only member of the "D6" family who had not appeared in the first four intermezzi, is first introduced in mm. 41–44 of the fifth (Example 8.10a) as a somewhat unstable individual; at mm. 43–44, he almost transforms himself into G6/5 (the five-eighth-note pitch succession C–D♭– E–G–B♭ is reiterated to form a 5-layer, but the sforzando on the second eighth note of m. 44 prevents D6+1 from disappearing entirely). This Protean character dances with G3/2 at mm. 129–31 (Example 8.10b); these measures feature not only G3/2 but also D3+1 and D6+1 (the 3-layer, and the 6-layer embedded in it, does not begin on a metrical downbeat, as in all of the earlier statements of G3/2, but one eighth note thereafter). Once again, G3/2's father, G6/4, appears and decisively puts an end to his flighty daughter's entanglement (mm. 133–34).

The sixth intermezzo draws a number of familiar characters together for a splendid finale. D6+2 plays a prominent role within the A sections, in which many second beats are dynamically and durationally accented (see Example

EXAMPLE 8.11. *Metrical dissonance in op. 4 no. 6*

8.11, and mm. 12–16, 39–41, and later corresponding measures). His brother D6+4 appears in mm. 3–4, 39–40, 55–56, 59, 71, and 75. In the first two of these passages, the two brothers tread the measure together (although D6+2 dances with greater energy), recalling the opening of the fifth piece. D6+2's little cousin D2+1, who already played a role within the first, second, and fifth intermezzos, is prominent within the "Alternativo" (especially at mm. 58–60 and 62–68 and later similar passages, with their offbeat density and durational accents). G6/4 appears, masked, at various points, beginning with the first measures (Example 8.11). The third beat of m. 1 is identical to the first; the incipient pattern repetition results in the initiation of a 4-layer. The four duplet eighth notes at the end of m. 2 create a third pulse of the 4-layer. The metrical 6-layer, meanwhile, keeps a low profile until m. 3. At mm. 8b–10, a reiterated melodic sigh creates a 4-layer, again in the absence of clear articulation of the metrical 6-layer. In mm. 24–25, a repeated harmonic pattern reawakens the 4-layer, the 6-layer again becoming dormant. Further appearances of G6/4, mostly masked, occur at the beginning of the "Alternativo" and at mm. 76–85.

We are granted only one tantalizing glimpse of the lovely G3/2 in the final intermezzo: in m. 72, a melody whose contour expresses a 3-layer (G5-A5-B5-E5-F♯5-G5) is superimposed on a continuing 2-layer. At mm. 5–6 (Example 8.11) and 98–99, however, there appear new generations of descendants of G6/4; in the former measures, one of these arises from the superposition of triplet and non-triplet eighth notes, and in the latter measures, another emerges from the grouping of triplet eighth notes into twos by the repetition of a falling octave pattern.[10]

An interesting twist in the metrical drama takes place close to the end. Measures 113–14 are a varied repetition of mm. 20–21 and, as in those earlier measures, G6/4 is present (albeit masked). In addition, however, Schumann places dynamic accents on the second members of alternate triplet groups, thus creating a diminution of the protagonist D6+2, and therewith bringing the G and D clans together once more.

Schumann's *Intermezzi* op. 4 represent a major advance over his earlier works in terms of the pervasive and cohesive use of metrical dissonance. Perhaps it is in this context that we can understand the numerous quotations from his earlier works (mentioned by numerous earlier authors): aside from the aforementioned quotations of "Hirtenknabe," Schumann alludes to the Piano Quartet in C Minor (in the fourth intermezzo, mm. 1, 6, 7–10, and 15–18), and to the "Abegg" Variations (in the sixth intermezzo, mm. 43–45 and 127–31). Although both of those works constitute important stages in Schumann's metrical odyssey, dissonance is there not nearly as pervasively and interestingly employed as in op. 4. Schumann appears to be taking stock of his progress as a composer and saying to himself and to his audience, "I've come a long way." ❦

Eusebius covertly glanced at Florestan, who had shown signs of agitation at the mention of the words "Meine Ruh ist hin." "Look, Florestan," he said soothingly, "the next section discusses the music of Chopin." At the sound of that name, Florestan repeatedly put his hand to his head and gazed worriedly about the room. Eusebius gently asked, "What is the matter, Florestan?" Florestan mumbled, "Where is my hat? I need my hat." With some difficulty, Eusebius pacified him, and read on:

"CHOPIN" (FRÉDÉRIC CHOPIN, VARIOUS WORKS)

Whereas metrical dissonance is not a hallmark of Chopin's style, his music contains numerous examples of metrical and hypermetrical dissonance.[11] Chopin's figuration owes much of its sparkling charm to metrical conflict. I offer only a few examples, extracted from the scherzos and études. In the Second Scherzo, some of the ornamented arpeggio figures that cascade up and down the keyboard are based on reiterated four-eighth-note segments, which create G6/4 in relation to the metrical 6-layer (1=8th). This dissonance is already suggested in the first arpeggiating figure in the work (mm. 49–52—Example 8.12a); the eighth notes within the dramatic downward arpeggiation of the D♭ major triad form groups of four (although there are not enough of these groups to establish G6/4 securely). The delicate arabesque outlining the dominant of C♯ minor in mm. 307–9 (Example 8.12b) more clearly exhibits the quadruple grouping and hence the dissonance G6/4, as do the ornamented E major arpeggiations of mm. 358–64 (Example 8.12c) and the climactic descending arpeggiation of V of B♭ in mm. 540–43 (Example 8.12d). The diminution of G6/4, G3/2, is also featured within some of the figuration, namely at the end of the Scherzo section (mm. 118–29—Example 8.12e). The contour of these figures establishes a 3-layer, conflicting with the 2-layer that reigned in the foregoing measures and that here continues to be conveyed by the left hand.

In the Third Scherzo, the shimmering descending eighth-note figures within the Trio involve hand shifts at four-eighth-note intervals, and the left-hand figure segments into four-eighth-note groups on the basis of pattern repetition, resulting, along with the metrical 6-layer, in G6/4. In the Fourth Scherzo, pattern repetition in the right hand of mm. 69–71 (D♯-C♯-A-E) results in four-

EXAMPLE 8.12. *G6/4 and G3/2 in Chopin's Scherzo op. 31*

eighth-note groups that conflict with the established metrical 6-layer. The climactic cascade at mm. 122–27 similarly divides into four-eighth-note groups, this time on the basis of a repeated contour rather than a repeated pitch pattern, resulting, in interaction with the metrical 6-layer, in subliminal and indirect G6/4 (1=8th).

Some of Chopin's études explore intriguing low-level dissonant relationships. At the opening of the second étude from op. 25, for instance (Example 8.13), the 2-layer (1=triplet 8th) established by left-hand quarter-note triplets is dissonant against the 3-layer formed by the right hand's reiterations of C5. Frequently, the 2-layer invades the right-hand part, so that it dominates the texture

EXAMPLE 8.13. *Metrical dissonance in Chopin's Etude op. 25 no. 2*

and G3/2 is submerged. In m. 3, for example, reiterations of E5, then B♭5 occur on alternate triplet pulses in the right hand, together with the left-hand quarter-note triplets. (The pianist can, of course, continue to articulate the 3-layer during such passages, so that the dissonance becomes perceptible to listeners.)

The fifth étude of op. 25 begins with displacement dissonance (Example 8.14a), and the first part of the B section continues that dissonance (although the displacement index grows from a sixteenth note to a triplet — Example 8.14b). The second statement of the B material (mm. 81–97 — Example 8.14c), however, is based on a scintillating grouping dissonance. The right-hand arpeggiations are composed of single notes and dyads, the dyads occurring on every third sixteenth-note pulse. The 3-layer (1=16th) created by these density accents conflicts with the 4-layer established by the beautiful "tenor" melody. The resulting dissonance (G4/3) casts a delightful sheen over the passage. At times, for example in mm. 82 and 84, the right hand's 3-layer encroaches on the left-hand melody; in these measures the final note of the melody (the resolution of the first-beat suspension) is surprisingly postponed, so that the measure ends with a three-sixteenth-note pulse (not aligned with the right hand's 3-layer) instead of the expected quarter-note pulse.

EXAMPLE 8.14. *Metrical dissonance in Chopin's Etude op. 25 no. 5*

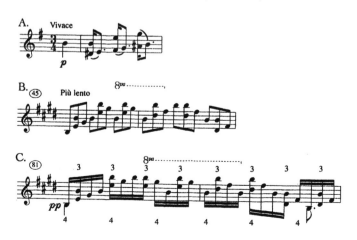

EXAMPLE 8.15. *G3/2 and its resolution in Chopin's Mazurka op. 17 no. 1*

Chopin's metrical dissonances are by no means restricted to his figuration. His dance pieces are rich in brief, yet striking examples that do not involve figuration. The earliest mazurkas contain much displacement dissonance produced by dynamic accentuation of metrically weak beats, sometimes D3+1 (1=quarter), as in op. 6 no. 2, mm. 1–4, sometimes D3+2 (for example, in op. 6 no. 1, mm. 4–7), sometimes both in juxtaposition (op. 6 no. 4, mm. 1–8). Such antimetrical accentuation is, of course, typical of the mazurka.

A particularly interesting example of grouping dissonance occurs in the B section of the Mazurka op. 17 no. 1 (Example 8.15). In mm. 41–50 and 53–58, the left hand consists of an "oom-pah" pattern that forms a 2-layer dissonant against the right-hand melody (in which a 3-layer is formed by varied repetition of a rhythmic pattern). As the phrase ends approach (mm. 52 and 60), Chopin expands the left hand's "oom-pah" pattern to "oom-pah-pah," thus creating the potential for resolution into the primary consonance. At the first phrase ending, however (mm. 51–52 — Example 8.15a), the right hand refuses to collaborate in the resolution; instead of continuing its 3-layer, it lapses into repetition of the rhythm "quarter-eighth-eighth," thus taking over the 2-layer previously articulated by the left hand. This "layer exchange" subverts metrical resolution at this phrase ending. At the next phrase boundary, on the other hand (mm. 59–60 — Example 8.15b), the right hand does maintain its 3-layer and joins the left hand in a definitive metrical resolution. The earlier evasion of metrical resolution makes the resolution at the end of the B section all the more satisfying. In sum, although Chopin employs metrical dissonance more sparingly than Schumann, he does so with skill and subtlety. ❦

Eusebius noticed that Florestan had fallen asleep. He left him to his slumber and continued reading silently:

"RÉPLIQUES" (ROBERT SCHUMANN,
SCHERZO IN F MINOR)

Summary

1. Main recurring dissonances: D6+5 and D3+2 (1=8th) in the Scherzo, G3/2 and D2+1 in the Trio.
2. Families of dissonances operative in the movement: D6+5 and the tighter relative D3+2.
3. Recurring juxtapositions or superpositions: aside from the trivial superposition of the above related displacement dissonances, none.
4. Proportion of primarily consonant and primarily dissonant passages: mostly dissonant.
5. Amount of subliminal dissonance: much subliminal dissonance in the Scherzo sections, very little in the Trio.
6. Frequency of change of metrical state: very frequent in the Scherzo (for the most part, every two or three measures), infrequent in the Trio (only three significant changes over 47 measures).
7. Basic metrical narrative: in the Scherzo section, a metrical and an antimetrical placement of 6/3 consonance vie for supremacy, the former placement being victorious in the end. The Trio provides contrast by clearly articulating the metrical layer throughout and by presenting relatively weak dissonances. The narrative of the movement as a whole is thus a variant of "D-C-D"; the middle section is not fully consonant, but much more weakly dissonant than the outer sections.

Schumann composed his original version of the Piano Sonata op. 14, entitled *Concert sans orchestre*, in 1835–36. It was to be a five-movement work with two Scherzos. Apparently at the request of the publisher, he excised one of the Scherzos, which Brahms published in 1866 along with the abandoned finale to the Piano Sonata op. 22.[12] The decision to excise the movement was probably a wise one, for, as Anton Kuerti points out, it would have resulted in a potentially tedious succession of three F-minor movements.[13] In the revised sonata, only two F-minor movements—the last two—occur in a row.

I imagine that Schumann excised the movement only reluctantly, for it would have created interesting metrical relationships within the sonata. A variant of its most prevalent dissonance, D3+2 (1=8th), for example, plays a significant role in the remaining Scherzo, where the augmentation D6+4 appears at the opening and at various other points (for example, mm. 16–18 and 35–38). A diminution of one of the dissonances of the Trio of the excised movement, D2+1, underlies the third variation of the slow movement. Aside from these contributions to the unity of the sonata, however, the excised Scherzo is an ex-

EXAMPLE 8.16. *Indirect D3+2 and D6+5 in Robert Schumann's* Scherzo in F minor

tremely interesting and beautiful piece, which Schumann could not have discarded without much soul-searching.

At the opening (Example 8.16), a 3-layer established by changes of harmony, and a 6-layer formed by density changes (imitative entries), together result in an aural impression of perfect consonance. This apparent consonance is disrupted at m. 3, where a stammer—a reiterated diminished-seventh chord—displaces the initial 3-layer by one eighth-note pulse. At m. 4, with a similar sensation of disruption or intrusion, the initial placement of the 3-layer (and the 6-layer) returns, only to be dislodged again at m. 7. The listener is similarly tossed back and forth between two rival consonances—rival meters, one might say—throughout the Scherzo section. The effect is that of a highly animated, in fact, maniacal dialogue; the points where the shifted 3-layer intrudes on the metrically aligned passages, or where metrical layers are forcibly imposed on the antimetrical ones, sound like interruptions by an over-eager respondent. ❦

Eusebius mused, "Florestan's notation, with its alternation of beams that contradict, and beams that support the primary consonance, strongly suggests that he regarded the dialogue between meters as an essential aspect of the movement. Were the pianist to articulate the notated meter by stresses throughout the Scherzo section, the effect of a dialogue between meters would be much less pronounced, and the movement would lose much of its dramatic impact. The pianist should apply stresses to the metrical pulses only where Florestan requests them."

At times, the interlocutors even speak simultaneously, the nonaligned layers being superimposed rather than merely juxtaposed. At m. 10, for instance (Example 8.17a), changes of harmony strongly delineate the antimetrical 3-layer, but the quarter-note attacks of the inner voice weakly affirm the metrical 3-layer. At mm. 31–38 (Example 8.17b), high and low points within the left-hand pattern and a repeated arpeggiatory pattern in the right hand maintain the antimetrical 3-layer, while the metrical 3-layer is again announced by inner-voice melodic attacks. In addition, occasional dynamic accents support both layers (as in mm. 32–33). In mm. 40–42, staccatos highlight the pulses of the

EXAMPLE 8.17. *Direct D3+2 and D6+5 in the* Scherzo in F minor

metrical 3-layer, while the arpeggiating pattern of both hands articulates the displaced 3-layer. At mm. 58–61 (Example 8.17c), finally, the left hand's dynamic accents and arpeggiations and the right hand's registral accents (high points) continue to articulate the shifted 3-layer, while right-hand dynamic accents clarify the metrical 3-layer in preparation for metrical as well as harmonic resolution at the final cadence of the Scherzo section.

In more technical terms, the Scherzo section contains much indirect displacement dissonance (at each collision between the two "meters") and some direct dissonance of the same type. Furthermore, one of the apparent consonances is actually a subliminal dissonance. Interestingly, Schumann treats the antimetrical placement of 6/3 as if it were a dissonance; he frequently resolves it into the metrical consonance at phrase ends (mm. 3–4, 7–8, 18–19, etc.; see Figure 8.1).

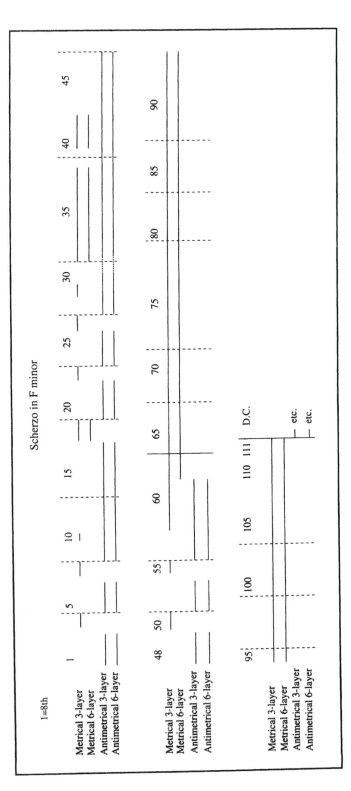

FIGURE 8.1. *Metrical map of Schumann's* Scherzo in F minor, *mm. 1–111*

EXAMPLE 8.18. *Metrical consonance and dissonance in the Trio of the* Scherzo in F minor

Its dominance at significant formal junctures notwithstanding, the metrical consonance is, within the Scherzo section, by far the weaker of the two metrical interlocutors. Because it occupies much less time than the "antimetrical consonance" and, unlike that consonance, is only rarely present in its full-fledged form (i.e., its 3-layer is only rarely associated with a 6-layer), the metrical consonance gives the impression of a speaker desperately attempting to "get a word in edgewise."

Within the Trio section, however, the metrical consonance succeeds in having its say, uninterrupted by its rival. The metrical 6- and 3-layers remain in effect throughout the Trio; the 6-layer is generally announced by dotted half-note attacks in the left hand, and melodic lines moving primarily in dotted quarters provide a consonant 3-layer (Example 8.18a).

The primary consonance does not, however, remain entirely uncontradicted in the Trio; a close listening reveals the presence of a number of subtle conflicts. The reiterated dyads within the right hand's accompaniment pattern result in a 2-layer, and the attacks of the right-hand doubling of the left-hand melody form a nonaligned layer of the same cardinality. The resulting disso-

EXAMPLE 8.19. *Return of the Scherzo section in the* Scherzo in F minor

nances are D2+1 (within the right hand) and G3/2 (in interaction with the left hand's melody). In mm. 80–84, the first portion of a restatement of the opening of the Trio (Example 8.18b), D2+1 continues in the right hand in a slightly more intense form (the attacks of the second 2-layer are now sustained during those of the first). The metrical 3-layer, after being stated with particular emphasis by dynamic stress in mm. 76–78, is not articulated in mm. 80–84, so that G3/2 is submerged. A new, diminished version of the latter dissonance, however, appears at this point (G1.5/1); the left hand presents an eighth-note pulse while the right hand continues in triplets. Sparks of the same diminution of G3/2 occur in mm. 96, 98, and 100, where both triplet and duplet eighth notes are presented in the upper register. Near the end of the Trio (mm. 104–7— Example 8.18c), D2+1 is augmented (thus being treated in a manner diametrically opposed to the other motivic dissonance of the Trio, G3/2): D6+3 is formed by dynamic accentuation of second beats. Thus, although the Trio is substantially less intensely dissonant and expresses the notated meter much more clearly than the Scherzo, it does remain subtly conflicted.

At m. 111, the antimetrical interlocutor of the Scherzo's metrical dialogue brutally bursts in, as if unable to contain himself any longer (Example 8.19). This intrusion has a "brutal" effect not only because of the indirect dissonance resulting from juxtaposition of differently placed 6- and 3-layers, but also because after m. 111 we anticipate a return of the opening of the Trio, in analogy to the corresponding m. 79.[14]

The second Scherzo section is, in metrical terms, much like the first; the state of constant mutual interruption of metrical interlocutors is reestablished, the antimetrical speaker apparently being unmoved by the reasoned appeal of the Trio. Near the end of the movement, the displaced layers contradict the meter with unprecedented ferocity. Measures 163–68 (Example 8.20) correspond to an earlier passage in which both metrical and antimetrical levels are articulated by dynamic accents (mm. 58–60—Example 8.17c). In this altered restatement, however, both hands express the antimetrical 3-layer by dynamic accents, the metrical layer being articulated only weakly (in mm. 165–68) by durational accents on the lower notes of the right hand.

The antimetrical interlocutor, then, very nearly has the last word—but in the final three measures his metrical respondent firmly quashes him. Schu-

EXAMPLE 8.20. *Conclusion of the* Scherzo in F minor

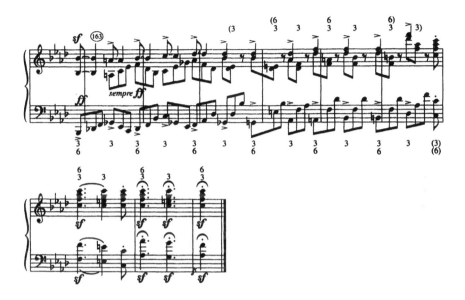

mann's fermatas and sforzandos request the pianist to strive for an effect of resolution into the notated meter. A broad and emphatic rendition of the final, metrically aligned measures should, in fact, be able to convey the impression that the notated meter wins the argument that has raged throughout the movement. ❦

Eusebius glanced at the sleeping Florestan and thought, with a sigh, "The metrical argument within this Scherzo reminds me very much of numerous recent occasions: me trying to bring Florestan into alignment with reality, he constantly interrupting with his ravings and not heeding me at all." He turned back to the manuscript and started as he encountered the name "Chiarina" over the following section of the manuscript. His eyes filled with tears and it was some time before he was able to continue his reading.

"CHIARINA" (CLARA SCHUMANN, PIANO TRIO OP. 17, SECOND MOVEMENT)

Clara Schumann employed metrical dissonance sparingly, but effectively in her compositions. The figuration in her early Piano Concerto, for instance, is occasionally seasoned with grouping dissonance. In the climactic triplet material in the piano part at mm. 123–25 of the first movement, harmonic changes occur on the first triplet of each group, reinforcing the metrical 3-layer (1=triplet 8th). In mm. 123–24, however, a recurring pattern—dyad followed by triad—over-

EXAMPLE 8.21. *Metrically dissonant figuration in the second movement of Clara Schumann's Piano Concerto op. 7, mm. 38–40*

lays the triplets with a duple layer. In m. 125, the 2-layer continues, now produced by a repeated pitch pattern; the 3-layer is not articulated here.

The second section of the second movement of the concerto, in which a
solo violoncello restates portions of the main theme to an elaborate piano accompaniment, contains a similar dissonance (Example 8.21). From m. 38 onward, the left hand's quarter notes reinforce the metrical 3-layer, but the right-
hand triplet figuration is generally grouped into twos by recurrence of a single
pitch (E♭ in m. 38), or by repetition of a pattern (e.g., "single note, chord"). The
metrical state is further enriched by the superposition of the cello's duplet
eighth notes on the piano's triplets, resulting in a diminution of the grouping
dissonance embedded in the piano part.

In the finale of the concerto, Clara Schumann employs displacement dissonance in an interesting manner. The first utterance of the violins and violas is a
syncopated reiteration of the dominant note (mm. 3–4), resulting in the dissonance D2+1 (1=eighth) against the trumpet's metrical layer. This dissonance
flares up in accompanying voices at various points in the movement. Its most
dramatic reappearance, however, is at the very end of the movement, where
piano and orchestra shout the tonic triad at each other, the piano on the quarter-
note beats, the orchestra on offbeat eighth notes (mm. 352–54). The movement
is thus effectively framed by D2+1.

Further interesting usages of metrical dissonance occur in Clara Schumann's songs, most strikingly in "Geheimes Flüstern" (op. 23 no. 3). In the
piano introduction, melodic attacks alternately suggest a 3-layer and a 2-layer
(1=16th). This indirect dissonance (G3/2) becomes direct as the voice enters in
m. 8; the voice continues the 2-layer of mm. 2, 4, and 6, while the piano persists
in the 3-layer of mm. 1, 3, 5, and 7-8. The dissonance is obviously intended to
mimic the "secret whispering" of forests and wellsprings.

Clara Schumann's most thoroughgoing usage of metrical dissonance occurs
in the Scherzo movement of her Piano Trio op. 17. A summary follows:

1. Main recurring dissonances: D3+1 and G3/2 (1=quarter).
2. Families of dissonances operative in the movement: none.

EXAMPLE 8.22. *Metrical dissonance in the Scherzo section of the second mvmt. of Clara Schumann's Piano Trio op. 17. © Amadeus Verlag, 1989. Used by permission of the publisher.*

3. Recurring juxtapositions or superpositions: D3+1 and G3/2.

4. Proportion of primarily consonant and primarily dissonant passages: the Scherzo is mostly consonant, the Trio mostly dissonant, so that in the movement as a whole, the two basic states are fairly equally represented.

5. Amount of subliminal dissonance: brief passages of subliminal G3/2 in the Trio, one of them being employed as a gesture of culmination near the end of the final statement of the Trio material.

6. Frequency of change of metrical state: the Scherzo is somewhat more volatile, alternating between consonance and weak dissonance every few measures. The Trio alternates fairly strong dissonance with weaker dissonance, changes occurring much less frequently than in the Scherzo (only at mm. 60, 75, 100, and 115).

7. Basic metrical narrative: in the Scherzo section, two dissonances are weakly announced. They are gradually intensified in the Trio, then restored to their original weak versions with the return of the Scherzo. The Scherzo section contains a nesting of this narrative; dissonance is very weak in the opening section, somewhat stronger after the double bar, then weaker again when the opening returns.

The Scherzo section contains some weak metrical dissonances, among them allusions to D3+1 (1=quarter) in mm. 3 (Example 8.22a), 9, and 11–12 (Example 8.22b), and hints at G3/2 in mm. 9–17 (Example 8.22b shows the beginning of this passage). It is in the Trio section, however, that metrical dissonance flourishes; here, Clara Schumann develops at length both of the dissonances weakly broached in the Scherzo section.[15] In mm. 35–51 (Example 8.23a), she dwells on G3/2; the dissonance is mainly subliminal through m. 46, the 2-layer reigning

EXAMPLE 8.23. *Metrical dissonance in the Trio section of the second mvmt. of Clara Schumann's Piano Trio op. 17. © Amadeus Verlag, 1989. Used by permission of the publisher.*

virtually without contradiction, but it surfaces in mm. 47–51, where harmonic changes and durational accents reinforce the metrical 3-layer. In mm. 51–55 (Example 8.23b), the composer develops D3+1, articulating the displaced 3-layer by second-beat dynamic accents and slurs in the violin (cf. m. 3, Example 8.22a). In mm. 55–58, she loosens the dissonance to D6+1, the loosening leading nicely into the resolution at the end of the section (mm. 59–60a). The section following the double bar (mm. 60b–75) provides contrast to the pervasively dissonant preceding section, containing only brief allusions to the two motivic dissonances. These include the weak G3/2 in mm. 60b–61, created by melodic new-event accents in the strings, and the hints at D3+1 in mm. 63 and 67, where a shifted 3-layer is suggested by second-beat durational accents. At m. 75, Clara Schumann begins the first of two restatements of the opening music of the Trio, which departs from the initial version in pitch, but not in metrical structure. A second restatement of the opening material of the Trio (following another statement, in mm. 100–115, of the weakly dissonant material of mm. 60–75) does deviate from the initial version in terms of meter; at mm. 119–22, a new passage articulates the 2-layer in an unprecedently strong manner (by chord changes) while the metrical 3-layer is not explicitly stated.

The movement illustrates not only subtle preparation of metrical dissonance to be enlarged upon later, but also the coordination of metrical progression and form. Most obvious, the Trio is set off from the Scherzo by its generally more prominent dissonance. Formal boundaries within the two main sections are also coordinated with changes in the metrical progression. In the Scherzo section, the double bar is highlighted by the proliferation of dissonance immediately after it. In the Trio, conversely, the double bar is followed by a marked decrease in degree of dissonance. ❦

Eusebius found the title of the next section puzzling; with wrinkled brow he read:

"VALSES CONTRE LES PHILISTINS" (ROBERT SCHUMANN, *FASCHINGSSCHWANK AUS WIEN*, OP. 26, FIRST MOVEMENT)

Summary

1. Main recurring dissonances: D3+2 (1=quarter).
2. Families of dissonances operative in the movement: none.
3. Recurring juxtapositions or superpositions: none.
4. Proportion of primarily consonant and primarily dissonant passages: the two states are present in approximately equal proportions.
5. Amount of subliminal dissonance: much subliminal D3+2.
6. Frequency of change of metrical state: change occurs with each new section of the rondo form. There are very few fluctuations of metrical state within sections.
7. Basic metrical narrative: alternation of consonance and dissonance, beginning with consonance and ending with last-minute reestablishment of consonance.

The first movement of the *Faschingsschwank* op. 26 contains some of Schumann's most prolonged and powerful metrical dissonances, as well as some dramatic hypermetrical conflicts.[16] Metrical dissonance in the movement falls almost exclusively into the category D3+2 (1=quarter). The antimetrical layer within each statement of the dissonance is produced either by durational accents (i.e. syncopation) or new-event harmonic accents on upbeats. Example 2.14 shows the first appearance of the syncopated version. This version returns in the coda (at mm. 465–90 and 547–51). A different form of D3+2, still involving syncopation, is found in mm. 409–40; here, one or more voices convey the metrical layer by durational accents while others present the syncopation, with the result that D3+2 lies on the surface. During mm. 86–126, 465–90 and 547–51, on the other hand, the dissonance remains primarily subliminal. The metrical layer is never articulated within mm. 465–90 and 547–51, where all downbeats are suppressed. In the latter section, very close to the end of the movement, the dissonance is particularly intense, the antimetrical layer being emphasized by dynamic accents. Within the section encompassing mm. 86–126, Schumann does permit the metrical layer to appear at a few phrase endings (mm. 102, 110, and 126—in the latter case, after intensifying the dissonance with dynamic accents—Example 8.24a). These reminders of the metrical layer on the one hand result in a sense of resolution appropriate to phrase endings, but with respect to the larger context they create indirect dissonance and, by aiding the listener in maintaining the metrical layer, contribute to the upholding of subliminal dissonance. The positioning of both mm. 86–126 and 465–90 after statements of the A section also helps the listener to maintain the metrical layer and hence a vivid impression of disso-

EXAMPLE 8.24. *D3+2 in the first mvmt. of Robert Schumann's* Faschingsschwank aus Wien *op. 26*

nance, for the A section contains much downbeat emphasis by dynamic, durational and density accents.

Schumann dramatically anticipates the second version of D3+2 (where the displaced layer is created by harmonic changes) in mm. 117–18 (Example 8.24b). Since this is a phrase ending, one might expect metrical resolution, which did occur at the two preceding phrase ends. Instead, Schumann emphatically initiates a harmony on the last beat of m. 117, and reiterates it softly within m. 118, thus continuing the antimetrical layer rather than abandoning it at the cadence. In m. 340 (Example 8.24c), he again initiates harmonies on third beats and restates them (now in a higher register) on the following downbeats. Harmonic change thus delineates an antimetrical 3-layer (while durational accents on the downbeats convey the metrical 3-layer). The dissonance resolves in mm. 405–8, where significant harmonic changes are again coordinated with the metrical layer.[17]

Some of the metrical conflict within the first movement of op. 26 takes place at a higher level. The major part of the movement is based on four-bar hypermeasures; as in many other works by Schumann, the four-bar hypermeter arises at least in part from a generic root that is of obvious relevance to the

Faschingsschwank: from the Viennese waltz. The movement is a succession of waltzes, influenced by those of Franz Schubert.[18]

Whereas Schumann's Schubertian waltz models virtually never deviate from four-bar hypermeter, Schumann disrupts that hypermeter quite frequently, at times only in a subtle manner, at times very dramatically. In the first two waltzes (mm. 1–24 and 24–62, respectively), he creates high-level displacement dissonances by dynamically accenting the metrically weak measures of four-bar hypermeasures. The resulting dissonances are D12+3 and D12+9 (1=quarter). In the second waltz (the B section), he disrupts the hypermeter more drastically. After m. 37, there is some ambiguity as to the placement of high-level downbeats (hyperdownbeats). The restatement of mm. 37–38 a sixth higher in mm. 39–40 results in the possibility of hearing the beginning of m. 39 as a new hyperdownbeat (equivalent to the downbeat of m. 37), or alternatively as the third beat of the hypermeasure initiated in m. 37. The result of this ambiguity is the hypermetrical dissonance D12+6 (see Example 8.25a). At the end of the B section there is hypermetrical irregularity of a different kind; Schumann expands the final hypermeasure from four to six measures by repeating the cadential measures (mm. 57–62), resulting in the indirect hypermetrical dissonance G18/12.

The disruptions of the initially regular four-bar hypermeter within the B section are of a mildness that one could describe as "Eusebian." A more violent "Florestanian" disruption is shown in Example 8.25b. The section from which the excerpt is taken (mm. 150–228—the D section, or fourth waltz) adheres slavishly, in fact monotonously, to four-bar hypermeter until m. 211. At that point, Schumann suppresses an expected downbeat and hyperdownbeat, then states two dynamically accented dominant ninth chords. In retrospect, mm. 211–12 are perceived not as initiating a new hypermeasure, but as concluding the hypermeasure that began in m. 207, for the recapitulatory m. 213 definitely initiates a new hypermeasure. Thus, the intrusive ninth chords stretch the hypermeasure beginning in m. 207 to six measures. Bringing together strong pitch dissonance, metrical dissonance (G3/2), and hypermetrical dissonance, mm. 211–12 explode the placid waltz character of the preceding music.

Further examples of hypermetrical disturbance, both Eusebian and Florestanian, occur in the coda of the first movement. Amidst its many four-bar hypermeasures, the coda contains one that is five, and one that is six measures in length (mm. 504–8 and 478–83, respectively). These expansions beyond the normal four-bar length result in indirect hypermetrical grouping dissonance. Stronger disruptions occur within the last few measures. At m. 549, Schumann displaces a downbeat and hyperdownbeat, creating the dissonances D3+2 and D12+2. Both the displacement and the succeeding repetition of the cadence of m. 548 blur the hypermetrical boundary, making it possible to hear a greatly expanded hypermeasure spanning mm. 545–52. The resolution to tonic in m. 552 not only completes a hypermeasure, but at the same time initiates one. This compression of two potential hyperbeats into one is a fitting final gesture for this conflict-ridden movement.[19]

EXAMPLE 8.25. *Hypermetrical dissonance in the first mvmt. of the* Faschingsschwank aus Wien

The frequent and prominent metrical and hypermetrical dissonances in the first movement of the *Faschingsschwank* may carry extramusical meaning. In order to uncover it, we must take a short excursion to Vienna, the city in which most of the work was composed.[20] In early October of 1838, Robert Schumann moved from Leipzig to Vienna. He did so with some reluctance, for he had been happy in Leipzig, and his journal, the *Neue Zeitschrift für Musik*, was securely established there. But once he had moved, he found many aspects of life in Vienna very pleasant. In his letters to Clara Wieck and in other writings, he praised the scenic beauty of the environs, the "festive rushing" in the streets, the impressive steeple of Saint Stephen's, the beautiful women, and the public opulence.[21] Furthermore, he appreciated certain aspects of cultural life in Vienna. He enjoyed meeting the various prominent musicians who lived in or passed through Vienna, and was impressed with the high quality of some of the theatrical and musical performances. Finally, he reveled in a sense of spiritual proximity to his revered Viennese predecessors, Beethoven and Schubert. He made a pilgrimage to their graves soon after his arrival in Vienna, where he picked flowers for Clara and found a pen that he reverently reserved for special occasions. Following an urge to become acquainted with someone who had been close to Franz Schubert, he visited the composer's brother, who gave him access to a treasure trove of Franz's manuscripts.[22] Such experiences, especially the latter, were uplifting and life changing.

Schumann's positive reactions toward life in Vienna were, however, counterpointed by intensely negative ones. He observed a number of serious problems in cultural and artistic circles. He wrote in the *Neue Zeitschrift*, "In Vienna, they are afraid of anything new, anything that goes beyond the run-of the-mill [*alten Schlendrian*]; in music, too, one desires no revolution there."[23] This resistance to the new and unfamiliar became ever more obvious to him during his stay in Vienna. He complained of the xenophobic attitude of the Viennese: "The Viennese are, in general, extremely suspicious of foreign musical greats (except, perhaps, the Italian ones)."[24] When he wrote this sentence, he had Mendelssohn in mind, whose music was generally not popular in Vienna at this time. He also, however, had some personal experience of Vienna's suspicion of foreign musicians. His own music was even less well received there than Mendelssohn's; in a letter written from Vienna in 1837, Clara Wieck had mentioned only one proponent of his works and referred to all other indigenous musicians as Schumann's enemies.[25] Furthermore, Schumann was informed soon after his arrival that because he was a foreigner, he would not be permitted to let his name stand as editor of his journal if it were published in Vienna.[26]

Schumann became aware that the Viennese narrow-mindedness arose in large part from the existence of certain powerful cliques. In a letter to his family of 10 October 1838, he wrote: "You would hardly believe what petty factions, coteries, etc. exist here; to become well established, one must possess a serpentine character, of which, I believe, there is little within me."[27] A particular clique to which he referred frequently in his writings was that controlled by Tobias Haslinger. He wrote to Clara on Easter Monday 1839, "Sedlnitzky [the director of the Censorship Department] is angry with me; I had written about the performance of *St. Paul*, and since I am leaving, I wrote for once according to the facts and in my own fashion about the Haslinger clique, not, of course, roughly and inimically, but rather jovially and wittily."[28] Schumann's remarks were not as benevolent in tone as he would have had Clara believe: "There exists here a clique, the descendant of that which once booed *Don Giovanni* and the *Leonore* Overture . . . a clique . . . as impoverished, as ignorant, as incompetent in terms of judgment and achievement as any in Flachsenfingen."[29]

Schumann also viewed with concern the censorship with which the Metternich regime sought to nip revolutionary tendencies in the bud. After a few months in Vienna, he fully recognized how difficult it was "to speak what one thought," and began to fear that the journal would never prosper in such an atmosphere.[30]

Schumann's letters indicate his planned courses of action in the face of these negative aspects of political and cultural life in Vienna. As far as political repression was concerned, his attitude seems to have been one of learning to live with it rather than one of attempting to change it. He was "careful in his speech and writing" so as not to annoy the censors and potentially embroil the recipients of his letters (especially Clara Wieck) in difficulties.[31] He also took steps to ensure that the journal would not offend the authorities. Soon after his arrival in Vienna, he wrote to Oswald Lorenz, who was running the journal in Leipzig during his absence: "Be very careful not to accept anything that might give the Viennese censors reasons for displeasure. You have no idea what power they have; it reminds one of the time of the *Vehme*."[32]

Schumann's attitude toward the cultural problems was less passive; he was eager to attempt to alter the state of affairs through his journal. As early as 25 October 1838, he wrote to Clara Wieck:

The petty coteries should be blasted apart, the various factions brought closer together, but all of this in an open, honest manner. Vienna has means aplenty, as has probably no other city, but a leader is lacking, someone like Mendelssohn, who could fuse and rule over them. Also, they are glad to let themselves be led here; they listen carefully when something is expounded in the appropriate manner. Indeed, some of the finer individuals actually hope for a Messiah to whom they would immediately offer crown and scepter. Thus, there would surely be much for the journal to do here."[33]

Reading between the lines, one gathers that, the reference to Mendelssohn notwithstanding, Schumann himself hoped to become the Messiah who would save Vienna.

Schumann's determination to take action against the Viennese Philistines seems to have reached a peak late in 1838. In an aggressive vein, he wrote to Clara on 30 December 1838: "Later . . . I would like to, and must, strike into the midst of this pettiness in such a manner that their eyes shall be opened."[34] A few days thereafter (on 10 January 1839), he wrote to Karl Montag: "Later, when the journal is fully established here, which will probably be accomplished by the middle of the year, I shall strike into it all with a great sword."[35]

The inner and outer conflicts with tyranny and cultural demagoguery detailed above seem to me to be reflected in the metrical structure of the first movement of the *Faschingsschwank*. Musical meter with its regularly recurring downbeats and bar lines is a logical metaphor for a rigid cultural or political framework. The metrical scheme designated by the time signature and bar lines—and no less by a clearly audible four-bar hypermeter—could symbolize a repressive, restrictive system. Overriding of those schemes would then suggest rebellion against the system.

As we have seen, the first movement of the *Faschingsschwank* contains many passages in which the music is at odds with the metrical framework, some of these dissonances being relatively weak, some of them very powerful. Passages like that shown in Example 8.25b, in which the dance-like four-bar hypermeter of the preceding measures is smashed, may be translations into music of the violent, Florestanian language of some of Schumann's anti-Viennese remarks, particularly that referring to the symbolic sword with which he planned to strike into the midst of Vienna's complacent clans and coteries. ❦

Eusebius looked up from the manuscript and mused, "Was the first movement of the *Faschingsschwank* really a protest against the Viennese Philistines? It might have been! Our quotation of the *Marseillaise* in mm. 293–300 certainly bears out the author's suggestion that the movement has a rebellious connotation. The author's linking of metrical dissonance and protest is supported by Ernst Wagner's remark about the 'tyranny of meter,' which Florestan quoted when we were in Euphonia; this remark had suggested to us the metaphorical association between musical meter and repression on the one hand, and between the veiling of meter and freedom on the other." With a sigh, he added, "I suppose that all of Florestan's violent metrical dissonances partake of a spirit of protest against mindless constraints, of lashing out against complacent Philistinery—the spirit that animated him when he was well."

The crackle of paper as he turned to the next page of the manuscript awakened the sleeping Florestan. Anxious to engage his attention before it focused on something that would provoke him, Eusebius said to him, "Listen to this analysis of one of the works of our friend Brahms—in fact, of the sonata movement that we briefly discussed while we were walking through Euphonia with Hector Berlioz." Florestan sat up, and Eusebius read:

"KREISLER JUN." (JOHANNES BRAHMS, PIANO SONATA OP. 5, FIRST MOVEMENT)

A number of composers seem to have learned to handle metrical dissonance by studying Schumann's music. Stephen Heller is one obvious example. His adulation of Schumann is clearly evident from his letters to him, and his music provides further evidence of his reverence for Schumann's works.[36] His Rondo-Scherzo op. 8, dedicated to "Florestan and Eusebius," contains numerous Schumannesque metrical devices. In mm. 59–68, for example, Heller almost entirely abandons the triple meter on the surface; the passage is dominated by a clearly duple rhythmic figure. The Scherzo of Heller's Sonata op. 9, a work that Schumann reviewed positively, contains a great deal of metrical dissonance.[37] Heller opens the movement, for example, with displacement dissonance (D3+2), then briefly presents G3/2; a repeated descending octave in the right hand forms a duple layer while the left-hand chords continue to assert the metrical layer.

The first opus of another composer, Julius Schaeffer, is a set of *Fantasiestücke* for piano, also dedicated to Robert Schumann. The influence of Schumann is evident not only from the title but also from extended metrically dissonant passages. The middle section of the first piece, for example, is based on consistent D3+2 (1=8th). At times, dynamic accents keep the metrical layer alive, but inceptions of harmonies and melodic attacks always contradict the meter by falling on the third eighth note of metrical groups of three. The fourth piece contains not only long passages of D2+1 (1=16th), reminiscent of numerous Schumann pieces, but also some dramatic G12/8.[38]

The best-known younger composer who was influenced by Schumann's metrical structures is Johannes Brahms. Brahms studied Schumann's music carefully during September 1853, and came into personal contact with him in the following months.[39] His works written before this time are, to be sure, not devoid of metrical dissonance, suggesting that other music might have influenced him earlier.[40] The Scherzo of his Piano Sonata op. 1, for instance, is permeated by a figure consisting of sequentially descending thirds in eighth notes (mm. 3, 11, 23, etc., and especially 78–80); the thirds create a 2-layer within the prevailing six-eight meter. These allusions to a 2-layer neatly prepare the Trio, which is written in three-four meter. Walter Frisch mentions another relevant passage from this sonata, namely the G-major episode in the Rondo finale, where a 6-layer, and at times a 12-layer, are imposed on the nine-eight meter.[41] In the first movement of the Sonata op. 2, there is an interesting instance of G4/3 (1=triplet eighth). In mm. 40–41, 43–44, 46–47, 49–50, and corresponding later measures, Brahms reiterates a pitch pattern consisting of four triplet eighths, which is dissonant against the three-triplet durations intermittently set out by the right hand.

Frisch observes, however, that metrical dissonance is relatively rare in Brahms's early works and is employed systematically only in his works of the 1860s.[42] It is likely that the upswing in metrical dissonance in Brahms's music of the latter decade can be attributed to his newly acquired knowledge of Schumann's music. In the following paragraphs I briefly investigate the metrical structure of the first movement of the Piano Sonata in F Minor op. 5—a movement conceived during Brahms's stay with the Schumanns, and first performed for Robert Schumann.[43]

Summary

1. Main recurring dissonances: G6/4, D6+2 (1=8th).
2. Families of dissonances operative in the movement: "G6/4" (diminutions appear frequently).
3. Recurring juxtapositions or superpositions: G6/4 and D6+2.
4. Proportion of primarily consonant and primarily dissonant passages: mostly dissonant.
5. Amount of subliminal dissonance: much subliminal G6/4, some subliminal D6+2.
6. Frequency of change of metrical state: frequent throughout (for the most part, every two to four measures).
7. Basic metrical narrative: constant struggle between 6- and 4-layers.

EXAMPLE 8.26. *Metrical dissonance in the exposition of the first mvmt. of Brahms's Piano Sonata op. 5*

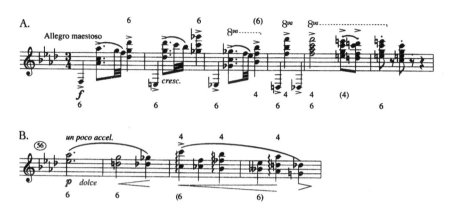

The movement appears to begin with an unambiguous establishment of the metrical 6-layer (1=8th); the initial three statements of the dramatic opening motive occupy six eighth-note pulses, or one measure, each (Example 8.26a). On the basis of harmonic change, however, a displaced 6-layer emerges as well; the third beat of the first measure introduces a new harmony, which is then maintained through the first two beats of the second measure. The same is true of m. 2 beat 3 through m. 3 beat 3, and, possibly, of m. 3 beat 3 through m. 4 beat 2. The interaction of these 6-layers results in subtle D6+4.

The situation from the end of m. 3 through m. 4 is, however, complicated by the repetition of a contour pattern ("high chord—low note"), which results in a 4-layer and in a hint at G6/4. The durational accent at the beginning of m. 5—the strongest such accent so far—temporarily brings the metrical layer to the fore and resolves the dissonances.[44]

In the second phrase Brahms elaborates on the dissonance broached in m. 4. Beginning in m. 7, the bass simultaneously presents two 4-layers, one formed by its durational accents (quarter notes among triplet eighths), the other by the repetition of the pattern "three triplets, quarter note." These layers result in D4+2, but also, more obviously, in G6/4. The right hand attempts to assert the metrical 6-layer against this pattern, and is at times successful (for example, in mm. 7–8, where the 6-layer is announced by dynamic accents and the repeated pattern "quarter, eighth, eighth, quarter"). Already in m. 8, however, the right hand exhibits a tendency to join the left hand in articulating the 4-layer; its six-pulse repeated pattern is curtailed in mm. 8–9 to the four-pulse pattern "quarter, eighth, eighth," which aligns with the 4-layer formed by the left hand's durational accents. In mm. 12–13, while the inner voices reiterate the six-pulse pattern from mm. 7–8 (thus articulating the metrical 6-layer), the right hand's dynamic accents and reiterations of D5 reinforce the same 4-layer.

Brahms continues to exploit G6/4 within the second theme area. The theme

EXAMPLE 8.27. *Metrical dissonance in the development section of the first mvmt. of Brahms's Piano Sonata op. 5*

begins with metrical consonance, but in mm. 49–50, harmonic changes, melodic attacks, and dynamic accents strongly articulate a 4-layer in the absence of the metrical 6-layer, resulting in indirect and subliminal G6/4. In mm. 58–59 (Example 8.26b) and 64–65, again after several measures of consonance, the right hand asserts a 4-layer by a series of registral accents and by repetition of a two-quarter-pulse pattern of falling fifths; again, indirect and subliminal G6/4 is formed. A few consonant measures close the exposition.

The metrical narrative of the exposition clearly centers on the struggle of the metrical 6-layer to assert itself against the rival 4-layer. The development section brings this narrative to a climax (Example 8.27a). It opens, interestingly enough, with two measures in common time (mm. 72–73). The 4-layer, now a metrical layer in terms of surface structure, is clearly articulated by the imitation of a four-pulse-long motive (a motive first stated in m. 16), and by durational accents. ❦

EXAMPLE 8.28. *Metrical dissonance in the coda of the first mvmt. of Brahms's Piano Sonata op. 5*

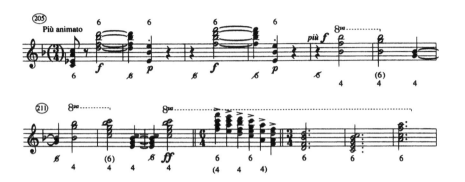

Eusebius looked up and remarked, "Johannes must have glanced at our sketch-books when he visited us! This passage is strikingly similar in terms of motivic and metrical structure to my violin and piano sketch in the third sketchbook (Example 5.5a), which we later transformed into the second section of the fifth Intermezzo from op. 4 (Example 5.13)."

The triumph of the 4-layer is, however, short-lived; m. 74, a five-four bar, juxta-poses a four-pulse segment with one of six pulses (the segments being delineated by harmonic change), and thus accomplishes a "modulation" back to the 6-layer. Not that the 4-layer is out of the picture after this point; it rears its head at intervals throughout the remainder of the movement. A large segment of the development section is based on the version of G6/4 that originated in the second phrase of the first theme (cf. mm. 7–16 and mm. 78–87). A later climactic passage, at mm. 119–22 (Example 8.27b), allows the 4-layer to dominate again; changes of har-mony project the 4-layer, while the metrical 6-layer is not clearly articulated. This passage is reminiscent of the first statement of G6/4 in the movement (mm. 3–4).

During the recapitulation (beginning at m. 131), Brahms suppresses some of the exposition's instances of G6/4, either by altering or by omitting measures; he replaces the hemiolic mm. 3–4 with consonant measures (mm. 133–34), and omits the dissonant material of mm. 7–16. The subliminal G6/4 of mm. 49–50 does reappear (in mm. 171–72), as does the falling fifth material shown in Example 8.26b (mm. 180–81 and 186–87). The coda contains one more flare-up of the 4-layer; in mm. 209–13 (Example 8.28), each chord occupies four eighth-note pulses, resulting in subliminal G6/4.

A secondary character within the metrical narrative of the movement is the dissonance D6+2. The first allusion to this dissonance occurs at mm. 9–10 (si-multaneously with continued development of G6/4); in m. 9, Brahms places a dynamic and durational accent on the second beat, and in m. 10, a durational accent only. During the transition, where the material of mm. 9–10 is devel-oped, additional dynamic and durational accents on the second beat (mm. 27,

28, and 35–38) result in more D6+2. The dissonance is associated with different music in mm. 51–52 and 54–55, but reappears in its original guise during the development section (mm. 81 and 86). In the coda, Brahms dramatically brings this dissonance into association with G6/4—an association that he had already foreshadowed in mm. 9 and 49–52. The *Più animato* section at m. 205 (Example 8.28) begins with several measures of subliminal D6+2 (the metrical 6-layer being suppressed). The succeeding subliminal G6/4 emerges naturally from D6+2; the displaced half-note chord of m. 209, rather than being followed by another chord in the same metrical position (so as to continue D6+2), is followed by a chord of the same duration, resulting in subliminal G6/4 instead.

Having neatly slid from D6+2 into G6/4, Brahms proceeds to resolve the latter dissonance in a subtle manner. Measure 214 (intriguingly similar to the opening of the third movement of Brahms's Fourth Symphony!) is a finely sculpted "modulatory" measure. At the beginning of the bar, one is likely to hear a duple grouping of quarter notes, and hence a continuation of the 4-layer of mm. 209–13; the first significant harmonic change takes place on the third quarter note, the second triad being heard as an embellishment of the tonic. If one takes the whole measure into account, however, a triple grouping of the quarter notes probably makes more sense, for the second-most significant triad of the measure (V) falls on the fourth quarter. This important harmonic change divides the six quarter notes of the measure into two groups of three, and thus reestablishes the metrical 6-layer. After this measure, one is prepared for the clear and uncontradicted final presentation of that layer in the form of repeated dotted half-note attacks. The metrical 6-layer, threatened until the end by the 4-layer as well as by an antimetrical 6-layer, is finally triumphant. 🎕

Florestan (whose nap had done him good) whispered, "Johannes is a fine composer, and a good lad, too! So nice of him to look in on us here at Endenich!" Eusebius agreed, adding, "I am delighted to learn that he will write symphonies! It is a pity that we shall never hear them." He turned back to the manuscript and read aloud the following analysis of one of his most beautiful slow movements.

"EUSEBIUS" (ROBERT SCHUMANN, STRING QUARTET OP. 41 NO. 2, SECOND MOVEMENT)

Summary

1. Main recurring dissonances: D3+2, D6+3 (1=8th).
2. Families of dissonances operative in the movement: Dx+3, "G6/4" (G6/4 appears in the fourth variation, the high-level relative G24/16 at the end of the fifth).
3. Recurring juxtapositions or superpositions: none.
4. Proportion of primarily consonant and primarily dissonant passages: changes from section to section. The theme contains both states in equal proportion, the first variation is entirely and strongly dissonant, the sec-

ond almost entirely consonant, the third mildly dissonant, the fourth strongly dissonant, the fifth variation and the coda mostly consonant. The sections are thus clearly distinguished by metrical state.

5. Amount of subliminal dissonance: the D3+2 in the first variation is mostly subliminal. The fifth variation, in common time, could be considered subliminally dissonant against the primary metrical consonance of the movement. Otherwise, dissonance is on the surface.

6. Frequency of change of metrical state: frequent in the theme, infrequent (only at section ends) in the first variation. In the second variation, the A sections involve frequent change (approximately every two measures), whereas the B section (mm. 41–44) adheres to one state (consonance) throughout. Infrequent change characterizes the third and fourth variations. In the fifth variation, alternation between consonance and D4+1 is frequent (each measure). The coda involves only two changes of state — from consonance to dissonance in m. 111, and back to consonance in the final measure of the movement. To some extent, frequency of change of metrical state helps to characterize the individual sections of the movement.

7. Basic metrical narrative: the movement begins with intensification of dissonance (D3+2) in the theme, culminating in the pervasive dissonance of the first variation. Thereafter, the movement alternates between consonant and dissonant areas. The theme returns with its intensification process, but this time it is followed by the primarily consonant coda (with flareups of motivic dissonances at the very end).

The second movement of Schumann's Second String Quartet is marked "quasi Variazioni." "Quasi" is an appropriate designation: the various sections of the movement do not exhibit the close harmonic correspondence to the theme that one expects from a true set of variations. The "first variation" (mm. 16–32), for example, preserves very few aspects of the "theme." Some melodic fragments of the theme make an appearance (for example, the F4-Bb3 descent from the second violin part of m. 1–2 — compare the cello in mm. 17–18; and the Eb-F neighbor motive of mm. 1, 6, 12–14, and 16 — see the second violin part in mm. 17–19). A few large-scale melodic and harmonic features are preserved as well, such as the Eb octave coupling (compare the first violin part in m. 4 and the cello part in mm. 22–24), and the motion to the mediant at the beginning of the second part (flat mediant rather than diatonic mediant in Variation 1). The differences between the theme and the variations, however, by far outweigh the similarities. The first variation's first half, for example, ends on the dominant rather than the tonic (compare mm. 8 and 24). The second, third, and fifth variations (mm. 32–48, 48–64, and 76–89) are based on the first variation rather than the theme, and the fifth variation compresses the material of the first variation almost to the point of the unrecognizability. Nevertheless, the term "variations" is appropriate, for the movement is, to a large extent, a set of variations on the metrical states of the theme.

The theme presents several dissonances. It begins with allusions to D12+3

EXAMPLE 8.29. *Metrical dissonance in the theme and beginning of Variation 1 in the second mvmt. of Robert Schumann's String Quartet op. 41 no. 2*

and D6+3 (1=8th). In m. 2, a registral and dynamic accent on the second dotted-quarter beat hints at D12+3 (Example 8.29a). In mm. 3, 6, 7, and later measures, registral and/or dynamic accents occur on both of the weak beats, with the result that D12+3 is tightened to D6+3.

Much more significant throughout the theme, however, is D3+2. ❦

Eusebius looked up and said, "I recall making a revision to ensure that D3+2 would not be overshadowed by D6+3. In my first draft, the melodic contour of m. 14 was quite different; I approached the second and fourth beats by upward leaps of a sixth in the first violin part, creating pronounced registral accents and therewith the dissonance D6+3. I subsequently eliminated those leaps and therewith the statement of D6+3, thus allowing D3+2 to remain in the forefront of the metrical action."[45]

D3+2 is very weakly present at the opening, where the metrical 3-layer, established by the durational accents of the violins and the cello, is contradicted by the attacks of the viola. The dissonance, initially almost inaudible, becomes more intense later in the theme, where Schumann involves outer voices in the antimetrical layer, and increases the number of instruments participating in that layer. The enlistment of outer voices begins in mm. 2 and 4, where the cello contributes one antimetrical pulse. At the beginning of the second section (mm. 8 and 9), the violin, which so far has staunchly adhered to the metrical 3-layer, joins the second violin in presenting intrusive antimetrical attacks. Measure 11 is the culmination of the increasing outer-voice involvement; both cello and first violin participate in the articulation of the antimetrical 3-layer (as do the inner voices).

Measure 11 is also the climax of the textural intensification process—of the encroachment of the antimetrical layer on an increasing number of voices. In m. 4, Schumann expands the antimetrical ranks from the initial single participant (the viola in m. 1) by adding the second violin and, briefly, the cello (see Example 8.29a). In mm. 8–9 he gives the antimetrical layer to both violins, in mm. 10–11 to the violins and the cello, and in m. 15 (the first measure of Example 8.29b) to the three lower instruments. This process is reversed at the very end of the theme, where only the cello adheres to the displacement.

As the first variation begins (see Example 8.29b), the cello persists in the same displaced 3-layer, providing smooth continuity from the theme. D3+2 is much more pervasive in this variation, both in a vertical and a horizontal sense. Whereas in the theme at least one instrument articulated the metrical layer at all times, in the first variation all sounding instruments are, except at a few significant points, engaged in the displaced layer—initially groups of three instruments, then all four in mm. 22–24 (Example 8.30a). This takeover of the entire texture by the displaced layer, which results in a total suppression of the metrical layer and hence in the "submerging" of D3+2, is a continuation of the intensification process initiated in the theme.

Schumann cleverly leaves vestigial remnants of the metrical layer in place within the first variation, and thus occasionally brings D3+2 to the surface. He does so not at arbitrary points but at important formal boundaries. The first such event occurs at the end of the first half of the variation (m. 24), where the viola, with a stammer, breaks out of the antimetrical 3-layer and asserts the metrical one (Example 8.30a). This surfacing of G3/2 coincides with particularly pungent pitch dissonance. The second violin resolves the leading-tone D4 to E♭4 at the end of m. 23, and the viola, heading for the same resolution, trails behind the second violin, stating C5 against the second violin's D4, and D5 against its E♭4.

A more emphatic assertion of the metrical layer (and surfacing of G3/2) occurs at the end of the third phrase, just before the return of the opening of the variation (m. 28—Example 8.30b). This time, a displaced harmony—the E♭ triad—is sustained an eighth-note pulse longer than expected, and a corrective accent on the final beat of m. 28 reestablishes the metrical layer. Schumann retains the metrical layer during the first beat of m. 29, then again suppresses it in all instruments until the end of the variation. 🎵

EXAMPLE 8.30. *Metrical dissonance in Variation 1 of the second mvmt. of Robert Schumann's String Quartet op. 41 no. 2*

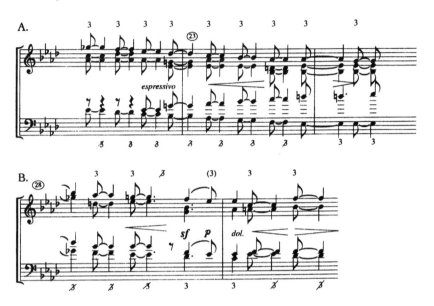

Eusebius remarked, "In my first draft, the displacement continued until the end of m. 28, and restoration of the metrical consonance occurred only in m. 29.[46] The revised resolution at the end of a measure is much more dramatic (because more unexpected), and thus much more strongly highlights the return of the opening material of the variation. The sforzando on the final dotted quarter of m. 28," he added, "also results in an allusion to the other significant dissonance of the movement, D6+3."

 The final cadence of the first variation, unlike the earlier cadences, is not associated with assertion of the metrical layer; Schumann saves metrical resolution for the second variation (mm. 32–48), which, in contrast to the first, is primarily consonant (Example 8.31). The attacks of the first violin consistently and unambiguously express the metrical 3-layer, while the other instruments generally articulate the eighth-note pulse. Only a few weak dissonances disturb this Eusebian idyll. In mm. 33–36, for example, allusions to antimetrical 3-layers in the second violin create intermittent weak D3+1 and D3+2 (Example 8.31). In mm. 38–40, D3+1 and D3+2 occur in more expansive form, the former dissonance created by attacks of the second violin and viola, the latter by those of the cello. This island of metrical dissonance effectively highlights the impending phrase ending; the resolution to V harmony at the cadence of m. 40 is coordinated with metrical resolution.

 In the third variation (beginning at m. 48), Schumann returns to the two main dissonances established in the theme and first variation. He alludes to

EXAMPLE 8.31. *Metrical dissonance at the end of Variation 1 and beginning of Variation 2*

D3+2 in mm. 49–52 (Example 8.32), 54 and 64, where registral accents within the sixteenth-note figuration, most frequently in the first violin, result in a suggestion of a displaced 3-layer. In mm. 55 and 63, the same dissonance is formed by durational as well as registral accentuation; the highest sixteenth notes are dotted—a striking departure from the otherwise unbroken flow of undotted sixteenth notes. Example 8.32 shows that D6+3 is also present in this variation. In mm. 48–54 and 60–61, the metrical 6-layer is conveyed by significant harmonic resolutions (usually the tonics within surface-level V-I progressions). In the former passage, Schumann creates an antimetrical 6-layer by regular alternation between instrumental groups containing the first violin (sometimes only that instrument), and groups lacking the first violin. In mm. 60–61, the antimetrical 6-layer arises from an alternation between maximally thick and thin textures.

Metrical connections between the third variation and earlier portions of the movement, then, are manifold. Another dissonance that is weakly presented in the third variation, on the other hand, provides links to the following variation, namely G1.5/1 (1=8th). The groups of six sixteenth notes in the violin parts occasionally divide on the basis of contour into subgroups of three sixteenths (for example, on the first and third beats of m. 49), while the plucked eighth notes of cello and viola maintain the expected two-sixteenth-note pulse.

The fourth variation (mm. 64–76) is dominated by G3/2, a relative of G1.5/1 (Example 8.33); an alternation between embellished I and V harmonies

EXAMPLE 8.32. *Metrical dissonance in Variation 3*

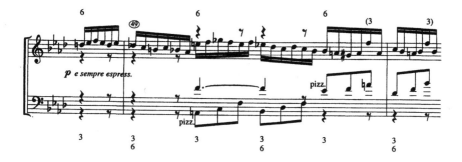

EXAMPLE 8.33. *G3/2 in Variation 4*

(over a tonic pedal) delineates the metrical 3-layer, while the cello attacks and melodic pattern repetitions in the upper instruments form a 2-layer. Aside from the connection with the G1.5/1 of the preceding variation, there are two additional subtle relationships between the fourth variation and the earlier sections. First, by various means—dynamic accents in the viola in m. 65 (the first measure of Example 8.33), durational accents and tenutos in the first violin in mm. 65–69, etc.—Schumann creates D6+3, which he already employed in the theme and third variation. In addition, the fourth variation includes allusions to D6+1, which is related to the D3+1 employed in the first variation; the hairpins in mm. 65 and 67 result in dynamic accentuation of the second pulses of three-eighth-note groups.

The metrical structure of the fourth variation, however, makes sense primarily in relation to the following music. The fifth variation, unlike all of the others, is in duple meter. The fourth variation's G3/2 is thus a "passing dissonance" between the triple consonance of earlier variations and the duple consonance of the fifth (Example 8.34).

The fifth variation is primarily consonant (4/2), with only a few allusions to D4+1 (created by registral accents in mm. 77, 79, and similar measures) and D4+3 (formed by dynamic accents in mm. 78 and 80), which are tightened to D2+1 at the end of the variation (m. 88). The statement of D2+1 coincides with

EXAMPLE 8.34. *Resolution of G3/2 at the beginning of Variation 5*

EXAMPLE 8.35. *Recall of motivic dissonances at the end of the second mvmt. of Robert Schumann's String Quartet op. 41 no. 2*

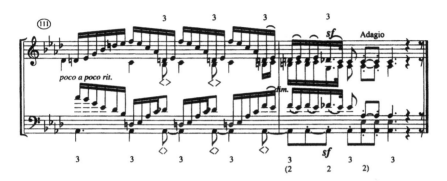

an interesting hypermetrical dissonance. The latter half of m. 88 and the first half of m. 89 constitute new material that expands the prototypical mm. 83–84. This expansion creates indirect G24/16 (three measures against two measures), an augmentation of the mid-level dissonance of the preceding variation (G3/2). The coincidence of G24/16 and D2+1 adds considerable tension to the final measures of the variation.

The fifth variation is followed by a return of the theme. The return is virtually identical to the opening statement, but there is an interesting addition in the form of the introductory E♭'s in the viola. The function of these two attacks may be to "modulate" from the duple meter of the fifth variation to the primary triple meter, for the first E♭ occupies two eighth-note pulses, the second, three. The two attacks also immediately reintroduce the main metrical dissonance of the movement, D3+2, for the second E♭ is displaced.

The following coda beautifully summarizes the metrical dissonances of the movement. Since it is based primarily on the third variation, it is not surprising that it alludes to D6+3. That dissonance is, however, considerably weaker in the coda, where its antimetrical layer is merely suggested by the slurring in the first violin and viola parts (mm. 105–10). Near the end, Schumann reminds us once more of the main dissonance of the movement; D3+2 makes a final appearance in the last two measures (Example 8.35), where dynamic accents appear on the third eighth notes of groups of three. The sforzando on the third eighth note of the final measure, however, in conjunction with the tempo and articulation change two eighth notes later, also suggests a duple partitioning of the eighth-note pulse and hence recalls G3/2, the dissonance of the fifth variation. 🎵

As Eusebius turned the page, Florestan remarked, "Your slow movement is indeed a beautiful one. It nicely leads into my third movement, too, in which I take up the second movement's main dissonance, D3+2, at a faster tempo (in mm. 5–6, 12–16, etc.)."

The next section, they saw, dealt with the music of a composer named Charles Ives, of whom they had never heard. As Eusebius leafed through the section, they caught sight of the musical examples. Florestan, appalled by the harsh harmonies of Example 8.37, shouted, "Is this the music of the future?" Eusebius attempted to soothe him by saying, "That example is indeed dreadful, but the others do not displease me as much. Please listen to the analysis before you excite yourself."

"BLUMENSTÜCK" (CHARLES IVES, "TWO LITTLE FLOWERS")

Even the early tonal songs of Charles Ives contain interesting metrical dissonances. The Lenau setting "Weil auf mir" of 1902 is notated in six-eight time, and the 12- and 6-layers (1=16th) suggested by the time signature are clearly articulated in the piano part. The remaining layer that one would expect, however—a 2-layer—is only latent; the six-sixteenth-note arpeggiating figure in the left hand of the piano consistently divides into two groups of three on the basis

EXAMPLE 8.36. *Metrical dissonance at the climax of Charles Ives's "Weil auf mir" (mm. 27–30).* © 1955 by Peer International Corp. International Copyright Secured. Reprinted by permission.

EXAMPLE 8.37. *G6/4 and G4/3 in Ives's "West London," mm. 13–14. From* Thirty Four Songs. © *1933 Merion Music, Inc. Used by permission.*

of contour, the 3-layer and the latent 2-layer resulting in subliminal G3/2. Duplet quarter-note attacks in the voice and the piano's right hand frequently reinforce the 3-layer. In the final, climactic phrase of the song, metrical dissonance becomes most intense; Ives adds a displacement dissonance to the subliminal grouping dissonance (Example 8.36). As voice and left hand continue the 3-layer, the right hand states octaves that occupy six pulses each; the resulting 6-layer is not, however, coordinated with the metrical 6-layer of the left hand. The displaced 6-layer, remote from the metrical context, suggests the "lonely hovering" of the beloved over the poet's existence to which the final line of text refers. 🐝

"You see, Florestan," remarked Eusebius, "this composer coordinates metrical dissonance with poetic meaning, just as we did." Florestan only grunted noncommittally, and Eusebius continued to read.

Even more adventurous dissonances are found in the radical later songs. In "West London," for example, the vocal line, derived from the hymn tune "Fountain," usually articulates the common time and hence the 4-layer (1=8th) of that tune by means of durational accents, occasionally by other means such as pitch recurrence and new-event or registral accentuation.[47] In the first section of the song, Ives superimposes various ostinatos on the vocal allusions to the tune, the pattern repetitions of each ostinato creating a variety of layers. The resulting metrical states are G6/4 (mm. 1–7), consonance (mm. 9–11), and G6/4/3 (mm. 11–14—Example 8.37). The remainder of the song is virtually consonant; Ives brings the piano into alignment with the voice and in the end, when the hymn tune is fully unveiled, even allows the piano to double the voice. The metrical progression is clearly tied to the form and content of the text. Ives assigns a different state to each couplet of Matthew Arnold's sonnet through the end of the octet, and sets the sestet apart from the octet by consistent consonance. The underlying metrical narrative of the song—the progress toward consonance—suggests progress from a time out of joint toward the "better time" mentioned in the final line. 🌸

Florestan admitted grudgingly, "I suppose the man does know what he is doing." Eusebius smiled and read on:

The lovely little song "Two Little Flowers," from the same period as "West London," is less adventurous in pitch structure, but no less interesting in terms of meter. A summary follows:

1. Main recurring dissonances: G8/7/4 (1=8th).
2. Families of dissonances operative in the movement: none.
3. Recurring juxtapositions or superpositions: none, aside from the obvious G8/7 and G7/4.
4. Proportion of primarily consonant and primarily dissonant passages: mostly dissonant.
5. Amount of subliminal dissonance: none. All dissonance is on the surface.
6. Frequency of change of metrical state: infrequent (change at mm. 9, 13, 23 only).
7. Basic metrical narrative: struggle between the 7-layer and the metrical 8/4 consonance; eventual resolution to 8/4.

The text, with its almost consistent iambs, suggests duple meter, and Ives roots the vocal melody securely in common time. He not only sets the text in such a way that metrical accents (on beats one and three) and textual accents coincide, but generally reinforces the metrical accents with registral and durational accents. In mm. 3, 6, 8, 19, 21, 23, 24, and 25, for instance, registral accents occur on downbeats, and in mm. 4, 6, 7, 9, 13, and 15, there are durational accents on first and/or third beats. Because of the placement of textual and musical accents, the metrical 8-layer and the subsidiary 4-layer (1=8th) are very clear in the voice. This is not to say that Ives allows the vocal line to convey these levels consistently; some of the fascinating weeds within the voice's metrical flowerbed are mentioned below.

The piano accompaniment, evoking the strumming of a guitar or the plucking of strings (the uppermost pitches in fact correspond to three of the open strings of a violin), begins with a pretense of setting up the metrical 8- and 4-levels; the registral accent on E5 appears at first to bisect a metrical group of eight eighth-note pulses (Example 8.38a). One might expect Ives to proceed by repeating the pattern encompassed by the opening measure, but this expectation is promptly defeated; the final eighth note of m. 1 instead acts as the beginning of a second group of seven eighth notes, and further repetition of the seven-note pattern results in a 7-layer, strongly dissonant against the metrical 8- and 4-layers.

The dissonance G8/7/4 is uprooted at several points within the song, the disruptions occurring within the voice, the piano, or both. The vocal line first deviates from its plodding 8/4 consonance at the end of the first stanza (mm.

EXAMPLE 8.38. *Metrical dissonance in Ives's "Two Little Flowers." From* Nineteen Songs. © *1935 Merion Music, Inc. Used by permission.*

9–10—see Example 8.38b), where durational accents and recurrence of D4 result in durations of five and nine eighth notes. Significantly, five plus nine equals fourteen (two times seven); Ives seems to be sowing the seeds of a rapprochement between the metrical strata of voice and piano. This strategy comes to fruition in mm. 13 and 14, where the voice's reiteration of the notes B4-G4-A4 suggests two pulses of a 7-layer, aligned with that of the piano. Some sensation of metrical dissonance, however, lingers in mm. 13–14; the durational accents of the voice part, falling on the A4's, result in a different 7-layer that is not aligned with that of the piano.

The disruptions of G8/7/4 in the piano part are more frequent and regular; beginning at m. 10 (Example 8.38b), they occur every four measures, in coordination with the four points of harmonic change that precede the harmonically more active final phrase, and also in coordination with the ends of couplets (mm. 14, 18, 22). From m. 14 onward, the disruptions result, like those already discussed, in a metrical rapprochement between piano and voice; tendrils from the vocal layers creep into the piano at each of these points, the prevailing 7-groups being curtailed to groups of four. The effect of these curtailments of the piano's 7-layer is the alignment of voice and piano at the first accented syllable of three successive couplets (*marigold, violet, lovliness [sic]*). Temporary resolution of dissonance thus articulates the form of the poem.

The incursions of the 4-layer into the piano part and the resulting temporary resolutions herald the subsequent definitive resolution of G8/7/4 into the primary consonance 8/4: in mm. 23–27—the final vocal measures, encompassing the "punch line" of the poem—piano and voice are perfectly in accord, both conveying the metrical layers (Example 8.38c). The postlude quickly reviews the song's basic metrical progression by briefly bringing back the 7-layer (indirectly dissonant against the immediately preceding consonance 8/4), then reverting to 8- and 4-layers (albeit displaced) in the final two measures.

There is an intriguing extramusical explanation for the prevalence of the 7-layer in the song: one of Ives's "little flowers," his adopted daughter Edith, was seven years old in 1921, the year in which the poem and the song were written![48] ❦

Eusebius pointed out, "Here is another link between this composer and us: he hides biographical details within his music, as we so often did in our youth." He looked ahead to the next section and said, "Ah, Florestan, here comes an analysis of one of your finest recent movements," and began to read.

"FLORESTAN" (ROBERT SCHUMANN, SYMPHONY NO. 3
OP. 97, FIRST MOVEMENT)

Summary

1. Main recurring dissonances: G6/4, D6+4 (1=8th).
2. Families of dissonances operative in the movement: "G6/4" (the diminution G3/2 and the augmentation G36/24 appear frequently).

3. Recurring juxtapositions or superpositions: the two main dissonances, G6/4 and D6+4.

4. Proportion of primarily consonant and primarily dissonant passages: about equal.

5. Amount of subliminal dissonance: much subliminal G6/4.

6. Frequency of change of metrical state: varies from section to section (e.g., increasingly frequent during the first theme, infrequent during the second theme).

7. Basic metrical narrative: constant struggle between 6- and 4-layers, the former, and metrical consonance, ultimately being victorious. Subplot: intensification of D6+4.

To superficial listeners, the first movement of Schumann's Third Symphony (chronologically, his fourth and final symphony) will appear to begin with two juxtaposed metrical consonances (see Example 2.5). The first six measures apparently establish the consonance 12/4/2 (1=8th). The 12-layer is created by a slow rising arpeggiation of the tonic harmony in the first violins and flutes (Eb5-G5-Bb5), the 4-layer by new-event melodic accents and durational accents in the first violin, cello, and double bass, and the 2-layer by new-event accents in the second violin and viola (not shown in Example 2.5). This apparent duple meter collides in the second phrase segment (mm. 7–13) with a different surface-level consonance, 12/6/2. The 12-layer is here formed by the attacks of a descending line in the melody (Ab-G-F-Eb), and the new 6-layer arises from harmonic changes and from durational accents in first violins and flutes.

More sophisticated listeners will not perceive this opening as being fully consonant. They will note that the collision of 6- and 4-layers at the intersection of these two surface-level consonances results in indirect G6/4. They might also observe that the initial 4-layer conflicts with the conductor's beats, which would, at the movement's quick tempo, express the metrical 6-layer. They would, furthermore, perceive m. 7 as the point of resolution of this conflict. Even without watching the conductor, I believe, the attentive listener would gain from m. 7 an impression of resolution, or at least relaxation, as a result of the broadening from a governing 4-layer to a 6-layer.

The score, of course, makes perfectly clear that the movement begins with subliminal G6/4, resolved at m. 7 into the primary consonance (with indirect G6/4 lingering during the first few beats of the consonance). At mm. 11–14, Schumann brings G6/4 to the surface; the 4- and 6-levels are presented simultaneously for the first time, the 4-layer being articulated by the attacks of the cello, bass, bassoons, and brasses, the 6-layer by durational accents in the remaining instruments. In mm. 13–18, the dissonance is again submerged; Schumann repeatedly juxtaposes 4- and 6-layers, but no longer superimposes them. The juxtaposition here occurs at much closer intervals than at the opening; the 4-layer is active in mm. 13–14, the 6-layer in mm. 15–16, and the 4-layer once again in mm. 17–18. Because of the increasing frequency of metrical change, mm. 1–20 give the impression of increasing instability.

This first section of the movement introduces two metrical dissonances aside from G6/4 that are significant later on: the displacement dissonance D6+4 and the hypermetrical dissonance G36/24. The former dissonance appears at the end of the section. Measure 19 reinstates the metrical 6-layer (by durational accents in the melody) while also alluding to the 4-layer (cello and bass). As the last quarter note in the bass of m. 19, however, is tied to a half note instead of a quarter, G6/4 fails to materialize, and a hint of D6+4 emerges instead.

G36/24, an augmentation of G6/4, arises from juxtaposition or superposition of four- and six-bar hypermeasures. It is possible to hear mm. 1–20 in four-bar segments, most of them marked off by prominent new harmonies: the dominant in m. 5, a tonic substitute in m. 9, an actual tonic in m. 13, another dominant in m. 17, and the tonic in m. 21. There is, however, some conflict against this four-square hypermeter. The initial motion from music dominated by the 4-layer to music dominated by the 6-layer, and the resolution of the initial subliminal dissonance, occurs in m. 7, so that one gains a strong impression of a hypermetrical boundary at that point. The beginning of another six-bar hypermeasure could be heard at m. 15, because of the confluence of the initiation of a prominent new harmony (V of V), of the first dynamic accent in the movement, of a registral accent in the high strings and woodwinds (created by a leap of a ninth!), and of a shift from 4- to 6-layer domination. The hypermetrical dissonance is weak at this point, but is worth noting because of its later importance.

The remainder of the exposition continues to dwell on the same metrical material, and begins to develop it. During the second section (the second part of the first theme area—mm. 21–56), Schumann continues the alternation between two surface-level consonances (or between subliminal dissonance and consonance). The alternation no longer proceeds at regular time intervals, so that the aforementioned sense of instability becomes somewhat more pronounced in this section. Like the first section, the second ends with a decrease in the durations occupied by individual metrical states (four measures of 12/4/2, then six measures of 12/6/2, then four measures of 12/4/2, eight of 12/6/2, four of 12/4/2, two of 12/6/2, four of 12/4/2, and four of 12/6/2).

Although the section brings no striking metrical innovations, some of the thematic metrical states come into sharper focus. The two rival surface consonances (and hence the primary consonance and subliminal dissonance) collide more sharply than ever before at mm. 47–52, where each state is associated with one of a pair of repeated segments. At the half-cadence at mm. 47–49 (Example 8.39a), Schumann makes use of the primary metrical consonance 12/6/2, whereas during the immediately following varied repetition he reshapes the cadence into a form governed by 12/4/2 (and, subliminally, G6/4—mm. 51–52). The hypermetrical dissonance suggested within the first section also becomes more prominent during mm. 21–56. Whereas four-bar hypermeter reigns between mm. 31 and 51, change of metrical state results in hypermetrical downbeats at mm. 25, 31, 51, and 57. These boundaries, in turn, result in the juxtaposition of four-bar and six-bar hypermeasures in mm. 21–31 and 47–56, and hence in indirect G36/24.

EXAMPLE 8.39. *Metrical dissonance in the exposition of the first mvmt. of Schumann's Symphony no. 3*

At the very end of the first theme area (mm. 53–56), Schumann introduces indirect G3/2, a diminution of G6/4; the reiterated rhythm of the cellos and basses suggests a 3-layer, which conflicts with the 2-layer of the surrounding measures. This distinctive dissonance was already broached by allusions to a 3-layer at mm. 25, 27, and 29. Its clearer emergence at mm. 53–56 sets the boundary between first theme and transition into relief.

The transition (mm. 57–94), largely modeled on the first theme, continues to alternate 12/6/2 and 12/4/2, and to present some indirect hypermetrical dissonance by juxtaposing four-bar and six-bar hypermeasures. Measures 73–76, for instance, constitute a four-bar dominant prolongation, mm. 77–82, a six-bar sequential passage, and mm. 83–86 represent the first of several four-bar hypermeasures delineated by melodic and harmonic recurrences. The latter portion of the transition entrenches itself ever more firmly into the primary consonance 12/6/2. One of the portions of the first theme that was dominated by 12/4/2 (mm. 21–24) is omitted from the transitional restatement; mm. 77–82, instead of restating mm. 21–24, go on to the material of m. 25, which is based on 12/6/2. The final measures of the transition (mm. 83–94) are virtually consonant. Only a hypermetrical displacement dissonance, D24+6, slightly ruffles the metrical surface; the displaced layer is produced by dynamic accents on the second downbeats of the four-bar hypermeasures at mm. 83–86 and 87–90.

The almost total elimination of metrical conflict at the end of the transition prepares the second theme area, which begins with the primary consonance (mm. 95–111). The initial bars of the second theme are, however, touched by hypermetrical dissonance. The melody of the second theme divides clearly into four-bar hypermeasures, but at m. 97 the local tonic of G unexpectedly appears in the cellos and basses under the dominant-prolonging winds. The adherence to the bass-note G for six measures results in conflict against the four-bar hypermeasures of the melody, and thus in an allusion to direct G36/24.

At m. 111, the long-absent 12/4/2, creating the usual indirect and subliminal G6/4, breaks out with a vengeance and remains in effect for no less than twelve measures (Example 8.39b). A four-bar prolongation of V of V of G minor (mm. 123–26), reverting to the primary consonance, ends with a brief allusion to D6+4, created by syncopation in first violins and high winds. At mm. 127–38, the second theme material reappears. This material, formerly consonant (except for a brief hypermetrical conflict), now absorbs the preceding dissonance D6+4, which is formed by added syncopation in the second violins and high winds (mm. 135–38). D6+4, then, thus far of peripheral significance, begins to gain ground. The following precadential section articulates first the primary consonance (mm. 139–52), then 12/4/2 (mm. 153–62). In the latter passage, the 4-layer is announced with unprecedented emphasis by dynamic accentuation in the brasses in mm. 157–58, and in all instruments in m. 159. The cadence at mm. 163–65 reverts to the primary consonance.

The rate of metrical change in the second theme is much slower than in the preceding sections; individual metrical states last much longer than before. This increased metrical stability lends most of the section an Eusebian quality, in strong contrast to the Florestanian character of the surrounding music.

The closing theme begins with a reappearance of D6+4 (mm. 165–72—Example 8.39c), which is resolved into the primary consonance at the end of each of two four-bar hypermeasures. The following reiterations of the authentic cadence remain metrically consonant. In order to prevent an effect of complete metrical resolution at the conclusion of the exposition, Schumann brings back 12/4/2 and its attendant indirect and subliminal G6/4 dissonances in mm. 177–80.

To summarize, the most pervasive dissonance of the exposition is G6/4. It is introduced in subliminal and indirect form, then surfaces at several points and is ultimately intensified by the use of dynamic accents. A hypermetrical augmentation of this dissonance appears intermittently. The displacement dissonance D6+4 is introduced very gradually, beginning with momentary allusions and culminating at a rather extensive statement within the closing theme.

Rather than analyzing the remainder of this long movement in comparable detail, I restrict the following discussion to a tracing of the further careers of the metrical states established within the first twenty measures.

G6/4, the key metrical player of the exposition, recedes into the background during much of the development section; Schumann, knowing that the recapitulation will of necessity feature this dissonance, avoids it during most of the development section. It does appear indirectly and subliminally during those portions of the development that allude to the first theme material (mm. 273–93 and 311–27). Furthermore, it is represented by relatives—by augmentations and diminutions already found in the exposition. The development section begins with intermittent G3/2. Allusions to this diminution already occurred during the exposition, as was mentioned, but in mm. 187–88 and 195–96 the 3-layer that creates the dissonance is articulated with unprecedented clarity by triad arpeggiations in bass instruments. The augmentation G36/24 appears frequently, for example at mm. 209–20 and the related mm. 247–72. Both points involve not only indirect but also direct hypermetrical dissonance. At m. 209, a series of six-bar hypermeasures intrudes into a context in which four-bar segments prevailed, resulting in indirect, then direct G36/24. The direct portion of the dissonance is shown in Example 8.40a. The six-bar units (shown in the example as 36-pulses) are delineated by large-scale harmonic changes (D major to G major), the four-bar segments (24-pulses) by surface harmonic patterns (D major to G minor in mm. 215–18 and D major to G major in mm. 219–22). This music is subsequently transposed (mm. 247–72), resulting in a similar progression from indirect to direct G36/24. The process of rendering an indirect dissonance direct, applied to G6/4 within the first section of the movement, is here extended to the augmentation of that dissonance as well.

The development of D6+4 is even more interesting. This dissonance, of secondary though increasing importance in the exposition, moves into the limelight early in the development section. The material comprising the parallel sections in mm. 215–22 (Example 8.40a) and 259–72 begins with D6+4, which is subsequently loosened to D12+10 at mm. 217 and 261, where ties appear only on alternate upbeats. Between the two parallel passages, at mm. 253–57, lies another prominent statement of D6+4, created by a 7–6 suspension chain. (This chain reappears at mm. 351–55.) D6+4 not only becomes more pervasive in the development section, but is also intensified by the frequent addition of dynamic and registral accents to the durational accents that previously created the antimetrical 6-layer (at mm. 299–301, 307–9, and 333–35).

Whereas I have discussed the development of the motivic grouping and displacement dissonances separately, the two types actually intersect at times within the development section. Schumann applies a typical developmental strategy—the bringing together of materials earlier stated separately—to the metrical dissonances. One such encounter between dissonances of different types occurs during the second of the two 7–6 chains mentioned above; at mm. 351–54, D6+4 is counterpointed by G3/2, the 3-layer resulting from new-event melodic accents in the second violin and viola. A dramatic juxtaposition of G6/4 and D6+4 occurs in the retransition (Example 8.40b). That section begins with a magical moment; against a static background of tremolos and sustained notes,

EXAMPLE 8.40. *Metrical dissonance in the development section of the first mvmt. of Schumann's Symphony no. 3*

the horns portentously present a metrically consonant version of the opening theme (mm. 367–70). From this form, there emerges the usual subliminally dissonant "duple" version of the theme, which now sounds like a distortion of the consonant form (mm. 371–73). Immediately thereafter Schumann launches into a suspension chain whose upbeat preparations are emphasized by dynamic accents (resulting in strong D6+4). Thus Schumann reminds us at a significant formal boundary of the primary metrical consonance and of the two main ways in which it is contradicted during the movement.

Another juxtaposition of D6+4 and G6/4 concludes the development section. The former dissonance appears in mm. 399–402, the displaced layer announced by cellos, double basses, trumpets and tympani. Subliminal G6/4 immediately follows, heralding the triumphant recapitulation.

A few words about the recapitulation and coda must suffice. The recapitulation is much like the exposition in terms of metrical structure. In terms of hypermeter, however, it differs significantly; several passages of the exposition that involved hypermetrical dissonance are not recapitulated (mm. 25–30, 51–56, and 77–87), so that the recapitulation contains less hypermetrical disturbance than the exposition. The recapitulation thus paves the way for the coda, which, not surprisingly, performs a resolving function.

The coda contains many statements of the motivic dissonances, followed by emphatic resolutions. The resolution of the indirect and subliminal G6/4 at mm. 531–33 is particularly interesting. Most G6/4's in the movement resolve at the end of a cycle; that is, the 4-layer continues until a pulse of the metrical 6-layer (i.e., a bar line) is reached. Schumann could easily have resolved the G6/4 at

EXAMPLE 8.41. *Hypothetical and actual resolution of metrical dissonance in the coda of the first mvmt. of Schumann's Symphony no. 3*

mm. 531–33 in the same manner, as is shown in Example 8.41a. Instead, he extends the chord of m. 533 to a six-pulse duration and follows it with a two-pulse duration (Example 8.41b). The displaced six-pulse duration results in an allusion to D6+4, and hence in another intersection of the two motivic dissonances.

D6+4 returns more explicitly at mm. 543–45, where its antimetrical layer results from durational and dynamic accents. The succeeding passage, in which the downbeats are emphasized by corrective durational and dynamic accents, firmly resolves the dissonance. At mm. 563–68, subliminal and indirect G6/4 appears for the last time, and is then resolved just as firmly as was D6+4; from m. 569 onward, the metrical 6-layer is conveyed without contradiction by durational, and often by dynamic, accents. Aside from a brief allusion to the high-level dissonance D12+6 in mm. 571–75 (in the form of passionate appoggiaturas in weak hypermeasures), Schumann maintains a state of metrical consonance until the end of the movement. 🌻

They sat awhile in silence, reveling in these ecstatic final measures, and entirely ignoring Dr. Richarz, who had entered the room with a cheerful "Good day, Herr Doktor Schumann" as Eusebius was finishing the section. The doctor noticed the empty tray near the open window, looked out, and shook his head when he saw what had happened to its contents. He wrote in his notebook, "He moves his lips as if talking to himself, seems to be suffering from aural hallucinations again, and has eaten nothing,"[49] then took his farewell. Eusebius turned to the final section of the manuscript and read:

"PIERROT" (ARNOLD SCHOENBERG, "VALSE DE CHOPIN" FROM *PIERROT LUNAIRE*)

In his essay "Brahms the Progressive," Arnold Schoenberg cites m. 49 from the finale of Mozart's String Quartet in D minor, K. 421, as an example of "poly-rhythmic construction."[50] In order to highlight this aspect of the excerpt, he renotates the various voices in different meters. The dynamic, registral and du-rational accents in the first violin line suggest to him a quadruple grouping of the twelve sixteenth-note pulses of Mozart's six-eight measures; thus he rewrites this line in three-four time. Mozart's dynamic accents on the fourth and tenth sixteenth-note pulses in the second violin part strongly imply a triple grouping of the twelve sixteenths; Schoenberg therefore notates this line in twelve-sixteen meter. In the viola part, Schoenberg adheres to Mozart's notated meter; the dotted-quarter beats of six-eight time are indeed reinforced by dynamic accents and by the repetition of a triadic pattern. While the cello attacks actually suggest six-eight time as well, Schoenberg renotates the cello part in two-four time, appar-ently carried away by his desire to demonstrate "polyrhythmic construction." In a second Mozart excerpt cited in the same essay, from the Minuet of the C-major Quartet, Schoenberg draws attention to a 5-layer (1=quarter) in the first violin line, created by the immediate repetition of a melodic segment. Schoenberg does not comment on the passage in detail, but it is apparent that he is again intent on illustrating "polyrhythmic construction"; the 5-layer is superimposed on a 3-layer in the lower voices, determined by the repetition of the rhythmic pattern "quar-ter note, quarter rest, quarter note."

Schoenberg's interest in metrical dissonance, already evident from the above analyses of Mozart excerpts, is even more amply demonstrated by his own music. I discuss only one example here: the "Valse de Chopin" from *Pierrot lunaire*.[51]

Summary

1. Main recurring dissonance: G6/4 (1=8th).
2. Families of dissonances operative in the movement: "G6/4."
3. Recurring juxtapositions or superpositions: none.
4. Proportion of primarily consonant and primarily dissonant passages: mostly consonant (17 dissonant measures out of 44).
5. Amount of subliminal dissonance: very little (m. 17 only).
6. Frequency of change of metrical state: fairly infrequent (changes at mm. 14, 18, 27, 32, and 41 only).
7. Basic metrical narrative: C-D-C-D-C-D; struggle between 6- and 4-layers appears to end with victory of the metrical 6-layer, but the 4-layer taints the ending.

The movement is based throughout upon the interaction of the metrical 6-layer and a 4-layer (1=8th). Initially, Schoenberg imposes a 12-layer on the eighth-note pulse, that interpretive layer being created by durational accents in the bracketed (most prominent) voices on the downbeats of mm. 2, 4, 6, and 8.

EXAMPLE 8.42. *Layers of motion in Schoenberg's "Valse de Chopin" from* Pierrot lunaire, *mm. 9–16. Used by permission of Belmont Music Publishers, Pacific Palisades, CA 90272. © 1914 by Universal Edition. Copyright renewed. All rights reserved. Used in the territory of the world excluding the United States by permission of European American Music Distributors Corporation, sole Canadian agent for Universal Edition.*

The metrical 6-layer is suggested by the successive durational accents on the downbeats of mm. 6 and 7 (in piano and voice, respectively), then clarified by durational accents and rhythmic pattern repetitions in mm. 9–16. The various repeated rhythms, as well as the durational accents on downbeats in the latter passage, are shown in Example 8.42.

In mm. 12–16, Schoenberg superimposes a 4-layer on the 6-layer, creating G6/4. The antimetrical layer is at first produced by the repetition of the dactylic pattern "2-1-1" (1=8th) in the piano (mm. 12–13), then by the repetition of "3-1" in piano and voice (mm. 14–17—Example 8.43). In m. 17, the 4-layer temporarily ousts the metrical 6-layer, rendering G6/4 subliminal. In mm. 18–19, however, the 6-layer conquers and in fact engulfs the 4-layer. In m. 18, Schoenberg adds a quarter note to the "3-1" pattern and reiterates the resulting rhythm ("3-1-2") in the voice part of m. 19. The pattern that created the 4-layer (3-1) thus becomes a component of a larger pattern that forms a 6-layer.

In mm. 19–20, the reiterated rhythm "4-2" in the piano reinforces and continues the 6-layer, and in mm. 21–22, while no layer larger than a 2-layer clearly interprets the eighth-note pulse, the dynamic accent in the flute briefly refers to the 6-layer. That layer is strongly reinforced in mm. 23–26 by the suggestion of a three-quarter-note "oom-pah-pah" accompaniment in the piano part and by the repetition of "3-1-2" in the clarinet (mm. 24–25).

In mm. 27–29, the climactic measures of the movement (Example 8.44), G6/4 reappears. The 4-layer arises, as in mm. 14–18, from the reiteration of a "3-1" pattern. The 6-layer is delineated by changes of rhythmic pattern rather than by repetition of pattern; in mm. 27–29, six-eighth-note durations (measures) are respectively occupied by steady sixteenth-note motion, then eighth-note motion, then sixteenth-note motion again (in the flute—not shown in the example).

After the climax, Schoenberg allows the 4-layer and the dissonance G6/4 to peter out. He abandons the 4-layer briefly at the beginning of m. 30, brings it back (now displaced in comparison to the climactic measures) for two more pulses as the voice reiterates the "3-1" rhythm, then eliminates it entirely for some time (see the last beat of Example 8.44). The 6-layer is, throughout mm. 30–41, created by various repeated patterns.[52] It is noteworthy that in mm. 30–41 pattern repetitions occur in pairs of measures, resulting in a 12-layer in addition to the 6-layer; this 12-layer is clearly evident in the piano part in mm.

EXAMPLE 8.43. *Schoenberg, "Valse de Chopin," mm. 14–19, piano and voice parts. Used by permission of Belmont Music Publishers, Pacific Palisades, CA 90272. © 1914 by Universal Edition. Copyright renewed. All rights reserved. Used in the territory of the world excluding the United States by permission of European American Music Distributors Corporation, sole Canadian agent for Universal Edition.*

30–31, 32–33, 34–35, 38–39, and 40–41. Mm. 36 and 37 have the same resultant rhythm and thus also contribute to the delineation of the 12-layer. Since the 12-layer is so clearly articulated in mm. 32–41, these measures recall the metrical consonance of the opening of the movement (12/6/2).

Schoenberg could easily have ended the movement as consonantly as he began it. Instead, he hints once more at G6/4; he alters the pattern of mm. 40–41 by the elimination of a quarter rest, resulting in the reiteration of a four-eighth-note pattern and hence in the suggestion of a 4-layer. The final two A♮'s also occupy four eighth-note pulses each (although the resulting 4-layer is not aligned with the earlier one). Thus the dissonance G6/4 faintly colors the ending —like a pale drop of blood on the lips of an invalid (Example 8.45). ❦

Florestan had become increasingly restless as he had looked over the musical examples for this section. As Eusebius looked on helplessly, he now sprang up and shrieked, "On these tones rests a destruction-seeking drive. These are chords of wild lust that disturb icy dreams of despair. Hotly jubilating, sweetly lan-

EXAMPLE 8.44. *Schoenberg, "Valse de Chopin," mm. 27–31, piano and voice parts. Used by per-mission of Belmont Music Publishers, Pacific Palisades, CA 90272. © 1914 by Universal Edition. Copyright renewed. All rights reserved. Used in the territory of the world excluding the United States by permission of European American Music Distributors Corporation, sole Canadian agent for Universal Edition.*

EXAMPLE 8.45. *Schoenberg, "Valse de Chopin," mm. 40–44, piano part. Used by permission of Belmont Music Publishers, Pacific Palisades, CA 90272. © 1914 by Universal Edition. Copyright renewed. All rights reserved. Used in the territory of the world excluding the United States by permission of European American Music Distributors Corporation, sole Canadian agent for Universal Edition.*

guishing, melancholy somber waltz, you shall haunt me forevermore!" As his increasingly incoherent shouts merged into a prolonged scream, he seized the manuscript and attempted to tear it in half, but desisted abruptly and fell silent as a bird landed on the window sill and gazed at him reproachfully. Florestan shrank back and whispered, "It is a vulture, waiting for my carcass." Their avian visitor snorted, "A vulture, forsooth! Do you not remember me? I am the Prophet Bird, and I beg you not to damage that manuscript, for I must return it unharmed to its author. In fact, since you appear to be finished with it, I had better collect it now. I trust you have enjoyed most, if not all, of it." As Eusebius looked on, Florestan walked slowly to the window and held the manuscript out to the Prophet Bird, who took it in his beak and, flapping his wings vigorously, departed through the window.

Epilogue: Morning Song

This epilogue is an attempt to recreate an effect of "metrical dissonance" in words by superimposing "noncongruent" layers of discourse. My aim is to suggest by such superposition the mental and emotional state of Robert Schumann in the asylum at Endenich in June of 1856. In one of the three strands, that which I have labeled "R" (for "Robert"), Schumann reminisces quite rationally about his recent past. I have counterpointed with this strand two others, occupied primarily by trains of thoughts that I imagine were, consciously or subconsciously, almost constantly active within Schumann at Endenich: one expressing a longing for Clara, the other, a longing for death. The former train of thought is here assigned to Eusebius ("E."), the latter to Florestan ("F."). The three brief utterances of the caretaker ("C.") make no impression on the main interlocutors; Schumann has withdrawn so completely into himself that no words from outside are able to reach him.

The superposition of these three strands is an obvious "surface-level" dissonance within the epilogue. The epilogue is also, however, characterized by a "subliminal" dissonance in the form of a superposition of three disparate functions and meanings. It can be read not only in the manner mentioned above but also as an appendix to the sixth chapter—as a list of passages from Schumann's songs in which emotional states are highlighted or musically represented by metrical dissonance. All of the utterances of Florestan and Eusebius are drawn from texts (in my translations) that Schumann set in a metrically dissonant manner. Interested readers may consult the footnotes for the location of the passages. I have not provided measure numbers, as very few editions of Schumann's songs include them; the passages can most easily be found by searching for the given German text excerpts.

Finally, the epilogue can be read as a metrical map of the third of the *Gesänge der Frühe*, op. 133; hence its title. Not every aspect of my dialogue relates to op. 133 no. 3; for example, the repetitions within the Florestan and Eusebius strands do not correspond to musical repetitions. The numbers above the "Robert" strand, however, are the measure numbers of that work, and each strand of the dialogue represents one of the layers of motion in the piece. The "Robert" strand stands for the metrical 9-layer (1=8th), which is active without interruption in the piece. The beginnings of most measures are strongly accented, either durationally (as in the pervasive dotted "crowing" motive), dynamically, or by significant harmonic change.[1] Even during the few brief passages where the accents delineating the metrical layer are relatively weak (as in mm. 20–22), the listener can easily maintain that layer. The "Florestan" strand represents a 9-layer shifted forward by three eighth-note pulses. This displaced layer originates in m. 9, where the durational accent within the bass's version of the "crowing" motive falls not on the downbeat (as it did in mm. 1–2 and 6–7) but on the second beat. The shifted 9-layer is later articulated by dynamic accents (in mm. 37, 42, 47, 49, and, very near the end of the piece, in mm. 60–61). The last chord, which registrally accentuates the second beat, constitutes a final allusion to the antimetrical 9-layer.

The "Eusebius" strand denotes a 3-layer, shifted by two eighth-note pulses. Hints at this layer appear in the bass of mm. 1–2 and the treble of m. 3. In mm. 4–6 it becomes virtually continuous, then fizzles out in m. 7. The same cycle occurs within each recurrence of the opening material (cf. mm. 23–29 and 43–46). Within the intervening developmental passages, there are additional instances of the shifted 3-layer (mm. 13–14 and 31–40). Since the shifted 3-layer disappears after m. 46, Eusebius ceases to speak at that point of the dialogue.

The caretaker's strand represents a more rarely appearing 6-layer, created in mm. 4–5, 16–17, 26–27, and 54–55 by pattern repetition; at the former three points, the right hand reiterates a contracted version of the "crowing" rhythm, and in mm. 54–55 the progression I–IV is repeated within three successive six-eighth-note segments.

Simultaneous utterances within the dialogue represent particular metrical dissonances; simultaneous "Robert" and "Florestan" lines represent the dissonance D9+3, coincidence of the lines of Robert and Eusebius represents D3+2, and coincidence of Robert's and the caretaker's lines stands for G9/6. The intersections of three interlocutors represent compound dissonances. The "Robert" strand on its own represents metrical consonance.

This *Gesang der Frühe* is, like most of Schumann's very late music, quite sparing and conservative in its use of metrical dissonance. Nevertheless, metrical dissonance is an important and pervasive feature.

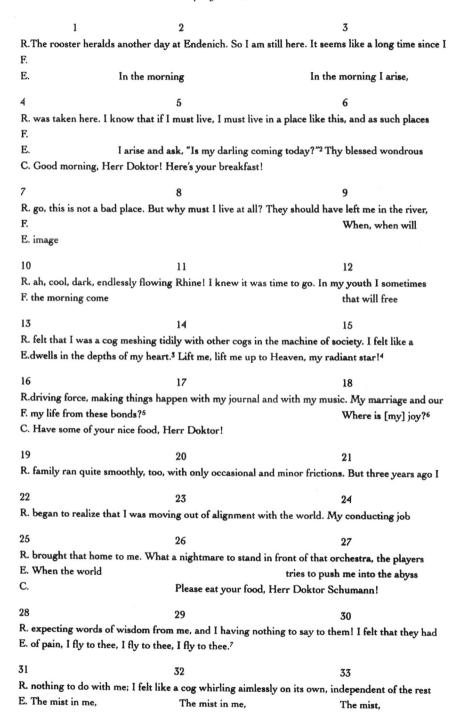

	1	2	3

R.The rooster heralds another day at Endenich. So I am still here. It seems like a long time since I

F.

E.   In the morning   In the morning I arise,

   4   5   6

R. was taken here. I know that if I must live, I must live in a place like this, and as such places

F.

E.   I arise and ask, "Is my darling coming today?"² Thy blessed wondrous

C. Good morning, Herr Doktor! Here's your breakfast!

   7   8   9

R. go, this is not a bad place. But why must I live at all? They should have left me in the river,

F.   When, when will

E. image

  10   11   12

R. ah, cool, dark, endlessly flowing Rhine! I knew it was time to go. In my youth I sometimes

F. the morning come   that will free

  13   14   15

R. felt that I was a cog meshing tidily with other cogs in the machine of society. I felt like a

E.dwells in the depths of my heart.³ Lift me, lift me up to Heaven, my radiant star!⁴

  16   17   18

R.driving force, making things happen with my journal and with my music. My marriage and our

F. my life from these bonds?⁵   Where is [my] joy?⁶

C. Have some of your nice food, Herr Doktor!

  19   20   21

R. family ran quite smoothly, too, with only occasional and minor frictions. But three years ago I

  22   23   24

R. began to realize that I was moving out of alignment with the world. My conducting job

  25   26   27

R. brought that home to me. What a nightmare to stand in front of that orchestra, the players

E. When the world   tries to push me into the abyss

C.   Please eat your food, Herr Doktor Schumann!

  28   29   30

R. expecting words of wisdom from me, and I having nothing to say to them! I felt that they had

E. of pain, I fly to thee, I fly to thee, I fly to thee.⁷

  31   32   33

R. nothing to do with me; I felt like a cog whirling aimlessly on its own, independent of the rest

E. The mist in me,   The mist in me,   The mist,

34   35   36
R. of the machine. Within me, too, everything was going awry. I had suffered long ago from
E.   The mist in me, the mist in me—transfigure it, my radiant star, into

37   38   39
R. premonitions of such a breakdown. Now I knew that it was beginning to happen. I knew that I
F. Madness gnaws at my soul.[8]
E. light, into light.[9]   The mist in me,

40   41   42
R. must be put away. I asked her to have me put away. She would not do it until in desperation I
F.   If only I could finally see that hour, finally see that hour,
E.transfigure it.

43   44   45
R. tried to put myself away. Now I am here, a displaced person, a defective cog that had to be
E.   Nobody   Nobody   Nobody

46   47   48
R. discarded before it damaged its neighbors. I am alone. She cannot come to see me. They are
F.   If only I could finally see that hour, finally see that hour
E. Nobody remembers me there.[10]

49   50   51
R. afraid that I would injure even her. But I could not harm my Clara, my light, my star! Please
F. in which I would cease to see![11]

52   53   54
R. come, dear one, and hold me close. I need to feel that I am in accord at least with thee. In thy
C.   All right, Herr Doktor,

55   56   57
R. arms I shall enjoy a blessed sensation of release. Thou shalt look into my eyes and thou
F.   When I am buried,
C. I'll take that tray now.

58   59   60
R. shalt say, "Thou sad, pale man!"[12] And thou shalt smile at me as I blissfully slip out of
F. When I am buried,   When I am buried,   When I am buried,

61   62   63
R. this world. Ah, come to me, dear one, come to me, Chiarina, and grant me Auflösung. . . .[13]
F. then the tale shall be ended,   ended.[14]

Glossary

Throughout the glossary, "consonance" refers to metrical consonance and "dissonance" to metrical dissonance.

Antimetrical layer: an interpretive layer that conflicts with at least one metrical layer

Augmentation: the progression from a relatively low-level to a higher-level version of a particular dissonance

Cardinality: an integer n denoting the constant number of pulse-layer attacks subsumed by each pulse of an interpretive layer. Each interpretive layer can be characterized by this integer (i.e., as an n-layer).

Compound dissonance: dissonance produced by the combination of more than two conflicting interpretive layers

Contextual intensity: intensity determined by the manner of presentation of a given dissonance in context

Cycle: a segment of a grouping dissonance demarcated by its periodic points of alignment

Deintensification: the process of weakening a specific strong dissonance, or of weakening dissonance in general across a given musical passage

Diminution: the progression from a relatively high-level to a lower-level version of a given dissonance

Direct dissonance: dissonance resulting from superposition of layers of motion

Displacement dissonance: the association of layers of equivalent cardinality (i.e., congruent layers) in a nonaligned manner; labeled with a "D" followed by the cardinality of the layers, a plus or minus sign (denoting displacement), and the displacement index

Displacement index: the constant number of pulse-layer attacks that separates the metrical and antimetrical layers of a displacement dissonance

Grouping dissonance: the association of at least two interpretive layers whose cardinalities are not multiples/factors of each other; labeled with a "G" followed by a ratio of the cardinalities involved

High-level (or hypermetrical) dissonance: dissonance formed by the interaction of large-scale (hypermetrical) layers of motion

Indirect dissonance: dissonance resulting from the juxtaposition rather than superposition of layers of motion

Inherent intensity: intensity of dissonance determined by the characteristics of the given dissonance type

Intensification: the process of rendering a particular dissonance more clearly perceptible, or of rendering dissonance in general more clearly perceptible across a given musical passage

Interpretive layer: a layer of motion that moves more slowly than the pulse layer and allows the listener to "interpret" the raw data of the pulse layer by organizing its pulses into larger units

Layer of motion: a series of approximately equally spaced pulses

Loose [displacement] dissonance: a displacement dissonance in which a relatively small number of metrical pulses is contradicted

Loosening: progression from a tight displacement dissonance to a looser relative; accomplished by multiplication of the cardinality by an integral factor, with preservation of the displacement index

Low-level dissonance: dissonance formed by the interaction of micropulses

Metrical consonance: a state of maximal alignment of layers of motion, existing when all pulses of all interpretive layers coincide with pulses on all faster-moving layers; labeled by a ratio composed of the cardinalities of the interpretive layers involved

Metrical dissonance: nonalignment of layers of motion

Metrical layer: one of the layers that form the primary metrical consonance of a work

Metrical map: diagram of the metrical progression of a work or movement

Metrical progression: the succession of consonances and dissonances within a given work or movement

Micropulse: an intermittently appearing layer of motion moving more quickly than the pulse layer

Mid-level dissonance: dissonance at levels between the two extremes of micropulse and hypermeter; formed by the interaction of metrical and antimetrical layers

Preparation: allusion within primarily consonant passages to dissonances that will be fully established later

Primary consonance: the consonance created by the primary metrical layer in interaction with the pulse layer

Primary metrical layer: the most prominent metrical layer in a work, generally (but not always) the layer designated by the upper integer of the time signature and rendered visually apparent by the bar lines

Pulse layer: the most quickly moving pervasive series of pulses in a given work or section

Resolution: progression from dissonance to consonance

Resultant rhythm: the rhythm formed by the summation of the pulses of a collection of superimposed interpretive layers

Simple dissonance: a dissonance composed of the minimum number of layers (a pulse layer and two conflicting interpretive layers)

Strong dissonance: clearly perceptible dissonance

Subliminal dissonance: dissonance formed by the interaction of at least one explicitly stated interpretive layer and at least one conflicting layer that is only implied (by the context and by the notation). The implied interpretive layer within such dissonances is generally the primary metrical layer.

Submerging: the process of rendering a surface-level dissonance subliminal; the dissonance begins in a form involving explicit articulation of all constituent layers but then, by the elimination from the musical surface of the constituent metrical layer, becomes subliminal

Surface-level dissonance: dissonance formed by at least two explicitly stated interpretive layers

Surfacing: the process of rendering explicit a subliminal dissonance; the dissonance begins in a subliminal form (without articulation of the constituent metrical layer) but then, by the addition of an explicitly articulated metrical layer, becomes obvious on the musical surface

Tight [displacement] dissonance: a displacement dissonance in which a relatively large number of metrical pulses is contradicted (as opposed to loose dissonance)

Tightening: progression from a loose displacement dissonance to a tighter relative; accomplished by division of the cardinality by an integral factor, with preservation of the displacement index

Weak dissonance: subtle, not immediately obvious dissonance

Notes

CHAPTER ONE

1. Euphonia is a fictitious town in the Harz Mountains in Germany, devoted entirely to musical pursuits. It was invented by Hector Berlioz, who in the *Gazette Musicale* for April 28, 1844 described the activities in that town during the twenty-fourth century. Berlioz's description is translated and reprinted in Barzun, *Berlioz and the Romantic Century*, 2:330–35. I am assuming that the musical activities in the town in 1854 were much the same as they were to be in the twenty-fourth century. (The Rhythmic Quarter is my contribution to Berlioz's fantasy, suggested by his fairly extensive discussion of rhythmic matters in the aforementioned essay.) Florestan and Eusebius are fictitious personae invented by Schumann, reflecting, respectively, the extroverted and passionate, and the introverted and gentle sides of his own personality. They make frequent appearances in his early critical writings and in his early music, sometimes in published works (for example, in *Carnaval*), even more often in the autographs. (Schumann originally ascribed the individual pieces of the *Davidsbündlertänze*, for example, either to Florestan or to Eusebius.) Throughout the first section of this chapter, actual quotations from the written works of the various speakers are italicized. Translations are mine unless otherwise indicated.

2. Barzun, *Berlioz and the Romantic Century*, 331.

3. The excerpt shown in Example 1.1 is found, along with the commentary paraphrased here, in Robert Schumann, "Phantasien, Capricen u[sw.] für Pianoforte," *Gesammelte Schriften*, 3:97 (1838). It appears to be Bergson's intention that the seven-eight measure displace the remainder of the bass line by one eighth note.

4. Barzun, *Berlioz and the Romantic Century*, 331.

5. Hauptmann, *The Nature of Harmony and Metre*, 344.

6. Robert Schumann, "Das Komische in der Musik," *Gesammelte Schriften*, 1:184–86 (1835).

7. Robert Schumann, "Die dritte Symphonie von C. J. Müller," *Gesammelte Schriften*, 1:115 (1835). Schumann's example lacks the natural before the E.

8. Schumann mentions a negative remark of Fétis's about Berlioz's music in *Gesammelte Schriften*, 1:127. For further information on Fétis's ambivalent view of Berlioz, see Barzun, *Berlioz and the Romantic Century*, 1:92, 105, 151, and 2:70.

9. Fétis, "Du developpement future de la musique." Mary Arlin's paper "Metric Mutation and Modulation: The Nineteenth-Century Speculations of F.-J. Fétis" (delivered at the meeting of the Society for Music Theory in Tallahassee on 1 Nov. 1994) brought Fétis's articles and some of Berlioz's related remarks to my attention.

10. Fétis, "Du developpement future de la musique," 326. William Caplin pointed out to me that Fétis's example is derived from the last movement of Beethoven's Piano Concerto op. 19 (compare mm. 1–4 and mm. 261–65).

11. Ibid., 300.

12. Ibid., 326.

13. Ibid., 327.

14. Berlioz, "Feuilleton du *Journal des Débats*, November 10, 1837," reprinted as "Berlioz on the Future of Rhythm" in Barzun, *Berlioz and the Romantic Century*, 2:336–39.

15. Mary Evans Johnson mentions this passage as an example of "metrical repositioning" in "Characteristic Metrical Anomalies." Her term encompasses both of Fétis's mutation types.

16. Young Riemann's argument comes, for the most part, from his later work *System der Musikalischen Rhythmik und Metrik*, 203–5. The Beethoven passage is treated in the same manner by the French theorist Mathis Lussy. See his *Traité de l'expression musicale*, 26–27, and Edmond Monod's summary of Lussy's views on renotation (including a citation of Beethoven's op. 27 no. 1) in *Mathis Lussy et le Rythme Musical*, 78.

17. Riemann, *System*, 101–11.

18. Ibid., 110.

19. Example 1.9b and the commentary are drawn from ibid., 89–90.

20. Hauptmann's reference to syncopation as a conflict between two nonaligned layers is found in *The Nature of Harmony and Metre*, 341.

21. For Riemann's discussion of these conflict types, see *System*, 111–21.

22. See Riemann, *System*, 118: ". . . it would be wrong, if during such configurations one were to cancel the meter and instead were simply to observe the rhythmic organization marked by the motivic lengths. Just as the changing significance of these immediately repeating figures is determined only by the unswerving adherence to the metrical organization, so does their contradiction of the harmony endow them with additional new meanings."

23. Ibid., 121.

24. Robert Schumann, *Gesammelte Schriften*, 2:64 (1836).

25. Ibid., 3:101 (1839).

26. For the references to Kittl's *Scherzi* and Hiller's *Etudes*, see ibid., 4:37 (1841): "A frequent unclarity of the phrase rhythm such that there appears to us to be somewhat too much or too little especially at the cadences of some sections." See also ibid., 1:80 (1835): "I have various complaints about [Hiller's] cadences, at which I almost consistently find that there is something extra or something missing."

27. Robert Schumann, "Phantasien, Capricen u[sw.] für Pianoforte," *Gesammelte Schriften*, 3:101 (1839): "To be sure, we sometimes encounter apparently disturbed phrase rhythms in the masterworks, which, however, immediately resolve themselves" ("die sich aber zur Secunde wieder ausgleichen").

28. Robert Schumann, "Symphonie von H. Berlioz," *Gesammelte Schriften*, 1:125 (1834).

29. "Berlioz on the Future of Rhythm," in Barzun, *Berlioz and the Romantic Century*, 2:338.

30. Cooper and Meyer, *Rhythmic Structure of Music*, 81, 90, 106–15, 165.

31. Berry, *Structural Functions*, 318–19, 325–26, 359.

32. Ibid., 324–26, 365–71. Berry also uses other terms such as "metrical incongruity" and "polymeter" to describe metrical conflict.

33. Their analysis of the opening of the finale of Haydn's Quartet op. 76 no. 6 is a good example; Lerdahl and Jackendoff, *Generative Theory of Tonal Music*, 90–96.

34. An example of conflicted grouping structure is their Example 3.23, in connection with which they state that a grouping into fours is preferable on the basis of slurring, but they do not deny the presence of a grouping into threes on the basis of motivic parallelism (repetition of a pitch pattern).

35. Lester, *Rhythms of Tonal Music*, 48, 77–126.

36. See especially Schachter, "Rhythm and Linear Analysis: Aspects of Meter," 1–60.

37. Ibid., 26–28, 50–51, 36, respectively.

38. Schachter's discussions of these displaced passages are found in ibid., 33–35 and 53–58, respectively. For a more recent discussion of processes involving hypermetrical displacement, see William Rothstein, "Beethoven with and without 'Kunstgepräng,'" especially 186–93.

39. Cowell, *New Musical Resources*, 50.

40. Cowell elsewhere discusses both types of metrical conflict addressed in this volume, but does not apply consonance-dissonance terminology to them; ibid., 64–65, 70–71.

41. Seeger, "On Dissonant Counterpoint," 25–31.

42. Schillinger, *System of Musical Composition* (New York: Carl Fischer, 1941).

43. Schillinger, *Encyclopedia of Rhythms* (New York, 1966).

44. The following excerpt illustrates the imprecision of Colin's analogy: "The various resultants (3:2 or 4:3) correspond to the acoustical ratios of the harmonic overtone series. This means that the rhythmic resultant of 4:3 is slightly more dissonant than the rhythmic resultant of 3:2. The former corresponds to the perfect 4th and the latter to the perfect 5th." Ibid., I.

45. Yeston, *The Stratification of Musical Rhythm* (New Haven: Yale University Press, 1976).

46. Ibid., 39–54.

47. Ibid., 79–102.

48. Ibid., 102–12.

49. Wallace Berry, *Structural Functions*, 362.

50. Krebs, "Some Extensions of the Concepts of Metrical Consonance and Dissonance," *Journal of Music Theory* 31/1 (1987): 99–120.

51. Hlawicka, "Die rhythmische Verwechslung," and "Musikalischer Rhythmus und Metrum."

52. Cohn, "Metric and Hypermetric Dissonance," and his "Dramatization of Hypermetric Conflicts."

53. Imbrie, "'Extra' Measures"; Epstein, *Beyond Orpheus*, 131–32; Rothstein, "Beethoven with and without 'Kunstgepräng'"; Krebs, "Rhythmische Konsonanz und Dissonanz," 29–32.

54. Among studies dealing with Brahms's metrical conflicts are Frisch, "The

Shifting Bar Line"; Frisch, *Brahms and the Principle of Developing Variation*, 57–58, 93–95, 112, 115–16, 138, etc.; and Agmon, "Rhythmic Displacement in the Fugue of Brahms's Handel Variations." Another relevant study of the music of Brahms is David Lewin's "On Harmony and Meter in Brahms's Op. 76, No. 8." In the course of his analysis, Lewin not only analyzes metrical structure but also brilliantly develops pitch/meter analogies, assigning "tonic," "subdominant," and "dominant" qualities to particular hypermeters, and showing how a modulatory pitch passage is also modulatory in metrical terms.

55. For relevant analyses of works by Wagner and Debussy, see Krebs, "Dramatic Functions of Metrical Consonance and Dissonance in *Das Rheingold*," and "Rhythmische Konsonanz und Dissonanz," 33–36, respectively.

56. August Reissman, *Schumann* (Berlin, 1865), 152; Dahms, *Robert Schumann*, 268; Gertler, *Robert Schumann in seinen frühen Klavierwerken*, 74–78; Daniel Mason, "Robert Schumann," in Oscar Thompson, *The International Cyclopedia of Music and Musicians* (New York, 1946), 1683.

57. Knayer, "Robert Schumann als Meister der rhythmischen Verschiebungen," 177–79, 201–3, 231–33.

58. Kohlhase, *Die Kammermusik Robert Schumanns*, 2:30, 35, 50, 66, 105, 125.

59. Appel, "Robert Schumanns Humoreske für Klavier Op. 20," 289–305.

60. Edler, *Robert Schumann und seine Zeit*. In his discussion of the incomplete *Jugendsinfonie* in G minor, he points out various metrical idiosyncrasies that anticipate the composer's mature style (118). Within an analysis of the *Fantasy* op. 17, he refers several times to the significance of syncopation, which "sometimes remains in effect over such long stretches that the perception of the measures is in danger of being lost" (144). He mentions the metrical and hypermetrical complications in the second movement of the First Symphony (152), the finale of the Piano Concerto (161), the first movements of the String Quartets (166), the Scherzo of the Second String Quartet (168), and the second Trio of the Piano Quartet (172), among others.

61. Gerhard Dietel, '*Eine neue poetische Zeit*,' 267.

62. Schnebel, "Rückungen—Ver-rückungen," *Musik-Konzepte, Sonderband Robert Schumann I* (1981), 4–89.

63. Rosen, *The Romantic Generation*, 655, 684, 688.

64. Honsa, "Synkope, Hemiola und Taktwechsel in den Instrumentalwerken Schumanns"; Mary Evans Johnson, "Characteristic Metrical Anomalies."

65. Kaminsky, "Aspects of Harmony, Rhythm and Form," 34–35, 39, 157–58.

CHAPTER TWO

1. In earlier writings, I employed the term "level of motion" rather than "layer." Here, I require the term "level" for other purposes and thus replace it with "layer" (which recalls Yeston's term "stratum").

2. See chapter 1, notes 12, 19, and 20.

3. Roeder, who employs the model in the discussion of nontonal music in "Interacting Pulse Streams," uses the term "pulse stream" for individual layers. This term suggests an emphasis on the horizontal continuity of the phenomena in question, whereas "layer" suggests an emphasis on the vertical dimension—on the metrical states that result from combined streams. For the other sources cited here, see chapter 1, notes 33, 45, and 52. Not all twentieth-century theorists subscribe to a "layer" model. Christopher Hasty, for instance, attempting to "rescue" meter from its historical role of inexpressive "grid" in

Meter as Rhythm, rejects stratification (see, for example, pp. 154 and 201). As I hope to show, the stratification model of meter does not necessarily preclude expressiveness.

4. Lerdahl and Jackendoff, *Generative Theory of Tonal Music*, 17.

5. My categories of phenomenal accent are drawn primarily from Joel Lester's *Rhythms of Tonal Music*, 18–40.

6. In the examples, pulses that are relatively weakly articulated are shown by integers in parentheses. (Time signatures in parentheses indicate that the time signature is not actually present within the cited excerpt.) When a pulse is not articulated at all, I draw a stroke through the corresponding integer. In simplified examples, some numbers for pulses that appear to be absent may lack strokes; this situation indicates that the pulse is articulated in the full score.

7. In some editions, even more of the accents are missing, namely the first and third in the second measure of the example (m. 9). These, however, are present in the *Stichvor-lage* housed at the Staatsbibliothek zu Berlin—Preußischer Kulturbesitz (Musikabteilung mit Mendelssohn-Archiv), Mus. ms. autogr. R. Schumann 29.

8. Yeston gives many examples of layers arising from subsurface melodic change in chapter 3 of *Stratification of Musical Rhythm*, 55–76.

9. For a detailed discussion of such grouping devices, see Lerdahl and Jackendoff, *Generative Theory of Tonal Music*, 36–39.

10. Maury Yeston draws attention to layers formed by various types of pattern repetition (*Stratification of Musical Rhythm*, 50–54). My article "Some Extensions" deals almost exclusively with layers formed by pattern repetition. Several authors have pointed out that the separation between accentuation and grouping is not necessarily a sharp one; Yeston states that "the beginnings of repetitions of patterns become points of accent" (p. 85), and Joel Lester similarly observes that initiation points of patterns carry an accent (*Rhythms of Tonal Music*, 37).

11. Lester makes this point in *Rhythms of Tonal Music*, 40.

12. The special significance of harmony in forming metrical layers has been noted by many earlier writers, including Lerdahl and Jackendoff (see their Metrical Preference Rule 5f, *Generative Theory of Tonal Music*, 84) and William Rothstein (see "Beethoven with and without 'Kunstgepräng,'" 173). Albert S. Bregman discusses the tendency of dynamic accents ("loud sounds") to group together (i.e., to form layers) in *Auditory Scene Analysis*, 648.

13. I do not include the possibility of aligned presentation of interpretive layers of identical cardinality because I consider such a situation as a single interpretive layer created by the collaboration of a number of musical means. Albert S. Bregman discusses the significance of such "collaboration" in the formation of auditory streams in *Auditory Scene Analysis*, 651–52.

14. Lester, *Rhythms of Tonal Music*, 50. Lester uses the term "level" rather than "layer."

15. This definition, again, excludes the possibility of associations of layers of identical cardinality (which could, of course, never produce dissonance).

16. Kaminsky, "Aspects of Harmony, Rhythm and Form," 27. Note that the term "grouping" is here employed with a meaning different from that used in the earlier discussion of layer formation.

17. The coffee-bean diagrams in this chapter are modeled on the dot diagrams in Lerdahl and Jackendoff, *Generative Theory of Tonal Music*.

18. Yeston, *Stratification of Musical Rhythm*, 140; Horlacher, "The Rhythms of Reiteration," 174.

19. Kaminsky, "Aspects of Harmony, Rhythm and Form," 27.

20. Where there is no metrical framework, the layer initiated earlier usually functions as the referential layer.

21. Bo Alphonce makes the distinction between forward and backward displacement in "Dissonance and Schumann's Reckless Counterpoint," par. 4–6 and 10–11.

22. Note that Dx–a and Dx+b, the sum of a and b being x (the cardinality), are the respective "backward" and "forward" labels for a given displacement dissonance. Thus, D3+2 and D3–1, D4+3 and D4–1, etc., where the displacement indices of each pair add to the cardinality, are alternate designations for the same displacement dissonance.

23. I have adopted the term "resultant" from Yeston, *Stratification of Musical Rhythm*, 77.

24. There are other types of families of grouping dissonances. Pairs of the type Gx/y, G(x+y)/y, for instance, are closely related; the resultant of the dissonance with the higher numerator is similar, but reiterates y. Thus, the resultant of G5/3 is "3 2 1 3 1 2 3," while that of G8/3 is "3 3 2 1 3 3 1 2 3 3." Yeston constructs families of grouping dissonances on the basis of inclusion relations, modeled on Allen Forte's pitch-class set complexes (ibid., 143–47). I do not dwell on these families here since they do not seem to be significant in Schumann's music.

25. I coined the term "indirect dissonance" in "Some Extensions," 103. A number of writers had, however, previously acknowledged the possibility of metrical conflict in the horizontal dimension. Fétis's discussion of five-four meter as a horizontal association of triple and duple meter, and his extrapolation to other juxtapositions of meters in regular alternation, hints at the idea of indirect metrical conflict ("Du developpement future de la musique," 353). Charles Seeger considers the possibility of horizontal as well as vertical dissonance, describing the latter as much more strongly dissonant ("On Dissonant Counterpoint," 27). Wallace Berry refers to horizontal as well as vertical "noncongruity," giving an example of juxtaposition of three- and four-quarter-note groups at the opening of the second movement of Beethoven's Eighth Symphony (*Structural Functions in Music*, 362–65).

26. Yeston refers to this tendency in *Stratification of Musical Rhythm*, 31, 96.

27. See, for example, Charles Rosen, *Romantic Generation*, 684–85.

28. This analysis differs slightly from that in Kaminsky's Example 1.5b, in which the 3-layer is continued through m. 68 ("Aspects of Harmony, Rhythm and Form," 34–35).

29. "Grille" means "whim" or "quirk."

30. If the pulse unit were determined by the underlying pulse of the lowest-level dissonances in the given work, the numbers associated with higher-level dissonances within the same work would be cumbersomely large. I therefore admit fractional values into the labels of low-level dissonances.

31. The term "hypermeter" is derived from Edward T. Cone's term "hypermeasure," designating a metrical unit of greater length than a notated measure; see his *Musical Form and Musical Performance*, 79. For more recent developments in hypermetrical theory, see Rothstein, *Phrase Rhythm in Tonal Music*; and Kramer, *The Time of Music*, esp. 83–107. Some rhythmic theorists have questioned the existence of hypermeter, or meter at high levels (for instance, Lester, *Rhythms of Tonal Music*, 158–69), and would thus question the existence of hypermetrical dissonance as well. Others, for example, Richard Cohn (in "Dramatization of Hypermetric Conflicts," 188–206), have convincingly demonstrated that dissonance at high levels not only exists but can have great dramatic impact.

32. John Daverio draws attention to some of the subtleties of hypermeter in this passage in *Robert Schumann*, 14–15.

33. William Rothstein notes that the conclusion of an exposition with a three-bar group was a "generic norm by Beethoven's time"; see "Beethoven with and without 'Kunstgepräng,'" 175n. Even if this particular hypermetrical irregularity was a norm, Schumann employs it here in an unusually interesting manner.

34. In the autograph of the first edition of this symphony, held at the Archive of the Gesellschaft der Musikfreunde in Wien (A289), m. 84, there notated as two measures of two-four time, is deleted. Its deletion, revoked in the second edition, would have removed the hypermetrical dissonance.

35. Charles Colin suggests this point in his introduction to *Encyclopedia of Rhythms* (New York, 1966. Rpt. New York: Da Capo Press, 1976), p. L: "You will notice as the rhythms become more dissonant, their total durations are longer."

36. This principle is also operative in the domain of pitch; the intervals of a major seventh or minor second are, in tonal contexts, very strongly dissonant because they so closely approach the most stable intervals, the unison and the octave.

37. Richard Cohn demonstrates this aspect of grouping dissonance intensity in "Metric and Hypermetric Dissonance," 13.

38. Albert S. Bregman's observation, in *Auditory Scene Analysis*, 649, that "continuous sounds hold together better as a single stream than discontinuous ones do," suggests another possible way in which sustention affects contextual intensity. A succession of sustained sounds will be more clearly perceived as a stream than one containing gaps; therefore, dissonances whose layers consist of sustained sounds will be more clearly perceived and hence more intense than those whose layers are "gapped."

39. The above statements do not apply if dynamic or harmonic new-event accents are involved; I regard those as creating intense dissonance no matter where and how they arise.

40. Not all combinations of three or more layers of different cardinality result in compound grouping dissonance, for when any two of the cardinalities are multiples/factors of each other, they result in consonant relationships. Thus, the superposition of a 2-layer, a 3-layer, and a 6-layer does not result in compound dissonance, but only in a combination of G3/2 and the two consonances 6/3 and 6/2.

CHAPTER THREE

1. See Daverio, *Robert Schumann*, 22.

2. Macdonald, "Schumann's Earliest Compositions and Performances," 259–83; and Daverio, *Robert Schumann*, 22, 29, 47, 68.

3. Daverio, *Robert Schumann*, 47.

4. Schumann's comment on Hummel's *Method* is found in his *Gesammelte Schriften über Musik und Musiker*, 1:15 (1834).

5. Schumann saw a painting similar to this vision while he was transcribing Paganini's G-minor Caprice, and was subsequently haunted by that painting; Robert Schumann, *Tagebücher*, 1:404.

6. Discussions of the influence of Paganini on Schumann are found in Daverio, *Robert Schumann*, 63, and Boetticher, *Robert Schumanns Klavierwerke, Teil II*, 56.

7. See Daverio, *Robert Schumann*, 71. Evidence of Schumann's familiarity with Bach's *Partitas* is to be found in *Gesammelte Schriften über Musik und Musiker*, 2:36–41. Schumann lists a number of movements from this collection as studies in particular technical difficulties.

8. Schumann mentions finding the pen in *Gesammelte Schriften über Musik und Musiker,* 3:203 (1840).

9. Mary Evans Johnson refers to the influence of Beethoven's rhythmic style on Schumann in "Characteristic Metrical Anomalies," 250. Arnfried Edler believes that Schumann consciously adopted "humoristic" metrical dissonance from the Scherzo movements of Beethoven; see *Robert Schumann und seine Zeit,* 144. Schubert's influence on Schumann has been studied in detail by Marie-Luise Maintz in her "Studien zur Schubert-Rezeption Robert Schumanns."

10. John Daverio discusses the influence of Schubert's chamber music on Schumann in *Robert Schumann,* 49–52.

11. Robert Schumann, *Gesammelte Schriften über Musik und Musiker,* 2:11–13. Maintz, in "Studien zur Schubert-Rezeption Robert Schumanns," 282, mentions the similarity between "Arlequin" from *Carnaval* and Schubert's op. 33 no. 2 (although, as she points out, Schumann displaces Schubert's rhythm by a quarter note), and between the rhythmic pattern of *Papillon* no. 6, mm. 7–14, and Schubert's op. 33 nos. 4, 6, and 9 (the similarity is especially close in Schubert's sixth dance). I cite additional Schubert waltz quotations, not mentioned by Maintz, in connection with my analysis of the first movement of Schumann's *Faschingsschwank aus Wien* in chapter 8. A further item of evidence of Schumann's interest in Schubert's waltzes is his fragmentary set of variations on Schubert's *Sehnsuchtswalzer* (op. 9 no. 2), which Schumann absorbed in part into his own op. 9, the *Carnaval.*

12. Mary Evans Johnson discusses Schumann's fondness for the inherent duple/triple conflict in the waltz in "Characteristic Metrical Anomalies," 38–39, 302.

13. Heinrich Schenker briefly discusses the metrical structure of the passage from op. 110 in *Beethoven, die letzten Sonaten, Sonate As Dur op. 110: Kritische Einführung und Erläuterung,* ed. Oswald Jonas (Vienna: Universal Edition, 1972), 58.

14. See chapter 1, note 7.

15. For the dating of the Concerto sketches, see Boetticher, *Robert Schumanns Klavierwerke, Teil I,* 28, and *Teil II,* 10. These sketches occupy a large part of the first and third of the six sketchbooks housed at the Universitäts-und Landesbibliothek (ULB) at Bonn.

16. Boetticher, *Robert Schumanns Klavierwerke, Teil I,* 99–104. Schumann's Foreword and preparatory exercises are found in Robert Schumann, *Studien op. 3 und Konzertetüden op. 10 nach Capricen von Paganini,* ed. Hans Joachim Köhler (Leipzig: Edition Peters, 1981), 4–12.

17. The Piano Quartet remained unpublished during Schumann's lifetime and was issued only in 1979 by Heinrichshofen's Verlag, Wilhelmshaven (ed. Wolfgang Boetticher). One of the ideas from the Trio of the second movement seemed to Schumann to embody romanticism, and he quoted it in several of his later works. For one such quotation, see Example 2.1. Boetticher lists other examples in the introduction to his edition of the Quartet (p. vii).

18. Schumann associated the ending of this Caprice with the described image of Paganini; Robert Schumann, *Tagebücher,* 1:404.

CHAPTER FOUR

1. Clara was playing the *Emperor Concerto* in January of 1854. She performed it on 21 January in Hanover; see Knechtges-Obrecht, "Clara Schumann in Düsseldorf," 215.

2. Kirnberger, *Art of Strict Musical Composition*, 235–36.

3. The idea that metrical anomalies are embellishments of the normative meter is broached by Mary Evans Johnson in "Characteristic Metrical Anomalies," 249.

4. I suggested at the end of "Some Extensions" that such reduction might be a worthwhile pursuit. I have since come to a different conclusion.

5. Some of these processes have been touched upon by earlier authors. Cooper and Meyer show an intensification process in Dufay's *Missa Sancti Jacobi* (*Rhythmic Structure of Music*, 113–15), and Walter Frisch discusses intensification of a different type in "Metrical Displacement in Brahms," 154. Peter Kaminsky's analyses indicate his awareness of several metrical processes. For example, in his analysis of the Trio of Schumann's *Davidsbündlertanz* op. 6 no. 6 in "Aspects of Harmony, Rhythm and Form," he mentions the intensification of dissonance by addition of dynamic accents nine measures into the Trio (p. 57). He also analyzes the offbeat accents in the tenth and eleventh measures of the Trio as a development of those in mm. 2 and 4—a hint at a process which I shall discuss later as "tightening" (p. 57). In his analysis of op. 6 no. 1, he refers to an augmentation of a simple syncopation (p. 67).

6. The accents on the right-hand E♭ and A♭ in mm. 12 and 13, respectively, are missing in the Clara Schumann edition but are present in the Henle edition.

7. I have already applied the term "resolution" to metrical events at several points of this volume. Several earlier authors have also applied the term in this metaphorical sense, notably Cooper and Meyer in *Rhythmic Structure of Music*, 111, 115, 165, and Wallace Berry in *Structural Functions in Music*, 359.

8. Peter Kaminsky points out that the end of the Préambule does not completely resolve the D2+1 dissonance; "Aspects of Harmony, Rhythm and Form," 39.

9. One might argue that the new bass line introduces a new interpretive layer: durational accents on the second beat result in a displaced 3-layer and in the dissonance D3+1. Especially after m. 70, however, this layer is barely audible; the low-point registral accents in the bass on the downbeats of mm. 71–74 render the metrical 3-layer much more perceptible than the displaced layer.

10. This is the basic argument of Christopher Hasty's book *Meter as Rhythm*; his approach to the "rehabilitation" of meter is, to be sure, very different from mine.

CHAPTER FIVE

1. Schumann preserved his sketches and other autographs very carefully. It is partly for this reason that a large number of them have survived. The most significant collections are located at the Manuscripts Division of the Universitäts- und Landesbibliothek (ULB) in Bonn, the Deutsche Staatsbibliothek zu Berlin—Preußischer Kulturbesitz (Musikabteilung mit Mendelssohn-Archiv), the Schumann-Haus in Zwickau, the Heinrich-Heine-Institut in Düsseldorf, the Archive of the Gesellschaft der Musikfreunde in Wien, the Bibliothèque Nationale in Paris, and the Pierpont Morgan Library in New York (Robert Owen Lehman Collection). The extant documents include some sketches (for example, six sketchbooks housed at the ULB in Bonn, and sketches for the String Quartets op. 41 housed at the Deutsche Staatsbibliothek zu Berlin), and numerous fair copies and *Stichvorlagen*. Although they have not received nearly as much attention as Beethoven's, these sources have been studied by a number of authors. The first author to write extensively about them was Wolfgang Gertler, who in his *Robert Schumann in seinen frühen Klavierwerken* made some perceptive comments

about the sketches for the *Papillons*. Wolfgang Boetticher discussed many of the autographs in *Robert Schumann, Einführung in Persönlichkeit und Werk* and, more recently, in his studies *Robert Schumanns Klavierwerke, Teil I: Opus 1–6* and *Robert Schumanns Klavierwerke, Teil II: Opus 7–13*. Linda Correll Roesner, in her dissertation "Studies in Schumann Manuscripts: With Particular Reference to Sources Transmitting Instrumental Works in the Large Forms," investigated many of the technical aspects of Schumann's compositional process (ink colors, correction techniques, etc.) and also demonstrated numerous large-scale consequences of Schumann's revisions. Jon Finson, Akio Mayeda, Claudia Macdonald, and Rufus Hallmark have also done exemplary source-based work on particular bodies of Schumann's output. A transcription of the sketchbooks housed in Bonn, by Reinhold Dusella, Matthias Wendt, Reiner Leister, and others, is in progress, and will appear as a supplement to the *Neue Robert-Schumann-Gesamtausgabe*, beginning in 1998.

2. The Österreichische Nationalbibliothek in Vienna holds a photograph of the earliest manuscript of the discarded finale of op. 22 (PhA 1519); the autograph itself is in a private collection. The fair copy is housed in the Archive of the Gesellschaft der Musikfreunde in Wien (A288). The inserts for the fair copy are not contained in the Gesellschaft autograph; that for m. 99, labeled "a" in red crayon (just as is the point of insertion in the Gesellschaft copy), is at the Deutsche Staatsbibliothek zu Berlin — Preußischer Kulturbesitz (Musikabteilung mit Mendelssohn-Archiv), Mus. ms. autogr. R. Schumann 36 no. 6 (verso), brace 2. The manuscript of the complete sonata, still with the original finale, is also at the Deutsche Staatsbibliothek (Mus. ms. autogr. R. Schumann 38). "Brace" will henceforth be abbreviated "br." The abbreviation "st." (for "staff") will be used when a manuscript page contains both braces of staves and single staves (in which case single staves will be counted rather than braces).

3. Linda Correll Roesner discusses this revision in "Brahms's Editions of Schumann," 252–60. She points out that Brahms, when preparing the movement for publication in November 1866, preserved two statements of the dissonant material—those beginning at mm. 337 and 367—that Schumann had decided to excise; the penciled "gilt" (stet) beside those two deleted passages is in Brahms's, not Schumann's, hand.

4. Deutsche Staatsbibliothek zu Berlin — Preußischer Kulturbesitz (Musikabteilung mit Mendelssohn-Archiv), Mus. ms. autogr. R. Schumann 19, p. 33, br. 1, mm. 6–7. The pagination of this manuscript is confusing; there are numbers in light pencil at the top right-hand corners of each recto page, and different numbers in dark pencil below. Since the latter numbers are continuous throughout the manuscript, I cite only them.

5. The second of the six sketchbooks held at the ULB Bonn is a collection of short dated sketches relating to Schumann's early works. The term "musical diary" seems appropriate for this sketchbook. The passage mentioned here is transcribed in Krebs, "Schumann's Metrical Revisions," 41.

6. Deutsche Staatsbibliothek zu Berlin, Mus. ms. autogr. R. Schumann 19, p. 18, br. 2, m. 5 to br. 3, m. 2.

7. The fair copy is housed at the Heine-Institut in Düsseldorf (no. 78.5025). The revision discussed here is found on p. 3.

8. The three versions are found in ULB Bonn, Schumann 8, p. 4, br. 1–2; p. 6, st. 1–3; and p. 6, br. 4–6. The latter draft is very similar to the final version, although only outer voices are notated.

9. Bibliothèque Nationale, Paris, ms. 320, p. 8, br. 1, m. 3 to br. 2, m. 3.

10. The crossed-out anticipatory third F/D at the end of m. 5 foreshadows the displaced figuration of the final version.

11. The sketch on p. 38 of Schumann 15 shows an F as the uppermost note on the downbeat of m. 4. The F should, of course, be a D, tied from the preceding bar (as shown in my transcription).

12. The sketches for the *Abegg Variations*, op. 1, contain an example of change of dissonance type. In an early sketch of mm. 45–48 (ULB Bonn, Schumann 13, p. 55), Schumann featured the dissonances G4/3 and G3/2. In later sketches of the passage (ULB Bonn, Schumann 13, pp. 6 and 17), he began to weed out the 3-layer, then added a shifted 4-layer, thus replacing the original grouping dissonances with the displacement dissonance D4+1. For transcriptions of the relevant sketches, see Krebs, "Schumann's Metrical Revisions," 40. An additional example of a revision that altered the type of dissonance is found in the third *Davidsbündlertanz*, mm. 43–44. In the autograph (Archive of the Gesellschaft der Musikfreunde in Wien, A281, p. 5, br. 4, mm. 4–6), Schumann placed sforzandos on the third beats, creating the dissonance D3+2 (1=quarter). In the first edition of the work, he moved the sforzandos to the second beats, so that the dissonance changed to D3+1. This dissonance was anticipated in the autograph version of m. 42, where the sforzando was already on the second beat.

13. A more substantial example of the addition of layers to an existing dissonance comes from the slow movement of the Piano Quintet op. 44. Pages 25–27 of the fair copy (ULB Bonn, Schumann 5) correspond to the present mm. 132–64. The accompaniment pattern of the passage, however, was originally different from the present one: all instruments were to play a quarter-note triplet pattern, the triplets being grouped into twos by pattern repetition. The passage was thus permeated by weak G3/2. Schumann crossed out this material and wrote the present version as an appendix at the back of the manuscript. He preserved the duply grouped quarter-note triplets in the piano and gave eighth notes to the strings, thus adding low-level three-against-four dissonance to the existing G3/2.

14. At times, Schumann intensified existing dissonance by adding accents other than dynamic stresses. For example, in the first draft of the first movement of the String Quartet op. 41 no. 1 (mm. 52–55), he originally notated only the first violin part and a few notes of the second violin part (Deutsche Staatsbibliothek zu Berlin, Mus. ms. autogr. R. Schumann 19, p. 5, st. 5, mm. 3–6). The second violin part contained one tie across the bar, and thus hinted at the displacement dissonance D6+3 (1=8th). In the final version (Example 4.15b), Schumann gave the antimetrical durational accents to the cello, and stated three of them rather than one. Both the relocation of syncopation in a more prominent voice and its reiteration intensified the dissonance.

15. The sketch page (Schumann-Haus, Zwickau, 4648-A1, recto) begins with mm. 103–23 of the twelfth and final piece of the first edition, and mm. 101–21 of the tenth and final of the second (br. 1, m. 1 to br. 4, m. 1). The material on the remainder of the recto through br. 2, m. 3 of the verso corresponds quite closely to the tenth piece of the first version and the ninth piece of the second (although the note values are twice as large and the measures half as long as those of the editions).

16. Bibliothèque Nationale, ms. 329, p. 12v, br. 3, mm. 1–5.

17. This revision is found in the fair copy housed at the Heinrich-Heine-Institut, Düsseldorf, ms. 78.5025, p. 18. The page is reproduced in facsimile in Krebs, "Schumann's Metrical Revisions," 47.

18. ULB Bonn, Schumann 14, p. 5, br. 4.

19. Schumann apparently considered using the material shown in Example 5.11 as the opening theme of the finale. In the manuscript of op. 14 held at the British Library (Additional ms. 37056, p. 17), the passage appears in 6/16 meter, marked *prestissimo*. It is crossed out and followed on p. 18 by the present finale.

20. Archive of the Gesellschaft der Musikfreunde in Wien, A281, p. 17, br. 4, m. 11 to br. 5, m. 6.

21. The revised ending, on p. 52 of the third sketchbook, continues from the third measure (marked with an x) on the last line of p. 90. The displacement dissonance in the final version, incidentally, sounds more like D3+1 rather than D3+2. The reiteration of chords on second and third beats results in strong accents of harmonic change on the second beats, which overshadow the still active durational accents on the third beats.

22. This revision is reproduced in facsimile in Krebs, "Schumann's Metrical Revisions," 49. The autograph of the *Davidsbündlertänze* op. 6 and the pencil revisions in Schumann's copy of the first edition contain additional examples of deintensification of dissonance by removal of dynamic accents. In mm. 17–21 of the autograph of no. 13 (Archive of the Gesellschaft der Musikfreunde in Wien, A281, p. 17, br. 2), there are dynamic accents on the second beats. In the editions, Schumann retained these accents only in mm. 19–21, so that the dissonance D2+1 (1=quarter) lasts less long and the section as a whole is less dissonant. In the autograph (Archive of the Gesellschaft der Musikfreunde in Wien, A281, p. 18, br. 4), Schumann also placed dynamic accents on the second beats of mm. 113, 115, and 117, resulting, along with the ties from these beats to the following downbeats, in strong D4+2 (an augmentation of the earlier D2+1). In the editions, he excised the accents so that the dissonance becomes considerably weaker.

23. Wolfgang Boetticher refers to "this harmonically unacceptable rhythmic displacement" in *Robert Schumanns Klavierwerke, Teil I*, 68.

24. The passages from op. 6 no. 6 are in the Archive of the Gesellschaft der Musikfreunde in Wien, A281, p. 16, br. 3, mm. 3–4, and br. 3, mm. 7–8 to br. 4, mm. 1–4. Those from op. 6 no. 13 are in A281, p. 18, br. 4, mm. 4–12.

25. The fact that the passage is headed "Papillon" suggests that it was intended as a beginning.

26. Schumann's construction of pieces and movements by juxtaposing fragments originally composed independently, a process clearly evident from his autographs, has been discussed by a number of authors who have studied those documents, for example, by Gerhard Dietel in *"Eine neue poetische Zeit,"* 55, 57, and by Linda Correll Roesner in "Schumann's Revisions," 102, 107–9.

27. The opening theme was already worked out when Schumann sketched the m. 46 passage; the staff above the m. 46 sketch in ms. A285 at the Archive of the Gesellschaft der Musikfreunde in Wien corresponds to the first four measures of the finale (notated in 6/16 time). Most of the present weak-sixteenth accents in the theme are already present; only those on the present second beat of m. 1, and on the present second beats of mm. 3 and 4, are missing.

28. Heine-Institut, ms. 78.5025, p. 1.

29. In November 1853, the committee in charge of the Düsseldorf Musikverein had designated Julius Tausch as primary music director; Schumann was to conduct only his own works. Clara Schumann was infuriated by this decision. See Knechtges-Obrecht, "Clara Schumann in Düsseldorf," 212–13.

30. Revision of the discussion of metrical revision in op. 2 no. 1 (with dissonant layers removed): "Another instance of small-scale process achieved by a series of revisions is that in the first *Papillon* (see Example 4.5). The intermediate stages of the processes of intensification and deintensification were not present in our first two versions of the piece. In both, the inner-voice durational accents of mm. 4–6 were absent. In the first version, moreover, the second beats of mm. 9–12 were all dynamically accented. The gradual additions and deletions of accents that render the metrical process

in the final version so elegant were not fully worked out until our fair copy of the work." The early versions are in ULB Bonn, Schumann 15, pp. 93, 119. It is obvious that the version on p. 93 is later because it is labeled with a Roman numeral "I" (suggesting that its ultimate context had been determined), whereas the version on p. 119 is called "Walzer 6." In the fair copy (Bibliothèque Nationale, ms. 315), the passage appears on p. 3, br. 3.

31. The draft, probably dating from 1832, is housed at the Archive of the Gesellschaft der Musikfreunde in Wien (A283). The pages discussed here are reproduced in facsimile in Boetticher, *Robert Schumanns Klavierwerke, Teil II*, plates 6 and 19, and in my article "Schumann's Metrical Revisions," 52. Wolfgang Boetticher addresses the dating of the Fandango draft in *Robert Schumanns Klavierwerke, Teil II*, 147.

32. The drafting of the future op. 11 movement continues on the first two braces of a third page, with material anticipating the present mm. 175–90 (the opening of the development section), though with some gaps, and not yet in the final keys. The third brace on the final page of A283 begins with a blank measure, then contains material reminiscent of mm. 76–85 from the first movement of the Piano Sonata op. 14! The fourth brace appears to be intended as a continuation but does not correspond to any measures in either of the two versions of op. 14. The final two used braces on the page contain ideas for the introduction of the first movement of op. 11—the first phrase of the opening melody in the treble with a sixteenth-note bass accompaniment, then the second phrase in the bass, with treble accompaniment, all in A minor. The latter passage corresponds closely to mm. 14–19 of the present introduction.

33. It is not immediately obvious from the labels that D16+10 is a loose relative of D4+2. The relationship becomes clear if one inserts the "missing step" D8+2. D8+2 is an obvious loose relative of D4+2, and the similar relationship between D16+10 and D8+2 is evident from the equivalence of the differences between the respective cardinalities and displacement indices (the constant difference is 8).

34. The manuscript of the "Exercice" is in the Robert Owen Lehman Collection, on deposit in the Pierpont Morgan Library in New York. For information on the dating of this version, see Boetticher, *Robert Schumanns Klavierwerke, Teil II*, 10.

35. All but the first page of the "Exercice" manuscript retain this original notation (predominantly eighth notes rather than sixteenths). On the first page, Schumann crossed out the original *alla breve* time signature, replaced it with the present two-four signature, and added a second beam to all four-eighth-note groups.

36. Wolfgang Boetticher mentions many of the differences, including "new syncopated accents," in *Robert Schumanns Klavierwerke, Teil II*, 26–31, as does John Daverio in *Robert Schumann*, 64. Neither author discusses the metrical revisions in detail.

37. ULB Bonn, Schumann 14, p. 9, sk. no. 92; reproduced in Boetticher, *Robert Schumanns Klavierwerke, Teil II*, 38. This sketch must postdate the "Exercice" draft, as it is notated in sixteenth notes.

CHAPTER SIX

1. Peter Kaminsky notes that "metrical dissonance may be a significant factor in the articulation of form," and gives some supporting examples from the piano music of Schumann in "Aspects of Harmony, Rhythm and Form," 34. Other writers who have commented on the relation between form and particular interactions of layers or pulse streams are Richard Cohn in "The Dramatization of Hypermetric Conflicts," 200–205;

and John Roeder in "Interacting Pulse Streams in Schoenberg's Atonal Polyphony," *Music Theory Spectrum* 16/2 (Fall 1994): 231–49.

2. Deutsche Staatsbibliothek zu Berlin—Preußischer Kulturbesitz, Mus. ms. autogr. R. Schumann 19, p. 12, br. 5 and 7, and p. 14, br. 1 and 3.

3. The passage from the Second Quartet is shown in Example 5.2. For the passage from the First Quartet, see Deutsche Staatsbibliothek zu Berlin, Mus. ms. autogr. R. Schumann 19, p. 5, st. 14–15.

4. The first sketch is in the ULB Bonn, Schumann 15, p. 81, br. 3, mm. 3–5. The fair copy is housed at the Bibliothèque Nationale (ms. 315); the passage discussed here is on p. 5, br. 4–5.

5. Bo Alphonce discusses the "reckless counterpoint" of the latter passage in "Dissonance and Schumann's Reckless Counterpoint," *Music Theory Online* 0/7 (1994): par. 13–14.

6. See Krebs, "Alternatives to Monotonality in the Early Nineteenth Century," and "Some Early Examples of Tonal Pairing: Schubert's 'Meeres Stille' and 'Der Wanderer,'" in Kinderman and Krebs, *The Second Practice of Nineteenth-Century Tonality*, 17–33. William Kinderman, Kevin Korsyn, and Deborah Stein have also discussed tonal conflict in early-nineteenth-century compositions. See Kinderman, "Directional Tonality in Chopin," in Samson, *Chopin Studies*, 59–75; Korsyn, "Directional Tonality and Intertextuality: Brahms's Quintet op. 88 and Chopin's Ballade op. 38," in *The Second Practice of Nineteenth-Century Tonality*, 43–83; and Stein, "When Pieces Begin and End in Different Keys."

7. Deborah Stein discussed the significance of such enharmonically equivalent dyads in tonally dualistic music in the paper cited in the preceding note. For further discussion of such "enharmonic puns," see Stein and Spillman, *Poetry into Song*, 124–25 and 155–57.

8. Peter Kaminsky, in "Aspects of Harmony, Rhythm and Form," 53–63, gives some examples of the highlighting of important points within the pitch structure by means of metrical dissonance; he shows, for example, how the onset and resolution of metrical dissonance in Schumann's *Davidsbündlertanz* op. 6 no. 6 correspond to the rise and fall of arpeggiations.

9. I thank John Roeder for drawing my attention to the pitch component of the dual process.

10. For information on Schumann's activities as choral conductor, see Daverio, *Robert Schumann*, 397.

11. The original vocal line of this passage may have consisted of undisplaced half notes. The autograph at the Deutsche Staatsbibliothek zu Berlin—Preußischer Kulturbesitz, Mus. ms. autogr. R. Schumann 16/1, p. 78, br. 2, m. 7, shows that the quarter rest at the beginning of the measure was messily squeezed in. Furthermore, the quarter noteheads are unusually large, suggesting that they are filled-in half notes.

12. The autograph (Deutsche Staatsbibliothek zu Berlin, Mus. ms. autogr. R. Schumann 16/1, p. 130, br. 2 m. 9) shows that Schumann intended the piano part at "Philosophie" to be exactly as it is at the corresponding m. 9 (where there was no accent); he does not write out the latter measure but leaves it empty and labels it with an alphabetical label referring to the earlier corresponding measure—his usual practice when passages were to be restated without change. The accent is present in the later copyist's manuscript held at the Bibliothèque Nationale in Paris (ms. 326, pp. 5–8).

13. The autograph (Deutsche Staatsbibliothek zu Berlin, Mus. ms. autogr. R. Schumann 16/1, p. 110, br. 2) shows deletion of ties from the third beats in the introduction, and their replacement with ties from the second beats.

14. The autograph (Deutsche Staatsbibliothek zu Berlin, Mus. ms. autogr. R. Schumann 16/1, p. 74, br. 3, mm. 3–5) suggests that the displacement dissonance during the word "Wahnsinn" was an afterthought. The first right-hand note, F♯5, seems originally to have been an E; its notehead appears to have been enlarged so as to extend over the F♯ line. The second right-hand note, E5, was clearly added later, as is evident from its smaller size and from the fact that its stem, unlike those of the other notes, crosses over the eighth-note beam. Before these changes were made, the right hand would have played the unsyncopated eighth notes E5-D♯5-C♯5-B4-A♯4-Gx4, which would have sounded together with the left-hand eighth notes. It appears that the word "Wahnsinn" triggered Schumann's recasting of the right-hand part into a syncopated form.

15. Deutsche Staatsbibliothek zu Berlin, Mus. ms. autogr. R. Schumann 16/1, p. 118, br. 1.

16. The displacement was not present in the autograph of the tenth song (Deutsche Staatsbibliothek zu Berlin, Mus. ms. autogr. R. Schumann 16/2, p. 50); the high right-hand notes coincided with the bass notes. In the autograph of the eleventh song (p. 51), the displacement dissonance was considerably weaker; although antimetrical durational accents already suggested the displacement dissonance, the dynamic accents were lacking.

17. The text comes from Eichendorff's *Viel Lärmen um nichts*; it is sung within that novel by a recently married woman who longs for her childhood home. See Herwig Knaus, *Musiksprache und Werkstruktur*, 19.

18. Herwig Knaus refers to the representation of unrest by a syncopated accompaniment at other points within op. 39 in *Musiksprache und Werkstruktur*, 67. His book contains an excellent facsimile of the Berlin autograph of op. 39.

19. In the third volume of the Peters edition of Schumann's songs, the text is mistakenly given as "Ritter der Wildnis" ("knight of the wilderness").

20. Dietrich Fischer-Dieskau, *Robert Schumann*, 133, 140.

21. Thorough discussions of these conflicts are found in Dieter Schnebel, "Rückungen—Ver-rückungen," 4–89; Arnfried Edler, *Robert Schumann und seine Zeit*; and John Daverio, *Robert Schumann*. Schnebel refers to numerous events in Schumann's life, including the conflicts surrounding his courtship, that negatively influenced his mental health, and suggests that these events and Schumann's reactions to them find their expression in his use of displacement in concurrent works. He cites a letter from Schumann to his former theory teacher, Heinrich Dorn, in which he states that the Piano Sonata op. 14 (a work filled with displacement) is to be regarded as the artistic expression of the emotional strains arising from his courtship of Clara ("Rückungen—Ver-rückungen," 43). John Daverio argues that Schumann resolved the "musician/poet" dualism by adhering throughout his career to the "notion that music should be imbued with the same intellectual substance as literature" (p. 19), and also by engaging in music-critical writing (p. 130). Daverio (pp. 392–415) and Edler (p. 277) address the "bohemian/bourgeois" dualism. For discussion of the "subjective/objective" dualism, see Daverio, p. 13. He cites the following significant diary entry from 8 June 1831: "It sometimes seems to me as if my objective self wanted to separate itself completely from my subjective self."

22. Daverio, *Robert Schumann*, 394–95.

23. Schnebel, "Rückungen—Ver-rückungen," 16.

24. Schnebel makes this point in ibid., 46–47.

25. Bernhard Appel remarks on the comical aspect of certain metrical dissonances in the *Humoreske* op. 20 in "*Robert Schumanns Humoreske für Klavier op. 20*," 326.

26. The dreamlike, hovering nature of some of Schumann's metrical dissonances is

mentioned in Christian Knayer's "Robert Schumann als Meister der Verschiebungen,"
129, and in Dieter Conrad, "Schumanns Liedkomposition—von Schubert her gesehen,"
155.

27. Dieter Schnebel links Schumann's displacement dissonances with insanity in
"Rückungen—Ver-rückungen," 24–25, 37. On the latter page he employs the term
"schizophrenic music" with reference to the pervasively displaced 'Paganini' from *Carnaval*.

CHAPTER SEVEN

1. Martha von Sabinin had studied with Clara in Düsseldorf from November 1850
to March 1851, and had then taken up the position of *Hofpianistin* at Weimar. The two
women remained close friends. Knechtges-Obrecht, "Clara Schumann in Düsseldorf,"
200.

2. Wallace Berry discusses the "bringing out" of the meter and lists ways of doing so
in metrically ambiguous situations in *Structural Functions in Music*, 335–36.

3. For a similar argument, see Epstein, "Brahms and the Mechanisms of Motion,"
204.

4. The view expressed here diverges from that of Mary Evans Johnson, who feels
that solo performers must make a choice between metrical or antimetrical inflection. See
"Characteristic Metrical Anomalies," 297.

5. See Daverio, *Robert Schumann*, 246.

6. I thank William Rothstein for his penetrating remarks on Schumann's "Impromptu," which brought the distinctive string-quartet texture of the piece, and the
means of articulating its various metrical layers, into focus for me.

CHAPTER EIGHT

1. The reader is urged to consult scores of the works analyzed here. It was not possible to include all excerpts mentioned, and some excerpts are presented only in simplified form.

2. Schumann's remarks on Berlioz's irregular phrase rhythms are quoted in chapter
1 (see n. 28). Jacques Barzun gives some examples of Berlioz's use of metrical dissonance in *Berlioz and the Romantic Century*, 1:468n, 486.

3. Robert Schumann, *Gesammelte Schriften über Musik und Musiker*, 1:151.

4. At m. 322 the 4-layer is shifted by one eighth note, resulting in D4+2 in addition
to G6/4.

5. D6+4, brought about by dynamic accents in the horns, is much stronger than
D6+2 in these passages. D6+4 also appears at other points of the movement, for example,
in the statements of the *idée fixe* at mm. 123–25 and 304–7, and at the climactic passage
at mm. 327–29.

6. In the Berlin manuscript of the *Intermezzi*, there is a dynamic accent on the final
beat of m. 26 as well as mm. 24–25 (Deutsche Staatsbibliothek zu Berlin, Mus. ms. autogr. R. Schumann 29). There is also an accent on the second beat of m. 27, initiating the
dissonance D12+2. These accents are missing in the Clara Schumann edition.

7. The latter relationships are admittedly hardly audible, for the eighth-note unit increases in speed in the second intermezzo.

8. Measures 2–5 and 11–14 of the intermezzo are literally lifted from one of Schumann's early songs, entitled "Hirtenknabe" (Shepherd Boy); see Daverio, *Robert Schumann*, 33.

9. In the Berlin manuscript (Deutsche Staatsbibliothek zu Berlin, Mus. ms. autogr. R. Schumann 29), the second beats of mm. 65–66 are dynamically accented. These accents are missing in the Clara Schumann edition.

10. These dissonances could be named (rather cumbersomely) G1/.67 and G2/1.33 (1=8th).

11. Discussions of these features in Chopin's music are found in Rothstein, *Phrase Rhythm in Tonal Music*, 221–24 and 239–45; and Cinnamon, "New Observations."

12. Linda Correll Roesner provides information on Brahms's publications of these movements in "Brahms's Editions of Schumann," 251–60.

13. Anton Kuerti, liner notes for his recording of the work (Ace of Diamonds, SDD 2154, 1967), par. 7.

14. The dynamic accent on the second eighth note of a triple group in m. 109 foreshadows the return of displacement of the 3-layer, although the index of displacement is 1 rather than the 2 characteristic of the scherzo section.

15. Janina Klassen notes the metrical relationship between the sections beginning at m. 11 and m. 35, as well as other rhythmic relationships between Scherzo and Trio in *Clara Wieck-Schumann*, 238–39.

16. I do not agree entirely with Daverio's assessment, in *Robert Schumann*, 137, of the work as "less idiosyncratic" in style than the earlier piano music; this remark is, at least, not true of the first movement.

17. The passage in mm. 340–404 is a near-quotation of the Trio of the Menuetto movement of Beethoven's Piano Sonata op. 31 no. 3. Schumann no doubt quotes Beethoven because he is writing a "Viennese" piece. R. Larry Todd mentions this quotation in "On Quotation in Schumann's Music," 81, as does Olivier Alain in "Schumann und die französische Musik," 58. It is interesting to compare the two passages. Beethoven's new-event harmonic and the durational accents coincide with the downbeats, so that the metrical dissonance is much weaker than in Schumann's passage. As Frank Samarotto pointed out to me, there is *some* dissonance in the Beethoven excerpt; the low bass notes on upbeats result in antimetrical accents.

18. The first movement contains several quotations from Schubert's op. 33 (a work that Schumann, interestingly enough, described as "an entire Fasching" within his famous review of the work; *Gesammelte Schriften über Musik und Musiker*, 2:12). Schumann's mm. 253–56 are rhythmically and harmonically reminiscent of mm. 1–5 of Schubert's op. 33 no. 6. The dotted rhythm of Schumann's mm. 269–92 recalls the seventh waltz in Schubert's set, especially mm. 9–11. Schumann's mm. 340–48, finally, recall not only the aforementioned passage by Beethoven, but also the opening of the eighth waltz of Schubert's op. 33. Again, the quoting of Schubert is appropriate for a piece "aus Wien."

19. William Rothstein describes this phenomenon in *Phrase Rhythm in Tonal Music*, 52–56, using the term "metrical reinterpretation." I thank him for pointing out the metrical reinterpretation at the end of the first movement of *Faschingsschwank*.

20. The first, second, and third movements were completed in Vienna, probably in March 1839; see Robert Schumann, *Tagebücher*, 2:88–90. The finale was written after Schumann's return to Leipzig.

21. Robert Schumann, *Gesammelte Schriften über Musik und Musiker*, 3:195, 199 (1840). Translations are my own.

22. Ibid., 195–96.

23. Ibid., 1:51 (1838).

24. Ibid., 3:76 (1839).

25. Clara and Robert Schumann, *Briefwechsel,* 1:55.

26. Ibid., 259.

27. *Robert Schumann's Briefe: Neue Folge,* ed. F. Gustav Jansen (Leipzig: Breitkopf und Härtel, 1886), 119.

28. Clara and Robert Schumann, *Briefwechsel,* 2:463.

29. Robert Schumann, *Gesammelte Schriften ünd Musik und Musiker,* 3:76–77. "Flachsenfingen" seems to be a coined name suggesting a small-town cultural backwater.

30. *Robert Schumann's Briefe,* 151.

31. Clara and Robert Schumann, *Briefwechsel,* 1:337.

32. *Robert Schumann's Briefe,* 142. The "Vehme" was a secret court active in Westphalia until 1808.

33. Clara and Robert Schumann, *Briefwechsel,* 1:273.

34. Ibid., 337.

35. *Robert Schumann's Briefe,* 146.

36. Stephen Heller, *Briefe an Robert Schumann,* ed. Ursula Kersten, Europäische Hochschulschriften, Vol. 37 (Frankfurt: Peter Lang, 1988).

37. Robert Schumann, *Gesammelte Schriften über Musik und Musiker,* 3:186–89 (1839).

38. I thank Dr. Gerd Nauhaus of the Schumann-Haus in Zwickau for granting me access to Schumann's copies of the Heller and Schaeffer works.

39. Bozarth, "Brahms's *Lieder ohne Worte*," 370–71.

40. For discussion of other relevant influences, notably Beethoven, Haydn, and early music, see Frisch, "The Shifting Bar Line," 149–52, and Virginia Hancock, *Brahms's Choral Compositions,* 159.

41. Frisch, "The Shifting Bar Line," 139–63.

42. Ibid., 142–43.

43. Max Kalbeck, *Johannes Brahms,* 1:126.

44. It might be argued that one could, on the basis of apparent prolongation of C major harmony, combine the last beat of m. 5 with the first of m. 6 to form another duple group. I do not hear the passage in this manner. The C major harmony on beat three of m. 5 sounds like a passing chord within a typical fifth-species suspension resolution, not like the actual resolution of the preceding six-four chord; only on the first beat of m. 6 is the resolving C major harmony actually established.

45. Deutsche Staatsbibliothek zu Berlin—Preußischer Kulturbesitz, Mus. ms. autogr. R. Schumann 19, p. 20, br. 6, m. 3.

46. Deutsche Staatsbibliothek zu Berlin, Mus. ms. autogr. R. Schumann 19, p. 21, br. 2–3.

47. The hymn is reproduced in Clayton W. Henderson, *The Charles Ives Tunebook* (Warren, Michigan: Harmonie Park Press, 1990), 29.

48. Edith's dates are given in *Charles E. Ives: Memos,* ed. John Kirkpatrick (New York: W. W. Norton, 1972), 22. Information about Susanna, Edith's playmate, is found on p. 279. Her dates are not mentioned, but she was very likely of approximately the same age as Edith—perhaps eight, which could account for Ives's inclusion of an 8-layer.

49. This is an excerpt from Dr. Franz Richarz's entry for April 19, 1854 in his casebook on Robert Schumann, transcribed in *Robert Schumanns letzte Lebensjahre: Protokoll einer Krankheit* (Berlin: Stiftung Archiv der Akademie der Künste, 1994), 17. I thank Brigitte Berenbruch for the use of her copy of this publication (which is not widely available).

50. Arnold Schoenberg, "Brahms the Progressive," *Style and Idea*, ed. Leonard Stein and trans. Leo Black (Berkeley and Los Angeles: University of California Press, 1984), 437–38.

51. I discuss hemiola in the various versions of the fourteenth of the *George-Lieder* op. 15 in "Three Versions of Schoenberg's Op. 15 No. 14: Obvious Differences and Hidden Similarities," *Journal of the Arnold Schoenberg Institute* 8/2 (November 1984): 131–40. John Roeder studies interactions of pulse streams akin to metrical consonance and dissonance in two movements from *Pierrot* in "Interacting Pulse Streams in Schoenberg's Atonal Polyphony."

52. When he temporarily abandons G6/4 at m. 30, Schoenberg creates its diminution by superimposing triplet and duplet eighths.

EPILOGUE

1. The dotted motive at the beginning of op. 133 no. 3 conjures up the word "Kikeriki"—the sound that a German rooster makes.

2. "Morgens steh' ich auf und frage: kommt fein's Liebchen heut?" From op. 24 no. 1 (Heine).

3. "Dein Bildnis wunderselig hab' ich im Herzensgrund." From op. 39 no. 2 (Eichendorff).

4. "Heb' auf zum Himmel mich, mein schöner Stern." From op. 101 no. 4 (Rückert).

5. "Wann, wann erscheint der Morgen, der mein Leben löst aus diesen Banden?" From op. 74 no. 6 (Geibel).

6. "Wo sind deine Freuden hin?" From op. 142 no. 3 (poet unknown).

7. "Wenn mich in Jammerschlucht die Welt zu drängen sucht, nehm' ich zu dir die Flucht." From op. 101 no. 6 (Rückert).

8. "Wahnsinn wühlt in meinen Sinnen." From op. 24 no. 5 (Heine).

9. "Den Dampf in mir zu Licht, mein schöner Stern, verklären hilf." From op. 101 no. 4 (Rückert).

10. "Es kennt mich dort keiner mehr." From op. 39 no. 1 (Eichendorff).

11. "Wenn es endlich doch geschähe, dass ich säh' die Stunde, wo ich nimmer sähe!" From op. 74 no. 6 (Geibel).

12. "Du trauriger, blasser Mann!" From op. 48 no. 12 (Heine).

13. "Auflösung" means both dissolution (death) and resolution.

14. "Wenn ich begraben werde, dann ist das Märchen aus." From op. 127 no. 3 (Heine).

Bibliography

Agmon, Eytan. "Rhythmic Displacement in the Fugue of Brahms's Handel Variations: The Refashioning of a Traditional Device." *Studies in Music from the University of Western Ontario* 13 (1991): 1–20.

Alain, Olivier. "Schumann und die französische Musik." In *Sammelbände der Robert-Schumann-Gesellschaft I*. Leipzig: VEB Deutscher Verlag für Musik, 1961.

Alphonce, Bo. "Dissonance and Schumann's Reckless Counterpoint." *Music Theory On-Line*. 0/7 (1994): par. 1–19.

Appel, Bernhard. "Robert Schumann und der 'provençalische Ton.'" In *Schumann's Werke: Text und Interpretation*, ed. Akio Mayeda and Klaus Niemöller, 165–78. Mainz: Schott, 1987.

———. "Robert Schumanns Humoreske für Klavier Op. 20: Zum musikalischen Humor in der ersten Hälfte des 19. Jahrhunderts unter besonderer Berücksichtigung der Formpraxis." Ph.D. diss., Universität des Saarlandes, 1981.

Bareda, Margaret. "A Comparative Study of Metrical Displacement in Schumann's *Intermezzi* Op. 4 and *Waldscenen* Op. 82." Ph.D. diss., Indiana University, 1977.

Barthes, Roland. "Rasch." In *Musik-Konzepte, Sonderband Robert Schumann II*. Ed. Heinz-Klaus Metzger and Rainer Riehn, 264–74. München: edition text + kritik, December 1982.

Barzun, Jacques. *Berlioz and the Romantic Century*. 2 vols. 3d ed. New York and London: Columbia University Press, 1969.

Beaufils, Marcel. "Mythos und Maske bei Robert Schumann." In *Sammelbände der Robert-Schumann-Gesellschaft II*, 66–76. Leipzig: VEB Deutscher Verlag für Musik, 1966.

Berry, Wallace. *Structural Functions in Music*. Englewood Cliffs: Prentice-Hall, 1976.

Bischoff, Bodo. "Alte und neue Wege der motivisch-thematischen Arbeit in Schumanns 4. Sinfonie." *Traditionsbeziehungen bei Schumann: Robert Schumann-Tage 1986*, 22–35. Karl-Marx-Stadt: N.p., 1987.

Boetticher, Wolfgang. "Die Frühfassung des ersten Satzes von Robert Schumanns Klavierkonzert op. 54 und das Problem seiner Durchführung." *Festschrift Arno*

Forchert zum 60. Geburtstag, ed. Gerhard Allroggen and Detlef Altenburg, 216–21. Kassel: Bärenreiter, 1986.

————. Introduction to Robert Schumann, *Klavierquartett in c-moll*, v-viii. Wilhelmshaven: Heinrichshofen's Verlag, 1979.

————. *Robert Schumann, Einführung in Persönlichkeit und Werk*. Berlin: Bernhard Hahnefeld Verlag, 1941.

————. *Robert Schumanns Klavierwerke, Teil I: Opus 1–6*. Wilhelmshaven: Heinrichshofen's Verlag, 1976.

————. *Robert Schumanns Klavierwerke, Teil II: Opus 7–13*. Wilhelmshaven: Heinrichshofen's Verlag, 1984.

————. "Zur Kompositionstechnik und Originalfassung von Robert Schumanns III. Sinfonie." *Acta Musicologica* 53/1 (January–June 1981): 144.

Botstein, Leon. "History, Rhetoric and the Self: Robert Schumann and Music Making in German-Speaking Europe, 1800–1860." In *Schumann and His World*, ed. R. Larry Todd, 3–46. Princeton: Princeton University Press, 1994.

Bozarth, George. "Brahms's *Lieder ohne Worte:* The 'Poetic' Andantes of the Piano Sonatas." In *Brahms Studies: Analytical and Historical Perspectives*, ed. George Bozarth, 345–78. Oxford: Clarendon Press, 1990.

Bracht, Hans-Joachim. "Schumanns *Papillons* und die Ästhetik der Frühromantik." *Archiv für Musikwissenschaft* 50/1 (1993): 71–84.

Bregman, Albert S. *Auditory Scene Analysis: The Perceptual Organization of Sound*. Cambridge: MIT Press, 1990.

Chailley, Jacques. "Zum Symbolismus bei Robert Schumann mit besonderer Berücksichtigung der *Papillons* op. 2." In *Robert Schumann: Ein romantisches Erbe in neuer Forschung*, 57–66. Mainz: Schott, 1984.

Cinnamon, Howard. "New Observations on Voice Leading, Hemiola, and Their Roles in Tonal and Rhythmic Structure in Chopin's Prelude in B Minor, Op. 28 No. 6." *Intégral* 6 (1992): 66–106.

Cohn, Richard. "Metric and Hypermetric Dissonance in the *Menuetto* of Mozart's Symphony in G Minor, K. 550." *Intégral* 6 (1992): 1–33.

————. "The Dramatization of Hypermetric Conflicts in the Scherzo of Beethoven's Ninth Symphony." *19th Century Music* 15/3 (Spring 1992): 188–206.

Colin, Charles. Introduction to Joseph Schillinger, *Encyclopedia of Rhythms*. New York: Da Capo Press, 1976.

Cone, Edward T. *Musical Form and Musical Performance*. New York: W. W. Norton, 1968.

Conrad, Dieter. "Schumanns Liedkomposition—von Schubert her gesehen: Einwendungen zu Th. Georgiades 'Schubert, Musik und Lyrik.'" In *Musik-Konzepte, Sonderband Robert Schumann II*, ed. Heinz-Klaus Metzger and Rainer Riehn, 129–69. München: edition text + kritik, December 1982.

Cooper, Grosvenor, and Leonard Meyer. *The Rhythmic Structure of Music*. Chicago: University of Chicago Press, 1960.

Cowell, Henry. *New Musical Resources*. New York, 1930. Reprint with notes and an accompanying essay by David Nicholls. Cambridge and New York: Cambridge University Press, 1996.

Dahms, Walter. *Robert Schumann*. Berlin: Schuster und Loeffler, 1916.

Daverio, John. *Robert Schumann*. New York and Oxford: Oxford University Press, 1997.

Dietel, Gerhard. *"Eine neue poetische Zeit": Musikanschauung und stilistische Tendenzen im Klavierwerk Robert Schumanns*. Kassel: Bärenreiter, 1989.

Draheim, Joachim, "Schumanns Jugendwerk: Acht Polonaisen op. III für Klavier zu 4

Händen." In *Schumann's Werke: Text und Interpretation*, ed. Akio Mayeda and Klaus Niemöller, 179–91. Mainz: Schott, 1987.

Dusella, Reinhold. "Symphonisches in den Skizzenbüchern Robert Schumanns." In *Probleme der Symphonischen Tradition im 19. Jahrhundert*, ed. Siegfried Kross and Marie Luise Maintz, 203–24. Tutzing: Hans Schneider Verlag, 1990.

Edler, Arnfried. *Robert Schumann und seine Zeit*. Laaber: Laaber Verlag, 1982.

Epstein, David. *Beyond Orpheus: Studies in Musical Structure*. Cambridge: MIT Press, 1979.

———. "Brahms and the Mechanisms of Motion: The Composition of Performance." In *Brahms Studies: Analytical and Historical Perspectives*, ed. George Bozarth, 191–226. Oxford: Clarendon Press, 1990.

Fétis, François-Joseph. "Du developpement future de la musique: Dans la domaine de rythme." *Revue et Gazette musicale de Paris* 19 (1852): 281–84, 289–92, 297–300, 325–27, 353–56, 361–63, 402–4, 456–60, 473–76.

Finson, Jon W., and R. Larry Todd, eds. *Mendelssohn and Schumann*. Durham: Duke University Press, 1984.

———. *Robert Schumann and the Study of Orchestral Composition: The Genesis of the First Symphony Op. 38*. Oxford: Clarendon Press, 1989.

———. "The Sketches for Robert Schumann's C-minor Symphony." *Journal of Musicology* 1/4 (October 1982): 395–418.

———. "The Sketches for the Fourth Movement of Schumann's Second Symphony, op. 61." *Journal of the American Musicological Society* 39/1 (Spring 1986): 143–68.

Fischer-Dieskau, Dietrich. *Robert Schumann: Das Vokalwerk*. München: Deutscher Taschenbuch Verlag and Bärenreiter Verlag, 1985.

Frisch, Walter. *Brahms and the Principle of Developing Variation*. Berkeley and Los Angeles: University of California Press, 1984.

———. "The Shifting Bar Line: Metric Displacement in Brahms." In *Brahms Studies: Analytical and Historical Perspectives*, ed. George Bozarth, 139–63. Oxford: Clarendon Press, 1990.

Gertler, Wolfgang. *Robert Schumann in seinen frühen Klavierwerken*. Wolfenbüttel and Berlin: Georg Kallmeyer, 1931.

Graves, Floyd. "Metrical Dissonance in Haydn." *Journal of Musicology* 13/2 (Spring 1995): 168–202.

Green, Michael D. "Mathis Lussy's *Traité de l'expression musicale* as a Window into Performance Practice." *Music Theory Spectrum* 16/2 (Fall 1994): 196–216.

Gülke, Peter. "Zu Robert Schumanns 'Rheinischer Sinfonie.'" *Beiträge zur Musikwissenschaft* 16 (1974): 125.

Hallmark, Rufus. "A Sketch Leaf for Schumann's D-minor Symphony." In *Mendelssohn and Schumann*, ed. Jon W. Finson and R. Larry Todd, 39–51. Durham: Duke University Press, 1984.

———. "Die handschriftlichen Quellen der Lieder Robert Schumanns." In *Robert Schumann—Ein romantisches Erbe in neuer Forschung*, 99–117. Mainz: Schott, 1984.

———. *The Genesis of Schumann's 'Dichterliebe': A Source Study*. Ann Arbor: UMI Research Press, 1979.

———. "The Sketches for Dichterliebe." *19th Century Music* 1/2 (November 1977): 110–36.

Hancock, Virginia. *Brahms's Choral Compositions and His Library of Early Music*. Ann Arbor: UMI Research Press, 1977.

Hasty, Christopher F. *Meter as Rhythm*. New York and Oxford: Oxford University Press, 1997.

Hauptmann, Moritz. *The Nature of Harmony and Metre*. Trans. and ed. W. E. Heathcote, with a new foreword by Siegmund Levarie. New York: Da Capo Press, 1991.

Hlawicka, Karl. "Die rhythmische Verwechslung." *Musikforschung* 11 (1958): 33–49.

―――. "Musikalischer Rhythmus und Metrum." *Musikforschung* 24 (1971): 385–99.

Honsa, Melitta. "Synkope, Hemiola und Taktwechsel in den Instrumentalwerken Schumanns." Ph.D. diss., Universität Innsbruck, 1966.

Horlacher, Gretchen. "The Rhythms of Reiteration: Formal Development in Stravinsky's Ostinati." *Music Theory Spectrum* 14 (1992): 171–87.

Imbrie, Andrew. "'Extra' Measures and Metrical Ambiguity in Beethoven." In *Beethoven Studies*, ed. Alan Tyson, 45–66. New York: W. W. Norton, 1973.

Johnson, Mary Evans. "Characteristic Metrical Anomalies in the Instrumental Music of Robert Schumann." Ph.D. Diss., University of Oklahoma, 1979.

Jonas, Oswald. "Das Skizzenbuch zu Robert Schumanns Jugendalbum, Op. 68." *Neue Zeitschrift für Musik* 98 (1931): 579–83.

Kalbeck, Max. *Johannes Brahms*. 4 vols. Wien and Leipzig: Wiener Verlag, 1904.

Kaminsky, Peter M. "Aspects of Harmony, Rhythm and Form in Schumann's *Papillons, Carnaval* and *Davidsbündlertänze*." Ph.D. diss., University of Rochester, 1989.

Kapp, Reinhard. "Schumann nach der Revolution—Vorüberlegungen, Statements, Hinweise, Materialien, Fragen." In *Schumann-Forschungen III: Schumann in Düsseldorf, Werke, Texte, Interpretationen*, ed. Bernhard Appel, 315–415. Mainz: Schott, 1993.

―――. *Studien zum Spätwerk Robert Schumanns*. Tutzing: Hans Schneider Verlag, 1984.

Kersten, Ursula, ed. *Stephen Heller; Briefe an Robert Schumann*. Europäische Hochschulschriften, vol. 37. Frankfurt: Peter Lang, 1988.

Kinderman, William, and Harald Krebs, eds. *The Second Practice of Nineteenth-Century Tonality*. Lincoln: University of Nebraska Press, 1996.

Kirnberger, Johann Philipp. *The Art of Strict Musical Composition*. Trans. David Beach and Jurgen Thym. New Haven: Yale University Press, 1982.

Klassen, Janina. *Clara Wieck-Schumann: Die Virtuosin als Komponistin*. Kassel: Bärenreiter, 1990.

Knaus, Herwig. *Musiksprache und Werkstruktur in Robert Schumanns 'Liederkreis'*. Vol. 27 of *Schriften zur Musik*, ed. Walter Kolneder. München: Musikverlag Emil Katzbichler, 1974.

Knayer, Christian. "Robert Schumann als Meister der rhythmischen Verschiebungen: Eine Anregung für das Studium seiner Klavierwerke." *Musikpädagogische Blätter* 37 (1912): 177–79, 201–3, 231–33.

Knechtges-Obrecht, Irmgard. "Clara Schumann in Düsseldorf." In *Clara Schumann 1819–1896: Katalog zur Ausstellung*, ed. Ingrid Bodsch and Gerd Nauhaus, 189–229. Bonn: N.p., 1996.

Kohlhase, Hans. *Die Kammermusik Robert Schumanns: Stilistische Untersuchungen*. 3 vols. Hamburg: Verlag der Musikalienhandlung Karl Dieter Wagner, 1979.

―――. "Die klanglichen und strukturellen Revisionen im Autograph der Streichquartette op. 41." In *Schumanns Werke: Text und Interpretation*, ed. Akio Mayeda and Klaus Niemöller, 53–76. Mainz: Schott, 1987.

―――. "Quellenuntersuchungen zu den Streichquartetten op. 41: Über einen besonderen Akzenttypus bei Schumann." In *Schumann-Forschungen III: Schumann in Düsseldorf, Werke, Texte, Interpretationen*, ed. Bernhard Appel, 141–78. Mainz: Schott, 1993.

Koßmaly, Carl. "Über Robert Schumanns Clavierkompositionen." *Allgemeine musikalische Zeitung* 46 (1844), cols. 17–21, 33–37. Trans. Susan Gillespie. In *Schumann and His World*, ed. R. Larry Todd, 303–16. Princeton: Princeton University Press, 1994.

Kramer, Jonathan. *The Time of Music: New Meanings, New Temporalities, New Listening Strategies*. New York: Schirmer Books, 1988.

Krebs, Harald. "Alternatives to Monotonality in the Early Nineteenth Century." *Journal of Music Theory* 25/1 (1981): 1–16.

———. "Dramatic Functions of Metrical Consonance and Dissonance in *Das Rheingold*." *In Theory Only* 10/5 (1988): 5–21.

———. "The Interactions of Levels of Motion in Schoenberg's Middle-Period Music." Paper delivered at the symposium "Arnold Schoenberg: The Critical Years." University of Victoria, Victoria, B.C., 1991.

———. "Rhythmische Konsonanz und Dissonanz." *Musiktheorie* 9/1 (1994): 27–37.

———. "Robert Schumann's Metrical Revisions." *Music Theory Spectrum* 19/1 (Spring 1997): 35–54.

———. "Some Extensions of the Concepts of Metrical Consonance and Dissonance." *Journal of Music Theory* 31/1 (1987): 99–120.

Kross, Siegfried. "Die Schumann Autographen der Universitätsbibliothek Bonn." In *Studien zur Bonner Musikgeschichte 18. und 19. Jahrhunderts*, ed. Marianne Bröcker and Günther Massenkeil, 9–19. Köln: Volk, 1978.

Lerdahl, Fred, and Raymond Jackendoff. *A Generative Theory of Tonal Music*. Cambridge: MIT Press, 1983.

Lester, Joel. *The Rhythms of Tonal Music*. Carbondale: Southern Illinois University Press, 1986.

Lewin, David. "On Harmony and Meter in Brahms Op. 76 No. 8." *19th Century Music* 4/3 (Spring 1981): 261–65.

———. "Vocal Meter in Schoenberg's Atonal Music, with a Note on a Serial Hauptstimme." *In Theory Only* 6 (1982): 12–36.

London, Justin. "Metric Ambiguity(?) in Bach's Brandenburg Concerto No. 3." *In Theory Only* 11/7–8 (1991): 21–53.

Lussy, Mathis. *Traité de l'expression musicale: Accents, nuances et mouvements dans la musique vocale et instrumentale*. 5th ed. Paris: Heugel et Cie., 1885.

Macdonald, Claudia. "Schumann's Earliest Compositions and Performances." *Journal of Musicological Research* 7/2–3 (1987): 259–83.

Maintz, Marie-Luise. "Studien zur Schubert-Rezeption Robert Schumanns in der Instrumentalmusik." Ph.D. diss., Rheinische Friedrich-Wilhelm-Universität, Bonn, 1993.

Mason, Daniel G. *The Romantic Composers*. New York: Macmillan, 1906.

Monod, Edmond. *Mathis Lussy et le Rythme Musical*. Neuchâtel: Attinger Frères, 1912.

Mountain, Rosemary. "An Investigation of Periodicity in Music, with Reference to Three Twentieth-century Compositions (Bartók's *Music for Strings, Percussion, and Celesta*, Lutoslawski's *Concerto for Orchestra*, and Ligeti's *Chamber Concerto*)." Ph.D. diss., University of Victoria, 1993.

Musiol, Robert. "Der Takt bei Robert Schumann." *Neue Zeitschrift für Musik* 68/23–24 (12 June 1901): 309–10.

Nauhaus, Gerd. "Quellenuntersuchungen zu Schumanns *Paradies und die Peri*." In *Robert-Schumann-Tage 1985*, 68–75. Karl-Marx-Stadt: Rat des Bezirkes, 1986.

Ostwald, Peter. *Schumann: The Inner Voices of a Musical Genius*. Boston: Northeastern University Press, 1985.

Plantinga, Leon. *Schumann as Critic*. New Haven: Yale University Press, 1967.

Rahn, John. "D-Light Reflecting: The Nature of Comparison." In *Brahms Studies: Analytical and Historical Perspectives*, ed. George Bozarth, 399–404. Oxford: Clarendon Press, 1990.

Riemann, Hugo. *System der Musikalischen Rhythmik und Metrik*. Leipzig: Breitkopf und Härtel, 1903. Reprint. Niederwalluf: Dr. Martin Sändig, 1971.

Roeder, John. "A Calculus of Accent." *Journal of Music Theory* 39/1 (Spring 1995): 1–46.

———. "Interacting Pulse Streams in Schoenberg's Atonal Polyphony." *Music Theory Spectrum* 16/2 (Fall 1994): 231–49.

Roesner, Linda Correll. "The Autograph of Schumann's Piano Sonata in F minor Op. 14." *Musical Quarterly* 61 (1975): 123–27.

———. "Brahms's Editions of Schumann." In *Brahms Studies: Analytical and Historical Perspectives*, ed. George Bozarth, 251–82. Oxford: Clarendon Press, 1990.

———. "Schumann's Revisions in the First Movement of the Piano Sonata in G Minor op. 22." *19th Century Music* 1/2 (November 1977): 97–109.

———. "The Sources for Schumann's Davidsbündler Op. 6: Composition, Textual Problems, and the Role of the Composer as Editor." In *Mendelssohn and Schumann*, ed. Jon W. Finson and R. Larry Todd, 53–70. Durham: Duke University Press, 1984.

———. "Structural Revisions in the String Quartets Opus 41 of Robert Schumann." *Current Musicology* 7 (1968): 87–95.

———. "Studies in Schumann Manuscripts: With Particular Reference to Sources Transmitting Instrumental Works in the Large Forms." Ph.D. diss., New York University, 1973.

———. "Tonal Strategy and Poetic Content in Schumann's C-major Symphony, op. 61." In *Probleme der Symphonischen Tradition im 19. Jahrhundert*, ed. Siegfried Kross and Marie-Luise Maintz, 295–306. Tutzing: Hans Schneider Verlag, 1990.

Rosen, Charles. "Brahms the Subversive." In *Brahms Studies: Analytical and Historical Perspectives*, ed. George Bozarth, 105–19. Oxford: Clarendon Press, 1990.

———. *The Romantic Generation*. Cambridge: Harvard University Press, 1995.

Rothstein, William. "Beethoven with and without 'Kunstgepräng': Metrical Ambiguity Reconsidered." In *Beethoven Forum* IV, ed. Christopher Reynolds, Lewis Lockwood, and James Webster, 165–93. Lincoln: University of Nebraska Press, 1995.

———. *Phrase Rhythm in Tonal Music*. New York: Schirmer Books, 1989.

Samson, Jim, ed. *Chopin Studies*. Cambridge: Cambridge University Press, 1988.

Schachter, Carl. "Rhythm and Linear Analysis: A Preliminary Study." In *Music Forum* IV, 281–334. New York: Columbia University Press, 1976.

———. "Rhythm and Linear Analysis: Durational Reduction." In *Music Forum* V, 197–232. New York: Columbia University Press, 1980.

———. "Rhythm and Linear Analysis: Aspects of Meter." In *Music Forum* VI, 1–60. New York: Columbia University Press, 1987.

Schenker, Heinrich. *Beethoven, die letzten Sonaten, Sonate As Dur op. 110: Kritische Einführung und Erläuterung*, ed. Oswald Jonas. Vienna: Universal Edition, 1972.

Schillinger, Joseph. *Encyclopedia of Rhythms: Instrumental Forms of Harmony*. Introduction by Charles Colin. New York, 1966. Reprint. New York: Da Capo Press, 1976.

———. *The Schillinger System of Musical Composition*. 2 vols. New York: Carl Fischer, 1941.

Schnebel, Dieter. "Rückungen—Ver-rückungen: Psychoanalytische und musikanalytische Betrachtungen zu Schumanns Leben und Werk." In *Musik-Konzepte, Sonderband Robert Schumann I*, ed. Heinz-Klaus Metzger and Rainer Riehn, 4–89. München: edition text + kritik, November 1981.

Schoenberg, Arnold. "Brahms the Progressive." In *Style and Idea*, ed. Leonard Stein, trans. Leo Black, 398–441. Berkeley: University of California Press, 1984.

Schubring, Adolf. "Schumanniana No. 4: The Present Musical Epoch and Robert Schumann's Position in Musical History" [1861]. Trans. John Mitchell Cooper. In *Schu-*

mann and His World, ed. R. Larry Todd, 362–74. Princeton: Princeton University Press, 1994.

Schuhmacher, Gerhard, ed. "Notwendige Ergänzung." In *Zur musikalischen Analyse*, 525–48. Darmstadt: Wissenschaftliche Buchgemeinschaft, 1974.

Schumann, Clara, and Robert Schumann. *Briefwechsel: Kritische Gesamtausgabe*. Ed. Eva Weissweiler. 2 vols. Basel: Stroemfeld/Roter Stern, 1984–87.

Schumann, Robert. *Gesammelte Schriften über Musik und Musiker*. 4 vols. Leipzig, 1854. Reprint. Wiesbaden: Breitkopf und Härtel, 1985.

———. *Robert Schumann's Briefe: Neue Folge*. Ed. F. Gustav Jansen. Leipzig: Breitkopf und Härtel, 1886.

———. *Tagebücher*. Ed. Georg Eismann and Gerd Nauhaus. 3 vols. Leipzig: VEB Deutscher Verlag für Musik, 1971–87.

———. Vorwort, *Studien op. 3 und Konzertetüden op. 10 nach Capricen von Paganini*. Ed. Hans Joachim Köhler. Leipzig: Edition Peters, 1981.

Seeger, Charles. "On Dissonant Counterpoint." *Modern Music* 7/4 (June–July 1930): 25–31.

Simonett, Hans Peter. "Taktgruppengliederung und Form in Schumann's *Carnaval.*" Ph.D. diss., Freie Universität Berlin, 1978.

Stein, Deborah. "When Pieces Begin and End in Different Keys: A Conceptual Approach to Directional Tonality." Paper delivered at the conference "Alternatives to Monotonality," University of Victoria, February 17, 1989.

Stein, Deborah, and Robert Spillman. *Poetry into Song: Performance and Analysis of Lieder*. Oxford and New York: Oxford University Press, 1994.

Taylor, Ronald. *Robert Schumann: His Life and Work*. New York: Universe, 1982.

Todd, R. Larry. "On Quotation in Schumann's Music." In *Schumann and His World*, ed. R. Larry Todd, 80–112. Princeton: Princeton University Press, 1994.

Trautwein, Wolfgang, ed. *Robert Schumanns letzte Lebensjahre: Protokoll einer Krankheit*. *Archiv-Blätter 1* (March 1994). Berlin: Stiftung Archiv der Akademie der Künste.

Turchin, Barbara. "Robert Schumann's Song Cycles: The Cycle within the Song." *19th Century Music* 8/3 (Spring 1985): 231–44.

Wasielewski, Wilhelm Joseph von. *Robert Schumann: Eine Biographie*. 4th ed. Leipzig: Breitkopf und Härtel, 1906. Reprint. Wiesbaden: Breitkopf und Härtel, 1972.

Wendt, Matthias. "Zu Robert Schumanns Skizzenbüchern." In *Schumanns Werke: Text und Interpretation*, ed. Akio Mayeda and Klaus Niemöller, 101–19. Mainz: Schott, 1987.

Westergaard, Peter. "Some Problems in Rhythm Theory and Analysis." *Perspectives in New Music* 1/1 (Fall 1962): 180–91.

Westrup, Sir Jack. "The Sketch for Schumann's Piano Quintet Op. 44." In *Convivium Musicum: Festschrift für Wolfgang Boetticher zum sechzigsten Geburtstag am 19. August 1974*, ed. Heinrich Hüschen and Dietz-Rüdiger Moser, 367–71. Berlin: Verlag Merseburger, 1974.

Wetzel, Hermann. "In welchem Takte steht Schumanns 'Des Abends'?" *Allgemeine Deutsche Musikzeitung* 39/72 (5 July 1912): 731–33.

Willner, Channan. "More on Handel and the Hemiola: Overlapping Hemiolas." *Music Theory Online* 2/3 (1996): par. 1–20.

———. "The Two-Length Bar Revisited: Handel and the Hemiola." *Göttinger Händel-Beiträge* 4 (1991): 208–31.

Wolff, Viktor E. *Robert Schumanns Lieder in ersten und späteren Fassungen*. Leipzig: Breitkopf und Härtel, 1914.

Yeston, Maury. *The Stratification of Musical Rhythm*. New Haven: Yale University Press, 1976.

List of Cited Works by Robert Schumann

Page numbers in italics indicate that a musical example appears on the given page. Page numbers in boldface indicate substantial analytical discussions with numerous musical examples.

Index

Page numbers in italics indicate that a musical example appears on the given page. Page numbers in boldface indicate substantial analytical discussions with numerous musical examples.

Printed in the United States
135353LV00005B/115/A

9 780195 169461

2530768R00166

Printed in Great Britain
by Amazon.co.uk, Ltd.,
Marston Gate.